IS THE FASHION BUSINESS YOUR BUSINESS?

Books by Eleanor L. Fried
IS THE FASHION BUSINESS YOUR BUSINESS?
STARTING WORK

IS THE FASHION BUSINESS YOUR BUSINESS?

ELEANOR L. FRIED

ILLUSTRATIONS BY FRED ROMARY

THIRD EDITION

FAIRCHILD PUBLICATIONS, INC.

NEW YORK

Copyright © 1970, Fairchild Publications, Inc.

All right reserved. No part of this book may be reproduced in any form without permission in writing from the publisher, except by a reviewer who wishes to quote passages in connection with a review written for inclusion in a magazine or newspaper.

Standard Book Number: 87005-087-7

Library of Congress Catalog Card Number: 74-92455

Printed in the United States of America

DESIGNED BY VINCENT TORRE

To Rebecca

Contents

Chapter 1	Starting Points	3
Chapter 2	Trends and Structures of the Industry	6
Chapter 3	Designing	19
Chapter 4	Merchandising	55
Chapter 5	Planning and Promotion	95
Chapter 6	Publishing	128
Chapter 7	Engineering and Management of Apparel Production	148
Chapter 8	Top-Level Jobs	165
Chapter 9	For Women Only	178
Chapter 10	Is There a Fashion Career for You?	187
Chapter 11	Job Hunting	198

Special Notes of Appreciation for 1970 Edition	213
Suggested Readings	215
Index	219

IS THE FASHION BUSINESS YOUR BUSINESS?

Chapter 1

Starting Points

Most of us spend more than half our waking hours at work. The hours an individual spends on a job may be a joy or a burden, depending largely upon how well the individual's interests and abilities match the requirements and potentialities of the job.

Rarely is there one right job, and only one, for an individual. Any normally intelligent person could find job satisfactions and financial security in any one of a dozen or so occupations. My advice is to try first to understand your own interests, abilities, and personality needs, and second, to get as many facts as possible about career opportunities open to a person of your interests, abilities, and personality traits.

My purpose in writing this book is to indicate some of the career opportunities existing in the fashion industries. I have tried to indicate fields of work rather than specific jobs. If you select a field of work you give yourself more leeway to try out your abilities, to broaden your interests and experience, and to find opportunities that draw on abilities and experience gained through interrelated jobs. It is possible to start your career as a trainee in fashion designing and to develop into a merchandising executive. It is possible, too, to start as a sales trainee and later move into designing.

Is the Fashion Business Your Business? deals with occupations related to the design, production, merchandising, distribution, and promotion of apparel and related fashion products. I have omitted such functions as personnel management, accounting, and others that are equally important in all industries. I have tried rather to describe the fields of apparel and fabric designing, production, merchandising, fashion planning and promotion, and publishing. I have not attempted to cover in detail all the jobs that fall within the industry. In apparel production, for example, I have only mentioned such specific jobs as cutter, patternmaker, and sewing machine operator. I have emphasized management and engineering opportunities in apparel production, an area of career possibilities that needs greater attention because of the increased and increasing opportunities.

The reader is aware, I am sure, of federal legislation that prohibits discrimination in employment based on race, religion, or sex. This was an enormously important move to open up opportunities to groups who have faced discrimination in the past. Subtle discrimination still exists among some employers, and constant vigilance must ferret it out. To gain full advantage of this law, all parts of the community must marshal its resources—industry, schools and colleges, employment and vocational counseling agencies, and, where necessary, law enforcement agencies. The fact that no black people have been hired in a firm or even in that industry must *not* deter a qualified, interested black person from applying. Unquestionably it takes courage and initiative, but the individual seeking a career must make every effort to explore opportunities, unshackled by irrational hiring practices of the past. Opportunities for women are so affected by tradition that many do not take this part of the law seriously. Not only does the employer frequently reflect this, but also the girl who will not consider a field of work because it is traditionally male. Now is the time to break with tradition, concentrating on the demands of fields of work to see if they interest you and to weigh your qualifications in relation to them. The reader can assume that all the jobs and fields of work I describe are open to them on the basis of their qualifications alone.

Nor is the chapter "For Women Only" inconsistent with the statements in the previous paragraph. The men should read it, too. Both men and women must face the question, "Will marriage and family

Starting Points

mean that a woman must give up her interest in the field of work she has chosen and for which she has prepared herself?"

I have included some information about salary, although it should be remembered that pay rates vary from company to company, from city to city, and from time to time. The fashion industries offer satisfactory money rewards to individuals of ability, energy, and experience. Good pay is a by-product of good training, good experience, good job performance, and good breaks. The career beginner will be wise to concentrate on developing his abilities to meet the requirements of the job at hand, keeping in mind the fact that money is one of the satisfactions to be gained from working, but not the only one.

Instead of concentrating on the lives of those few who are leaders in their fields, I have felt it would be more helpful to relate case histories of people on the way up, their jobs, their preparation, their reactions. I have even accepted the possibility that all of them may not reach the heights. Perhaps they will achieve modest success, earn a good living, enjoy their work, and make a sound contribution to the industry and the community. There are degrees of individual ability and various levels of success. I consider this comforting rather than alarming. Achievement of a satisfactory way of life is an individual matter, not subject to exact measurements in dollars and cents, nor by titles in an organization.

Furthermore, I believe that regardless of specialization and mechanization there always will be room in the fashion industries for the individual's own ability, personality, interests, and initiative to mold, develop, and even to change the nature of the job itself.

Chapter 2

Trends and Structures of the Industry

Prospects for the fashion industry are bright. In 1968 the population of our country reached 202,000,000; by 1970 it reached 209,000,000; and by 1975 it is expected to be 228,000,000. Between 1960 and 1975, those in the age category of ten to nineteen years of age, as an example, will have increased by 37 percent. What a set of opportunities for the apparel manufacturers, merchandisers, and promoters!

Not only are there more of us, but our habits of living have changed over the years. The move of large numbers to the suburbs meant more casual, informal attire, more sportswear, more special-occasion clothes. This in turn influenced clothes worn in urban settings. The young people who wanted more gaiety, more color, more "far-out" clothes can take credit too for some of these changes in the late sixties. Compared to the staid tailored clothing that was the only garb men wore to their offices ten or fifteen years ago, we now find some sports jackets and even turtleneck shirts and no ties. The change in men's sportswear and evening clothes is truly startling. Raspberry and burnished gold sports jackets,

Trends and Structures of the Industry

silver evening coats, Edwardian shirts have added zest to an industry where change had been at a standstill.

The trek to the suburbs has affected merchandising, too. We don't want to travel to the cities to do the family shopping. Large department stores have opened branches, shopping centers have been growing in all the suburban communities. You can even buy clothing in a supermarket.

We want good design and styling in everything we wear. This includes underwear, foundation garments, nightwear, children's wear, shoes, bags, all the accessories as well as the dress or the suit that has always caught the designer's attention.

The children's wear industry has grown enormously. More children, yes. Improved styling and sizing, too, in the garments—and perhaps in the children. Styling of adult clothes has influenced children's. The little girl who wants a skirt or robe like her mother's can get one. If she's not quite a teen-ager but feels too old for the little-girl dresses, she will find something in a subteen or preteen department. Boys' wear manufacturers are more conscious of the design of their product than they used to be, and have hired designers to improve their styling.

Ease of communication makes the fashion business truly international, with crosscurrents of influence and design inspiration coming from all over the world. Paris openings are still exciting, world-wide events, but Paris is only one of the fashion centers. Italy (Rome and Florence) and Spain have been fashion influences for years. More recently England, Ireland, and the Scandinavian countries must be included. Africa and Asia influence fashion, too, even though they are not yet fashion centers.

Nor are the American designs confined to our own shores. In Copenhagen I interviewed the young assistant buyer of women's foundation garments in one of their large department stores. She knew as much about American brassieres as any alert assistant buyer in this country. In fact, she was taking a correspondence course given by a leading American manufacturer. Our well-known flair for advertising and the spread of brand names has developed this familiarity. In addition, several American manufacturers have opened branches or licensed native factories in foreign countries, making it easy to distribute the product abroad. An example is the Kayser-Roth Corporation, a merger of hosiery, outerwear, innerwear, and footwear manufacturing concerns. It services 140 foreign licensee manufacturing and distribution organizations in addition to exporting to 90 countries and territories throughout the world. In South Africa, for example, there is a licensee for the Cole of California Division of Kayser-Roth. The Cole swimwear patterns are sent to the South

African factory and are reproduced in fabrics imported from the United States and Europe.

Two Paris datelines appeared in the same issue of *Women's Wear Daily*, the fashion industry's leading paper. One story reported the arrival in Paris of American designers, stylists, manufacturers, and fashion writers to cover the collections of the high-fashion couturiers; the other told of the promotion of American ready-to-wear by Galeries Lafayette, a large Paris department store. The store's ten windows were turned over to American fashions to promote double the amount of U.S. apparel imported the year before. The store ran no advertisements. "We do not need publicity of any kind to sell American ready-to-wear," said the general manager.

Fabric research has brought new fashion excitement to all branches of the industry. Nylon, Dacron, Orlon, Qiana, to mention a few, are fibers with uses and wearing qualities of enormous significance to the producers of apparel and home furnishings. Production of man-made fibers jumped 29 percent in 1968, according to the Textile Economics Bureau. And cotton—with new finishes, new styling, new combinations with man-made fibers—has been used more imaginatively than ever before. Permanent press has meant that garments can be washed, dried, and worn immediately without pressing—science fiction come true for the housekeeper.

We want what *we* want. The customer who pays will be served. If she doesn't buy, the design will be discontinued. Take width of skirts. Some seasons the emphasis is on slim skirts, some on full skirts. But in any season you'll find some of both because there are enough buyers for both. At the same time advertising and promotion have made great strides in the industry. We cling to some brand names in clothing just as we have for years in toiletries. This is particularly true in foundation garments, brassieres, women's underwear, and men's shirts. This trend extends to dresses and men's suits, and is the result of conscious promotion of the manufacturer's name or brand.

We want our money's worth. Good value, good quality for the price. We're more demanding, more selective than during the wild buying spree right after World War II, when a higher percentage of income was spent for things to wear. During the last few years of inflation and relatively high employment, demand has increased for sportswear, evening wear, and luxury items. We're buying a wide variety of garments. Some branches of the industry, like children's wear and sportswear, have benefited. The women's coat and suit industry, on the other hand, has

Trends and Structures of the Industry

declined. But even with the variation for each branch of the industry, the over-all outlook is good.

RELATION TO THE NATIONAL ECONOMY

We are talking about big business. The manufacturing of apparel and textile products, based on value of shipments, amounts to $40 billion a year, the fifth largest of the manufacturing industries in the country.

Nor does this take into account the large retailing industry, the publishing firms and advertising agencies that combine to get the finished product to the consumer. In 1967 we spent 8.7 percent of our income

on clothing. After World War II the figure was 11 percent, but then it declined until 1963, when the trend was reversed. Between 1963 and 1967, the share of consumer expenditures for clothing rose from 8.2 percent to 8.7 percent. While this may not seem a startling change, the fact is that consumer spending for clothing and shoes increased more than 44 percent in the five-year period ending 1967. Part of this increase,

IS THE FASHION BUSINESS YOUR BUSINESS?

of course, was due to higher prices. General affluence and increased fashion consciousness contributed to this change.

FABRIC MANUFACTURING

Adam and Eve launched the clothing business with fig leaves. Later, primitive man found that animal skins could serve as clothing. Today the textile industry uses vegetable and animal fibers on a mammoth scale to produce modern fabrics. Scientists have produced man-made fibers called synthetics. The actual manufacture of the fibers into cloth is done by textile mills, an industry by itself. Some mills stop at the gray-goods stage, when the fabric is unfinished, ready to be designed or styled. The next step is taken by the textile converter. The converter may have the fabric designed in his own studio or buy designs from outside studios specializing in this service and then have it printed or processed in a mill. Other mills have a vertical setup, doing the complete job—starting with the raw fiber, finishing it, designing it, processing it, shipping it to the manufacturer or store. The marketing of the fabric may be done by the vertical mills, or by the converters and textile jobbers who specialize in this phase.

New York City is unquestionably headquarters for the textile industry. Although textile mills are located in New England and the South, New York City centralizes the styling, sales, and business offices for over 90 percent of the industry. Prior to the 1950's Worth Street was the home of the large textile firms, but since then they have moved to modern buildings in the midtown garment district, bringing them closer to their customers.

While there are small textile companies as well as large, the trend is clearly toward more mergers, the big companies getting bigger and in some cases going beyond fabric production into the manufacture of apparel or commercial factoring and financing, even retailing. An outstanding example is United Merchants and Manufacturers Inc., a combination of several fabric firms, weaving mills, finishing plants, commercial factoring and financing, and of a chain of retail clothing stores, Robert Hall Clothes, Inc., with 408 units. It is a leading supplier of fabrics for men's, women's, and children's apparel and for home furnishings. Its foreign manufacturing and merchandising operations have spread into Argentina, Brazil, Colombia, Uruguay, Venezuela, Canada, France, and Great Britain. It operates forty-six manufacturing plants in

Trends and Structures of the Industry

the United States and abroad, maintains sales and distribution offices in many cities, and employs approximately 35,000 people. Its volume of sales for 1968 was over $650 million, ample evidence that this is big business.

APPAREL MANUFACTURING

Finally the apparel manufacturer gets his hands on the fabric. Apparel manufacturing consists of several branches or industries within this large classification. Broadly they fall into women's wear, men's wear, and children's wear, with many subdivisions and much overlapping within those categories. A very small segment, the custom houses, are designers and tailors of garments for the individual customer. They are the extremely high-priced end of the business. But by far the major portion of the industry, for which the United States is world famous, is the massproduced garment. The manufacturer usually specializes in the low- or medium-priced or the better-priced lines. In general he has specialized, too, in the type of apparel, such as ladies' dresses, men's tailored suits, or children's outerwear. This has been changing as manufacturers have found it more stabilizing to diversify their products. The distinction between sportswear, dresses, coats, and suits has become increasingly fuzzy. Diversification brings flexibility to the manufacturer and can counteract problems of seasonality.

There are three types of firms in apparel manufacturing. The manufacturer designs, cuts, sews, and assembles the garment in his own organization. The jobber owns the fabric, designs the garment, has it sewn by a contractor. The contractor sews and assembles the cut garment for the jobber, and for those manufacturers who have more work than their own shops can absorb. A jobber or manufacturer may have several contractors working for him.

PRESENT TRENDS IN MANUFACTURING

The history of the apparel industry is the story of thousands of producers, most of them small, with the few really large firms growing even larger. Although more than half of the manufacturers and jobbers have an annual sales volume under a million dollars, they do not account for much of the business now. In 1966, for example, 52 percent of the firms had sales under $1 million, but they produced only 14 percent of the total industry sales volume. In contrast, 22 percent of the manufacturers had sales volumes over $2½ million, yet they accounted for 67 percent of the total industry sales volume. The contrast was even sharper in 1967, with 52 percent of the under $1 million manufacturers doing only 9.9 percent of total sales volume; 22 percent of the manufacturers in the over $2½ million volume produced 71.4 percent of total sales volume. Large companies have become mammoth, acquiring smaller companies, merging with others. Along with this goes wide diversification of product. The trend is for more large companies with greater diversification within them. Small companies will find it increasingly difficult to survive because financing will be too hard for them. Many will be acquired by the large companies and, depending on the new structure, the small company may be able to retain relative autonomy within the larger organization. This trend can be described best by pointing to specific examples.

Jonathan Logan Corporation had been well known for years as a major producer of junior dresses and sportswear. In 1955 the company did a $30 million volume of business annually, a phenomenal figure at that time. In an interview I had then with Mr. David Schwartz, president of the company, he told me: "In the years ahead a manufacturer of apparel might look forward to doing a $50 million volume of business." By 1969 the Jonathan Logan Corporation's annual volume of business was $250 million, five times that optimistic prediction. Its capital assets of plants and machinery alone amounted to $34 million.

The growth of this company is dramatic evidence of the changes in the industry. It has continued its acquisition of companies with greater diversification—producing dresses, sportswear, swimwear, coats, and rainwear—including the largest fully integrated knitwear plant in the country, starting with the raw goods and producing the completed garments in a large modern factory in the South and one in Ireland. The products are primarily in popular-priced categories, 30 percent in junior wear, 70 percent in misses. Mr. Richard Schwartz, the dynamic young president of the corporation, finds that the growth of the company has meant more sophisticated systems of planning and control. He says, "We're more like other businesses outside of the apparel industry now, with the volume and structure of the business creating the necessary changes. Responsibility must be delegated instead of reposing it in only one or two strong executives."

Jonathan Logan is now a public corporation listed on the New York Stock Exchange. The companies within the corporation operate auton-

Trends and Structures of the Industry

omously, retaining their own names, often brand names known to the public. Each president is responsible for all the functions of his company in styling, sales, production, distribution, and advertising. The central services of the corporation are primarily financial: the corporation can finance operations and make capital expenditures, which the individual company might not be able to do.

Another giant is the aforementioned Kayser-Roth Corporation, the largest apparel manufacturing concern in the world. Their twenty-one operating divisions employ 30,000 people. This merger of hosiery, outerwear, innerwear, and footwear manufacturing companies in men's and women's wear reached a sales volume of $450 million in 1969. A publicly announced projection of the company is to reach a volume in excess of $1 billion by 1975.

While Kayser-Roth considers itself the largest manufacturing concern, Genesco, Inc., claims to be the largest apparel and footwear manufacturing and retail complex in the United States, with sales in 1969 running at a rate of $1.1 billion. Projections for the future make it difficult to pinpoint who will carry the label of "largest," nor does it matter much when figures become so astronomic.

Still another example of growth and diversification by acquisition of companies is the Palm Beach Co., originally solely a manufacturer of men's wear and now deeply involved in the production of women's wear —dresses, sportswear, beachwear. And another is Vanity Fair Mills Inc., a leading manufacturer of women's intimate apparel. In 1969 it took the first step toward its new goal of becoming a total producer of all types of clothing for the family—men's, women's, and children's wear. It acquired a leading manufacturer of women's hosiery that was also producing some men's and women's outerwear. The chairman of the board indicated that this was just the start.

Yet the small manufacturer can play an important role. A 1969 article in the *Daily News Record,* the trade paper devoting major emphasis to the men's wear industries, reported on a convention of men's wear merchandisers and retailers. A leading independent retailer pointed out that for high fashion or a sudden change in fashion, even if it were just a fad but important to have in order to meet consumer demand, it was the small producer he turned to, as the large ones were not ready for it. The trend to boutiques with ordering in small quantities at more frequent intervals lends itself to production by the small manufacturer.

Some of the markets outside New York have grown in prestige and influence: Los Angeles is known for women's and children's sportswear and casual clothes and Chicago, Philadelphia, and Rochester for men's wear. Others, such as St. Louis and Dallas, are apparel centers as well, but New York is still far and away the most influential. For example, New York firms are responsible for producing between 60 and 70 percent of the total volume of dresses, children's wear, sportswear, foundation garments, and lingerie. Trimmings, embroideries, and all the accessory trades are centralized in New York. Many firms do their production outside New York but maintain executive, designing, buying, and selling offices in New York City. Some concerns have buying or selling offices (or both) in New York and headquarters elsewhere. Improvements in communication and transport have made it increasingly possible to separate production from headquarters offices.

The famous garment center in New York is a world of contrasts. Old-fashioned hand trucks with racks of garments weave in and out of streets and on the sidewalks, a hazard for the sauntering pedestrian. At lunch time Seventh Avenue is a social center, the busy street jammed with workers standing, chatting, making appointments, talking about their jobs. Inside the tall, modern buildings there are plush air-conditioned showrooms alive with sleek models, well-groomed stylists, fast-moving buyers. From Thirty-fourth Street north to Forty-second Street, from Avenue of the Americas west to Eighth Avenue, is the world's largest concentration of ready-to-wear business.

PRINCIPLES OF ENGINEERING

Good styling is essential. But if production of the garment is poor, the design can be ruined or the quality reduced to the point of no sales. Few of the old tailors and highly skilled dressmakers who were the backbone of the industry are left. Many of them were immigrants trained in childhood under the European apprenticeship system. We will never replace these masters of the handicraft. Our way of life does not allow the exploitation of child labor that produced these fine artisans. Instead, new machines have been devised and operations simplified so that today's novice may be trained to produce garments that approximate the quality standards of the old tailors.

The principles of engineering can be applied to the manufacture of apparel. This startles many people who accept without question the fact that engineering is essential in manufacturing automobiles and other hard goods. An engineer introduces the revolutionary principle of "what's

Trends and Structures of the Industry

the best way to get this done" instead of "the old way is good enough for me." His goal is to produce an item at lowest possible cost, in quantity needed, retaining high standards of quality. These principles apply to a dress, man's suit, car, bicycle, or kitchen sink.

More and more apparel producers, especially the large ones, have introduced engineering into their plants. Many of these plants, located throughout the country, are modern, attractive, and progressive, belying the picture of the overcrowded sweatshop too long associated with this industry.

UNION

Apparel manufacturing is a highly unionized industry. The International Ladies Garment Workers Union serves workers in the women's wear industry, the Amalgamated Clothing Workers of America those in the men's wear. In New York City, well over 90 percent of garment workers are union members. Even outside New York the percentage is high. The International Ladies Garment Workers Union claims 90 percent of all women's clothing workers throughout the United States and Canada as its members. For the most part supervisors are not included. The Designers Guild of Ladies Apparel, Local 30, I.L.G.W.U. is an exception. Designers in the coat and suit industry are eligible if they meet certain requirements.

The unions are justly proud of their impressive record of no major strikes since 1933. The I.L.G.W.U. reports no strike at all, with the exception of a dress strike in the New York area in 1958 that was settled amicably after a short period. The Amalgamated Clothing Workers has had no industry-wide strike since 1933, no strike with any large company, and only occasional short strikes against smaller companies, primarily for organizing purposes. Both unions are proud, too, of their broad educational and cultural programs. Both have well-established research departments. The I.L.G.W.U. has its own engineering department as well.

SEASONALITY

Apparel manufacturing is seasonal. Its seasonality is affected largely by purchasing power as reflected in consumer demand and the degree of integration between manufacturing and retailing. Stable, advanced buying on the part of retailers means manufacturers can plan their production realistically. Proof of this came during World War II. True, other factors such as scarcity and government restrictions played an important part. But retailers were forced to give long-term orders. Manufacturers knew how much to produce. Employment was practically year round.

Seasonality has diminished somewhat but is still prevalent, the amount varying in the different industry branches. Diversification of product has reduced seasonality. This is notable in the very large companies, where the company as a whole benefits from the diminished seasonality.

But within the divisions of the company, each producing specialized items, seasonality is still a factor. Efforts to shorten the work week and spread employment have reduced somewhat the seasonal extremes. A guarantee of all-year employment in this industry might stimulate better planning and fuller utilization of the labor force.

MARKETING

After the fabric has been produced and styled, after the manufacturer has designed and produced the garment, the marketing and merchandising specialists take over. Full production of the garment doesn't begin until the manufacturer has shown his "line" for the season and has some evidence that it will sell.

There is a big gap between the wholesaler and the customer. It is filled by buying offices, specialty shops, chain stores, department stores, and mail-order houses. But to the manufacturer or jobber it's the *buyer* who represents all of them and can determine his success or failure.

To visit the markets of the apparel industry would mean a fine cross-country trip. But New York is the mecca. Thousands of buyers invade New York to select from lines and to place orders. Some stores and groups of stores maintain their own central buying offices in New York. In addition there are resident buying offices established to serve individual stores throughout the country. Buyers use the buying service for advice in screening or selecting from the many lines that are available.

Retailing is a mammoth field. It is the second largest industry in the United States, with some 2 million stores. This, of course, includes many engaged in the retailing of products other than fashion. Yet large numbers have fashion merchandise and many specialize in it. Retailing of

Trends and Structures of the Industry

fashion merchandise includes specialty shops, chain stores, department stores, and the mail-order or catalogue firms.

There are independently owned stores, but here again, as with textile firms and apparel manufacturers, the trend toward mergers and acquisitions has affected the retail business, too. There are fewer independent stores than in the past and more of the large groups, such as Allied Stores Corporation, which keeps adding to its acquisition of independent stores across the country. The trend toward mergers was pointed up when two major department stores, the Dayton Corporation of Minneapolis and the J. L. Hudson Company of Detroit reached a merger agreement in 1969. This meant that the two companies operated a total of more than eighty department stores, branches, and specialty shops doing a volume of more than $800 million a year.

Defying bigness are the boutiques, growing at the same time that the larger organizations are expanding. They have multiplied rapidly within the last five years. The department stores recognize their appeal by establishing their own boutiques within their larger structure.

PROMOTION AND PUBLICITY

There are advertising agencies and publicity agencies to promote the garment and the fabric. Large companies may have their own departments. Sometimes an entire industry will have its own public relations program. The men's wear industry, for example, has used this method to promote the wearing of formal attire.

Fashion publications, trade magazines, and newspapers are an important part of the business. They stimulate interest in fashion, help in determining trends, and carry considerable weight in the final marketing of the merchandise.

CAREER OPPORTUNITIES

The growth of the apparel and textile industries and the retailing business means increased employment and career opportunities. The large companies realize that their continued expansion is dependent on trained, strong manpower to fill positions created by growth. They have established recruiting programs to meet those needs. Charles F. Myers, company chairman of the large textile firm, Burlington Industries, was

IS THE FASHION BUSINESS YOUR BUSINESS?

quoted in the *Daily News Record:* "A steady flow of young talent into our company is undoubtedly the most vital requirement for our continued growth and success."

Some large manufacturers and retailers give scholarship aid to individuals who seek higher education. Burlington Industries, under the auspices of the Burlington Industries Foundation, gives educational

loans, direct grants, and matched tuition as part of its education program. Abraham and Straus, the well-known department store, gives a 50 percent tuition refund to full-time employees taking a college business administration program.

Some companies offer summer trainee positions to young people interested in a career in this industry. The summer of 1968 saw a serious effort to establish retail internships in New York City to attract black college students into the industry. The Consumer Distribution Committee, comprising thirty department and specialty stores, national chain headquarters, and resident buying offices, in cooperation with the Retail Industry Affirmative Action Program of the New York City Commission on Human Rights, undertook this program. Thirty members of junior classes from ten predominantly Negro colleges in the South were recruited for meaningful summer training positions with the goal of developing future executives. The program was expanded for the summer of 1969 to forty students with nine more companies participating.

Career prospects match the growth of the fashion industry for those already in it, as well as for those the industry seeks to attract.

Chapter 3

Designing

CLOTHING protects and adorns us. The designer, then, must create apparel that is both functional and beautiful. The good designer is up with the times, behind the times, ahead of the times. He knows the problems and living conditions of the present day. He has studied and frequently researches for ideas from rich cultural periods of the past. He looks ahead to see trends in the future.

APPAREL DESIGN

Where does creating end and copying begin? Who are the originators? Who the copyists? What is new under the sun? Sometimes similar ideas appear simultaneously in far-flung places. There are cycles, too—broad shoulders, natural shoulder line, short skirts, long skirts, high waists, low waists—the fashion of thirty years ago is the fashion of tomorrow. The answer is not simple. For our purpose let us consider as a designer anyone who develops a "line" of garments to be shown to buyers or directly to customers. In many popular-priced lines the designer adapts higher-priced garments. Perhaps there is a change of collar, an adaptation of trimming or fabric. Even here there is judgment, selection required. At the other end is the highly individualized creative designer, experimenting, searching, initiating original ideas, even setting trends.

Sound principles of design apply to all garments and accessories. Originally designers concentrated on the woman's dress, coat, and suit, and the man's coat and suit. Now designers have entered every phase of the clothing industry. Opportunities beckon in these new areas where fewer experienced designers are available. Besides dresses, coats, and suits, we find corsets and brassieres, underwear, maternity clothes, sportswear and coordinates, blouses, skirts, swimwear, rainwear, snow wear, nightwear, knitted clothes, furs, men's shirts and sportswear, children's clothes, and all the accessories—hats, bags, shoes, belts, gloves, neckwear, embroidery. With good basic training and an open mind able to see design possibilities in any of these products, a beginner can approach the field with hope of finding a place.

For the men's wear industry, the late 1960's brought a lively new approach—some call it revolutionary. Wild color, new styles, the concept of the total wardrobe with special shirts to go with the new jackets were new to this industry. Well-known designers of women's wear, such as Pierre Cardin, Givenchy, Bill Blass, and Oleg Cassini, went into men's

wear designing with enthusiasm and now show their collections just as they do for women's wear. Although the man's tailored suit has not changed basically, even the most conservative manufacturers have added sports jackets to their lines. Certainly the changes in the men's sportswear field have opened the door for new ideas and more opportunities for designers.

New York is by far the largest center for designers. Here, too, the greatest number of designers seek jobs. Sometimes the very need for new designing blood and the dearth of available talent in other apparel centers may mean opportunities in those places.

Horizons are broader for those willing to consider opportunities wherever they occur. Many personal situations prevent relocating. Yet often the obstacle is mere habit or lack of interest in the world beyond one's home town. A young New York design student had the chance to work for a well-known Chicago manufacturer of foundation garments

Designing

as a trainee designer. It was a big decision to go that far from home. But on a trial basis during the college's work-in-industry period, she liked the job, liked foundation garments, liked Chicago. Equally important, the firm liked her. After graduation she returned to a permanent job with a bright future ahead.

Garment designers vary in methods they use. Usually the ideas are sketched and then worked out in either muslin or the fabric itself on a dressmaker form. Sometimes the pattern is made directly from the sketch. Some designers don't use a sketch but work directly on the dressmaker form or live model, draping, molding the fabric with the design evolving from that process. After the pattern is ready the fabric can be cut, draped, and sewn into the sample garment, fitted on the live model or dressmaker form. The designer studies it, checks it against the sketch or her original idea, adapts or changes where she thinks necessary. Then come practical discussions with the production department on costing and problems affecting the design when it goes through the mass production process.

Before all this, of course, comes the designer's "idea" stage, her research, shopping, fabric and trimming buying. The designer starts working on the line six months to a year before it appears in the stores. Typically, she designs four seasonal lines a year.

The beginner's job varies according to the designer's methods, the size of the firm and design room and the willingness on the part of the designer to train. The beginner may find she works better in one medium than another. Perhaps she prefers sketching to draping. The wise one will learn all methods and be flexible enough to adapt to the demands of different design departments. The functions of the design room may be broken down into several duties. In small houses one person may do them all; in larger ones, several may divide them.

Functions Performed in Apparel Designing

RESEARCH:

Search for ideas in museums, costume institutes, libraries, literature, old files of magazines from all countries.

STUDY THE MARKET:

Shop stores for ideas: to see what's selling; to get salespeople and customer reaction; to see competitors' products; to see what other price lines are showing.

Read trade publications: *Women's Wear Daily, Daily News Record,* specialized magazines for the industry branches.

IS THE FASHION BUSINESS YOUR BUSINESS?

Read fashion magazines.
Attend fashion shows.
Travel to fashion centers throughout the world.

SKETCH:
Trade sketch will include details of construction, i.e., darts, number of gores in skirts, type of sleeve.
Make rough sketches of ideas gleaned from museums, other sources of inspiration; of garments seen at fashion shows, shopping.
Make sketches of designer's finished garment and of completed line.

MODEL:
Model sample garment for designer before and after it is finished.
Model garments for manufacturer and buyers in showroom.

SELECT FABRICS AND TRIMMINGS:
Shop the fabric market.
See fabric and trimming salesmen at own office.
Order sample cuts for sample garments.

PREPARE THE SAMPLE GARMENT:
Cut the garment.
Drape and fit.
Make the pattern.
Sew the garment by machine.
Finish by hand as required.

ORGANIZE AND SUPERVISE THE DESIGN ROOM:
Train and supervise assistant, samplehands, other workers.
Plan and schedule work.

FIGURE COSTS:
Estimate cost of fabric, trimmings; number of operations to produce garment.
Estimate costs in relation to price ranges of garments produced.

WORK WITH THE PRODUCTION DEPARTMENT:
Work out problems of production in relation to the design of the garment.
Check duplicate garment. (A duplicate is the first copy of the sample garment produced in the factory.)

REQUIREMENTS FOR ENTERING THE APPAREL DESIGN FIELD

A good base would be a broad educational background in the arts, literature, history, psychology, sociology, communications. Specific train-

Designing

ing is essential in sketching, anatomy and figure proportions, draping, cutting, sewing, patternmaking, identification and use of fabrics.

You sew beautifully but "can't draw a straight line." Yet you *can* learn to sketch. You don't have to be an artist to put an idea on paper. A working or trade sketch can show your idea. It will include the pleats, placement of darts, waistline, neckline—all the details that make the design.

Your friend loves to sketch but doesn't know how to sew. She can learn the construction process—and must if she wants to be a designer. Inspiration often comes from draping the fabric; good fit from a good pattern. Both are essential elements in design.

Knowledge of all phases will better equip you to be a designer and to supervise a workroom. More job opportunities will be open to you, too, as a beginner. In a small place a designer may work alone, performing all the duties of the design room. At the other extreme is the largest children's dress manufacturer in the world with its staff of twenty-five designers. A typical design room has one designer with three or four workers helping her. A medium-sized New York firm making five separate lines of garments each season has four designers and a total of twenty-eight in the design workrooms. In a custom shop there is one designer. Some of the larger stores with custom departments employ as many as five designers.

READY-TO-WEAR DESIGN

By far the largest segment of the industry is the manufacture of ready-to-wear garments, from the inexpensive to the very high-priced brackets. Ready-to-wear manufacturers usually specialize in price line (such as $8.75–$14.75) and in type of garment, such as men's coats and suits, junior dresses, sportswear, foundation garments. For the most part four lines of garments are shown a year with the average manufacturer having thirty to sixty garments in each of his lines, though the large one may jump as high as two hundred. Spring and fall are the main seasons, although the resort line is extremely important as a style tester. Spring collections are shown in November, fall lines in May and early June. In September and October some manufacturers show their resort and holiday line and in January their summer numbers. These showings are the culmination of the designer's activity. The hustle and bustle of finishing the sample garments, of adjusting them to the models, of timing every-

IS THE FASHION BUSINESS YOUR BUSINESS?

thing to be ready for the showings is a hectic period affecting everyone in the design room.

These regular showings are important but there is much replacement, substitution, addition of numbers in each line. It's the designer's job to keep coming up with ideas. This is particularly true in the medium- and popular-priced lines. If a number doesn't sell, frequently it's pulled out and another substituted. "Who says a designer 'completes' her lines for the opening? I'm designing every day—not just for the season ahead but for right now," said a volume house designer.

Some young designers discover early a flair or interest for a particular kind of clothes. Perhaps it's cocktail gowns, sports clothes or children's wear. Many are glad to design any type of garment. Their interests are not highly specialized. Frequently a girl who thinks she wants only junior dresses finds a job designing children's wear or ladies' underwear and to her surprise likes it.

Certainly a specialized interest should be taken seriously. Unquestionably some design one type of garment more successfully than another. But overspecialization for one entering the field may limit his opportunities. With experience, as in any type of work, a certain amount of specialization is inevitable. The designer who has years of experience in a popular-priced dress house will find it much easier to get a job with good salary in a similar firm than in a high-priced line. Actually, a good designer can design a variety of garments. Proof lies with the custom designer, who frequently designs all the outergarments, undergarments, hats, and accessories for her customer. Some branches the neophyte may not even think of are seeking designers. Good design is important in foundation garments, children's wear, men's sport shirts, accessories as well as in chi-chi cocktail gowns. The beginner who is flexible, open to opportunities in various branches, may find her interests broaden and develop. She may discover that she likes to design clothes she hadn't considered—perhaps men's sport shirts, ladies' hats, belts.

The trainee may start as sketcher, model, draper, samplehand (she sews the first garment or sample of the design), assistant designer. She may assist in the showroom along with modeling and sketching. Some houses are willing to try a trained beginner as designer. Usually they make low-priced garments or have never had a designer before and want to experiment.

Rosenau Bros., a major producer of children's dresses, with its large design staff has had considerable experience with trainees. The firm has no formal training program. Degree of turnover and available space have

Designing

much to do with the timing of hiring. It looks for high school graduates who have had postgraduate training in apparel construction and art. The trainee assists an experienced designer in the huge modern Philadelphia plant. She cuts, sews, drapes, makes the pattern. Sometimes she shows

her own sketches and may be able to work them up herself. Gradually she is entrusted with work of her own. Then she is given better fabric to work with, can develop her sketch and have the pattern and sample garment made up without supervision.

CUSTOM DESIGN

The custom designer designs for the individual who wants (and can pay for) an exclusive garment created for her and fitted to her exact measurements. The custom designer may make one model for one customer. At most she will make a very few of the same design, each finished and fitted for a particular customer. Some garments are copies of the designs of famous European couturiers. The original garments are purchased from the couturier at a high price for this purpose. Expensive fabrics and high standards of workmanship add to the quality of the design.

In addition to small custom shops, there are high-fashion specialty stores that design exclusive collections each season, and custom departments in large specialty stores such as Henri Bendel, Bergdorf Goodman, Bonwit Teller, and Saks Fifth Avenue in New York. They display their collections in their own fashion shows given for their customers.

The custom designer may design all types of garments, or specialize, for example, in hats or gowns. In the men's clothing field the designer is a highly skilled tailor.

IS THE FASHION BUSINESS YOUR BUSINESS?

The beginner learns a great deal by observing the high standards of workmanship in the workroom and, as much as she can, the designer at work. She bastes, helps finish the garment mainly by hand. The high quality standards of the custom shop require more experience than would be needed in a ready-to-wear firm. Advancement is relatively slower, and pay relatively lower than in ready-to-wear. Yet for the person interested primarily in high fashion, who perhaps looks forward to having his own custom shop, this is excellent preparation. Experience gained here is good background for any branch of the design field.

PATTERN COMPANIES

Pattern companies design for the home sewer. Their designers are concerned—as are all fashion designers—with current trends in style, color, line, fabric. They must understand, or soon learn, something about pattern construction and fit. They must be able to interpret their ideas in practical ways that can be used by home sewers of different levels of ability. Some patterns will necessarily be more intricate and probably geared for an experienced sewer. Emphasis is always on designs that are not behind the current trend shown in retail ready-to-wear departments. The designer works with a sketch, sometimes with muslin, rarely with the fabric itself.

The design department of one well-known company produces 600 designs a year for its pattern magazine, published every two months, and for the pattern catalogue, which is revised every four months. The company's relatively small department in New York (a director, two designers, one draper, one expediter and scheduler) develops these designs, which are then produced in a large plant outside of New York.

The designer puts her ideas down in a rough sketch or croquis. (She may produce several before one is approved by the design director.) A free-lance artist illustrates the rough sketch. If it is an intricate design, the draper works it out in muslin before it is sent to the out-of-town plant, but in most cases the plant produces the pattern by interpreting the sketch alone.

The design department works closely with the art department to be sure that the final illustration clearly conveys the design to the reader. Important, too, is the relationship with the copy department, which writes instructions for use of the pattern.

Designing

A beginner with training can start as sketcher or patternmaker's assistant, working on the translation of idea into pattern.

THEATRICAL DESIGN

High standards are set for those wishing to enter the design field in theatre, ballet, opera, movies, or television. Required are not only skill in art and design, but specific knowledge of costume history and theatre techniques such as staging and lighting.

Applicants in this field must become members of the union, the United Scenic Artists of America (in California the costume designer must belong to The International Alliance of Theatrical Stage Employees). The union holds periodic examinations for those wishing to qualify. Applicants may, and should, take the exams over again if they do not pass. The union's committee on examinations revamps the requirements regularly. Usually there is a two-day exam, including a project that the applicant completes at home.

For the costume designer the examination will undoubtedly cover identification of historic periods of dress, regional clothes and folk costumes, knowledge of cutting and draping in period or modern clothes, and knowledge of fabrics and lighting. The costume designer gets an associate membership. The scenic designer meets additional requirements for full membership, including the requirements for costume design; he qualifies to work in both fields. Regardless of the number of openings, if an applicant passes the test he can become a union member. Union membership makes him eligible for a job and, once he's secured work on his own, guarantees standards of pay. Employers make their selections from the many union members who apply for the jobs. On the whole movies want established people with experience. A beginner will have to get experience elsewhere before getting into films. Minimum union rates in 1969 for a staff costume designer were $231 a week; for free lance $250; for motion picture features $390.25.

The union is the first to say that this is an overcrowded field with considerable unemployment and insecurity. On the positive side is the increased number of ballet companies, regional theatres, small theatre groups, off-Broadway and university theatres and summer stock. Simultaneously, union membership has grown, so competition for jobs is heightened.

There are many misconceptions of the costume designer's role in

IS THE FASHION BUSINESS YOUR BUSINESS?

television. Despite the glowing hopes of many, job opportunities are extremely limited. There is a relatively new category of employment, stylist, for those who work on TV commercials and are usually employed by advertising agencies (described more fully in Chapter 5).

Television designers, as in the other entertainment fields, must be members of the United Scenic Artists. Their task is unique because they're working for a "one-night stand," as well as for the electronic camera. It's a one-night stand because on live television a show is done just once. The clothes are more frequently rented or borrowed than designed, due to time and budget limits. It's the designer's job to select or design the clothes that are worn on the shows. He works with members of the cast, wardrobe handlers, producers, directors, manufacturers, stores, sponsors' agencies. He meets rigid deadlines and tight budgets. He's tactful even when it hurts—when the star is tired or forgets her lines and suddenly wants a different gown. His skill in handling temperament is as important (maybe more) than his ability to select and fit the dress. He's a good businessman, a good bargainer, too. He rushes from the studio to a costume house to a manufacturer's showroom to a rehearsal. He may work some nights each week.

A staff designer may be responsible for three or four shows a week—for which he sometimes gets screen credit. For each show he attends the "concept" meeting, where general ideas and story highlights are discussed. Then he reads the script and prepares a costume budget to be presented at a "production" meeting about two weeks before the show is scheduled. After the cost estimate is approved (probably cut!), he interviews the cast at rehearsal, finding out each member's interpretation of the role he's to play. Does the actor feel his part has cynical overtones? Will he be somber or gay?

If it's a period piece calling for costumes, the designer arranges to take the actors to a costume house. There he selects costumes, arranges for any changes, and supervises each fitting. When the budget allows, he may design the costume, choose the fabric, color, and trimmings, and have the costume house make it up from his sketch. He does no cutting or sewing, but he must understand construction so that if it doesn't fit he'll know what's wrong and can have it adjusted.

Most modern clothes and accessories are borrowed from stores and manufacturers who are given screen credit for this. Sometimes actors will wear their own clothes. The expediting of this, collecting and returning the garments by bonded messengers, is handled by the secretary and clerk.

Designing

The designer is there for the "run-through," the rehearsal before the dress rehearsal, to fit the garments and to show the actors how to wear them to best advantage. Then he goes into the control room to check his costumes on "monitor" (on the screen), observing the effect of the color and fabric under the lighting. Always the background of the story is in his mind. Perhaps it's the star's most important scene. She is against a dark background. Her dress must blend and yet give proper contrast. The policeman's badge is too shiny. The designer asks the wardrobe handler to wax it to remove the glare. He is there through dress rehearsal, always taking notes, ready to make changes. He stays during the director's final orders, and right up to air time, perhaps until the show is on.

One major network has only three full-time staff designers, another has six. In addition, free-lance designers are hired for particular shows by the network or directly by the sponsor.

The costume designer must be prepared for some periods of unemployment. A well-established designer said he had met unemployment periods in the past by selling fabric and wallpaper designs. Others take temporary jobs in quite unrelated work. Those who want this field must be as dedicated as actors, whose drive for the theatre far outweighs their need for security.

The beginner must face the limitations, but if he is dedicated and motivated, he can have a career in theatrical design. Courses in fashion design, draping, costume history, art history, drama, theatre arts, scenic design, and lighting are the base. Some of this he can study on his own. Beginners will have to gain experience in non-union jobs—in summer stock, off-Broadway theatres, small ballet companies. The salaries will be small, sometimes merely board and room. But they are showcases for the young designer determined to get into the field. He will get credits, besides experience. And the experience is excellent, often broader than costume designing alone.

He should read all the publications that tell of new shows, ballets, operas, and summer theatres. The Leo Shull Publications include an annual directory of summer theatres and the weekly paper *Show Business*, which lists all the new productions that are coming up. A similar paper is *Back Stage* and, of course, the well-known *Variety*.

Persistence and ability to work well with people are as important as talent in this highly competitive field.

TEXTILE DESIGN

The textile designer's duties differ somewhat from the garment designer's, since he is concerned with the finished fabric rather than the garment. Again, specialization of function varies with size of company.

Color, in the opinion of many, is the most important element in textile design. A leading designer in this field credits his reputation primarily to the imagination he's used with color. He introduced pastels upon pastels, a combination that surprised many. Yet it caught on, he said, because the shades were "right." Then, before people tired of it, he shifted to dashing colors. The same design with different colors has new elements.

In general most textile designers make a "croquis": an original sketch, the design motif. They match colors, make color combinations, and mix paints. They put their designs in "repeat," i.e., plan out the design for reproduction by tracing the original croquis and repeating it so that the engraver can put the paper on standard-size copper cylinders for reproduction in volume.

The textile designer for woven woolen fabrics may do his designing on a loom, weaving a sample cloth from strands of wool instead of painting the design on paper. The weaver designer must understand the possibilities and limitations of the power looms that will produce the designs in quantity in the mill. Similarly, the knitwear designer must be aware of and challenged by the knitting machines. Part of the knitwear designer's training period will be spent at the mill studying the machines. Both fields have shown sudden growth in recent years. Knitwear has become a major fabric in all apparel areas.

The textile artist may work for a textile design studio specializing in creating designs for textile converters, or for the textile converter or as a free-lance artist.

An increasing number of textile converters have their own studios, although most still buy at least half their designs from outside studios. The converter finds it expensive to maintain a studio large enough to satisfy all the design needs.

The textile design studios defy the trend toward bigness. They find it more economical now to be smaller. Undoubtedly, too, the increase in size and number of converters' studios has had its effect. One well-known studio with sixteen artists today is considered good-sized. The owner told

Designing

me that several years ago he would have had to maintain a staff of forty to be one of the large ones. He supplements his staff with twelve experienced free-lance artists who do mainly repeats.

The free-lance textile artist may sell his work to the textile converter and to the textile design studio. He may sell an original design, or an original design put into repeat as well, or the original design, the repeat, and colorings, too. The studio may ask only for repeats or for colorings for designs already created by the art department.

Functions of the Textile Designer

STUDY THE MARKET:

Shop fabric, garment, and home-furnishings markets and stores to see what's selling.

Read trade publications and fashion magazines.

Attend fashion shows of garments and fabrics.

Discuss needs and ideas with garment designers.

RESEARCH:

Search for ideas in museums, art galleries, libraries, old files of magazines from all countries.

Travel, to explore past and present ideas that can be adapted to fabrics.

ORIGINATE IDEAS FOR DESIGN:

Make croquis for printed, woven, woolen, cotton, silk, synthetic fabrics and for plastics.

Draw motifs of figures, florals, geometrics, etc.

Use any of the following media and tools to execute ideas: ruling pen, triangles, T-squares, brushes, tempera paints, dyes, inks, crayons, pencils, weaving by handloom.

COLOR:

Mix and match colors.

Make new color combinations.

Select colors.

REPEAT:

Plan the design for reproduction by tracing the original croquis and repeating it so that the engraver can put the paper on standard-size copper cylinders for reproduction in volume.

ORGANIZE AND SUPERVISE THE DESIGN STUDIO:

Train and supervise colorists, repeat artists, originators.

WORK WITH THE MERCHANDISING AND PROMOTION DEPARTMENTS:

Interpret and adapt ideas in relation to merchandising and promotion.

FIGURE COSTS:

Select color and motifs in relation to cost of reproduction and to the fabric price-line.

WORK WITH THE REPRODUCTION DEPARTMENT (MILL, PRINTING SERVICE, ETC.):

Check on reproduction of design at mill or reproduction plant. See "strike offs," the sample cuts of the original designs, to evaluate reproduction of color.

Work out other color combinations from the strike offs.

REQUIREMENTS FOR ENTERING THE TEXTILE DESIGN FIELD

Essential elements are a sense of color and the ability to draw. A broad educational background in the arts, literature, history, psychology, and sociology will provide a sound base. Specialized art training can develop drawing ability and use of color. The student's training should develop his creativity and also his ability to project his ideas into practical channels. Recommended are courses in fine-arts painting, flower painting, textile design, fabric identification.

TEXTILE DESIGN STUDIO

The textile design studio usually works on a wide range of designs for men's, women's, and children's garments, for draperies and furniture coverings, rugs, shower curtains, wallpaper. In some studios an artist may specialize—in draperies, for example—either because he has a flair, or because a large demand for that type of work from the studio requires specialization. In most studios each artist works on a variety of designs.

The beginner frequently starts as colorist, mixing color combinations, painting the penciled designs of the repeat artist. Gradually he learns to plan and lay out the design, to put it in repeat. He works mainly with his paint brush but uses a ruling pen and other types of pens and crayons. He may work on very small motifs where neatness and accuracy are stressed, or on larger designs where he can be "free" rather than "tight." Probably he will work on both. All beginners enjoy "originating," painting an original idea or croquis. He may get a chance to do originals at the beginning or, more likely, he'll work up to it after he has developed skill in handling color.

Designing

The pace is considered faster than in the converter's studio. The textile design studio must work quickly to meet the converter's need, to adapt and change the original croquis. Actually, converters' studios face similar pressures; theirs come directly from the stylists, designers, and piece-goods buyers who use the finished fabric.

The head designer may do little or no painting himself. He will suggest ideas, evaluate the work of his staff and supervise the studio. An important function is seeing the stylists from the converters to find out the designs they want and to sell his designs. He will be aware of current trends, and develop designs accordingly. The Oriental influence may be strong. He suggests to his originators that they work up something resembling saris. The studio's reference library and museums may stimulate them in planning the designs. Over half of all the original croquis must be redone or changed to meet customers' reactions. The same artist usually works through on the same design until it is completed.

TEXTILE CONVERTER'S STUDIO

The textile converter's studio performs the same functions, frequently with less time on original designs. Some converters specialize, perhaps in fabrics for drapery or for men's wear in woolens, cottons, silks, or synthetics. Their studios design for the specialty.

Other converters make fabrics for many end uses. If the studio is small, the artists will work on designs for them all. In larger studios there may be several departments, such as men's wear synthetics, men's wear cottons, women's sportswear, children's wear, draperies. An artist will be assigned to one department.

The department head is usually called a stylist who, like the head of the textile design studio, may not do any painting. He suggests ideas to his staff, supervises the work, and works with the merchandise department to plan the types of designs needed. If a textile artist assists the stylist, he may visit the textile mill where the fabric is processed to see the "strike off," the sample cut of the original design and repeat. Is the color right? Are the motifs clear? The responsibility here is like that of the garment designer who works closely with the factory to check on the duplicate garment. We will discuss styling in more detail in another chapter.

Later in the present chapter, the story of a young stylist will describe his development from the rank of textile artist.

Size of converters' studios varies from the small one with one designer or stylist and one assistant, to one of the world's largest, M. Lowenstein & Sons, Inc., with a studio staff of over 150 in New York City and 10 in Paris.

Opportunities for textile designers are highly concentrated in New York. More may develop in California, and perhaps other areas, too, as they become better known as apparel centers.

EARNINGS

Salaries run the gamut from $4,000 to $40,000 a year, with a few topflight designers soaring even higher. The low end, of course, is for the beginner, the trainee. Trainee salaries usually fall within the $4,000–$7,000 category, while the majority of experienced designers are in the $9,000–$15,000 bracket. Designers in the top brackets frequently have responsibilities beyond designing, in styling and coordinating and even in over-all administration of the business. Bonuses are given by many firms, usually at Christmas, based on profits or the employer's goodwill.

JOB TURNOVER

Does the Seventh Avenue designer have to look for a new job each season? No. Despite seasonality, large numbers of designers are employed all year round. Some small manufacturers will hire a designer for one season only. If the designer's line was successful, perhaps he'll be called back for the next season.

Manufacturers who want just a shot in the arm will hire a free-lance designer to add a few numbers to the line. Most designers find that insecurity and uncertainty outweigh the variety and freedom that accompany these jobs. For those who want the freedom that comes with free lancing there are some advantages. Free lancing is not for beginners, either in apparel or textile design.

The beginning years in any field of work are usually associated with job turnover. To explore this, we studied the three-year postgraduate record of a series of Fashion Institute of Technology classes. During the first three years out of school, one out of every four graduates remained on the same job he'd had at graduation. Most of the group (two-thirds) had held one, two, or three jobs. The rest (one-third) had had four or

Designing

more jobs. The majority (two-thirds of the group) had had no unemployment during the three years.

WHO ARE THEY?

The picture comes alive when we meet the people at work. Why did they select this field? What was their preparation? What are their jobs really like? Let me introduce you to some of them.

E.B. / Designer of Junior Dresses

It was always fashion. She edited a fashion column for the high school paper, devoured fashion magazines, made her own clothes. She knew she had taste, feeling for color. After her high school graduation, the family moved from a New York suburb to the Midwest. E.B. sold better dresses in a department store, modeled them in fashion shows, helped in the advertising department. A year later the family was back in New York. E.B. knew clearly what she wanted—to be a fashion designer.

But taste and determination weren't enough. How was she to get into a design room? She headed for manufacturers' showrooms. Slim and petite, she was a good junior model. She got jobs—but for months it was one job after another.

Finally she clicked in a sportswear house. Soon the boss let her sell in the showroom as well as model. After a year, he sent her to the stores to select high-fashion merchandise that could be adapted. He liked her taste, gave her a chance to work for his designer. Finally—E.B. was in the design room!

The designer liked E.B.'s ideas and color sense, and when she left to take a job at a junior house, she took E.B. along as assistant. E.B. had learned a lot in the three and a half years with the sportswear firm. She liked her new job, learned the jobs of the workers in the design room, and also learned some of the problems of supervising it. In six months she was offered a chance to design for a large firm making medium-priced junior dresses. It was a big step. She leaped for it.

She had spent five and a half years of related work getting closer to her goal. The business end, cost and merchandising, she had learned from her boss; dress construction from her design room. After three years at this job, at age twenty-six, there are still gaps in her technical knowledge of construction, where she has to rely on others. Although she knew how to make her own clothes, it wasn't professional. She learned how to make a dropped shoulder from those who worked for her. He art background and interests have stood her in good stead. She wishes she had also studied cutting, draping, and especially patternmaking. Now there's no time.

"Most beginners," she says, "don't realize there's a business involved. You can't say I'm going to make this dress just because it's pretty."

When you face the production department, you talk costs. Can this style be produced at this price line? On the other hand, sometimes a designer "has to get a dress out of her system." She thinks it won't sell, or costs too much to produce, but she wants to see it so much that finally she makes it. Generally it won't go on the line.

Out of 350 samples that E.B. made for the fall line, 200 were finally selected—and the selection rested mainly on her slim shoulders. Fall and summer are her main lines, but with a spring line, holiday line, and some transitional cottons for in between, she's designing at a fast pace all the time.

E.B. starts her line usually six months before delivery to the stores. She may spend two weeks doing research on color and silhouette. She has an extensive library at home of past and present copies of fashion magazines from here and abroad. She shops the stores to see the competition, the better price lines, what's selling. Ideas come from a flash of color in a movie, from museums, from buyers' comments and suggestions. The fabric itself is one of her main sources of ideas. Fabric and trimming selection is an important part of the job. About 80 percent of the fabrics in her lines is her own selection.

Her design room *must* work to keep up the flow of sample garments. A sketcher, cutter, patternmaker, finisher keep them rolling. Until recently she's had an assistant to supervise the design room and to drape. But she finds that a young assistant wants to design, too. E.B.'s the designer and doesn't want help in this. Result—turnover. Now she's trying it without one, even though it means more work for her.

The sketcher works out construction details, makes a finished sketch from E.B.'s rough one or from her idea draped on the dummy. The sketch goes to the patternmaker. If he thinks it necessary, part or all of the garment is draped. But often he can make his pattern directly from the sketch. The pattern is swatched with fabric and sketch, the garment is cut and sewed, then fitted on a live model. The fitting is very impor-

Designing

'tant. Then E.B. frequently makes changes that are incorporated into the pattern and sample garment.

Her line includes some "rehashes," good numbers from last year with small style changes, the main changes being in fabric or color. Instead of making a sample garment first, she may send the sketch and fabric for the rehash directly to one of her company's many factories, all outside of New York.

A duplicate, the first factory copy, is made for every garment. E.B. checks the duplicates before the "markers" are made. In the factory, the pattern parts are laid out on a paper of the same dimensions as the cloth to be cut. The pattern outlines are transferred to this paper, usually with a tracing wheel that cuts perforations along the outlines. This piece of paper is the "marker." It is placed on the layers of cloth ready for the cutter. From the markers, cuttings are made for volume production.

Her biggest thrill is to see a buyer or fashion editor wearing one of her dresses. Another is to have a dress selected for a magazine cover. She's had covers on *Seventeen* and *Glamour*. She's beginning to get some editorial mention in the magazines. Soon she hopes to see the firm's ads say "designed by E.B." This is one of the tangible steps in recognition. All that's the icing.

But it's hard work and plenty of strain. The toughest part is "contending with everyone": with the sensitive, older workers in her design room; with the machine-minded, cost-conscious production department; with the buyer who, "like the customer, is always right." Firmly she believes that since they all must work together, she can't afford to be temperamental. Those designers who think they're conferring favors by being nice to fabric and trimming salesmen have a poor attitude, she says. "We both need each other. Nobody is doing anyone a favor by being nice. It's just businesslike."

She feels the strain of competition. "A designer is only as good as her last dress." She can't slide along; she's always on her toes. She may get to work as late as 10 or 10:30 but frequently will stay till 8. Her husband's work requires irregular hours. They're sure only of Sunday together, snatch hours here and there during the week.

Her starting salary has mounted rapidly, along with her bonus, in these three years. With her bonus she's making no less than $25,000 a year. Her dream to be a designer doesn't match the reality. She had not anticipated the business problems, the tensions. But she likes the reality. She tries to hang on to some of her dreams; it's part of being creative.

Her job is always with her. Although she could have a longer vacation, she never takes more than two weeks. "I don't want to be away too long —can't tell what will happen."

M.K. / Designer of Junior Dresses

M.K. says a good break can be painful. When she broke her ankle skiing, her boss didn't want her back until the cast was off. She hobbled to another job. There she advanced from samplehand to assistant designer. For years she'd prepared for this goal.

Even before high school she thought of the work she wanted to do. The family was far from well-off. Her father was dead, her mother worked in the millinery industry. She didn't think she'd like clerical or secretarial work. She'd liked making paper doll-clothes, then real dresses for her dolls, finally clothes for herself. Besides, she thought this field paid more money than office work.

She selected a high school where she studied costume design, learned patternmaking and garment construction. Upon graduation she felt ready to work as helper in a design room, even as a samplehand. It was time, she thought, to earn money.

But her mother encouraged her to continue her schooling as better preparation towards her goal of designer. She went to the Fashion Institute of Technology, majored in apparel design. She particularly enjoyed such academic subjects as psychology and sociology. "They broadened my outlook, helped in my personality development." History of civilization opened her eyes to the world of painting. Museum work stimulated her. Since graduation she's taken evening courses in oil painting and literature.

She had six jobs in her first two and a half years in industry. Her first—as samplehand for a children's dress manufacturer—persuaded her to go into junior dresses, always her preference. After that she managed to find jobs as samplehand in "missy" and junior houses. Only once, for a month, did she get a chance to design. Her boss said, "You'll never make a designer."

She moved from a job when she felt she'd learned as much as possible or if she didn't like it. For one year she worked under an assistant designer, sewing the sample together. In the other places the designer had no assistant, so M.K. cut, draped, and made the pattern, as well as sewed the sample.

She regrets not one moment of this period: today, she is never at a

Designing

loss to show her assistant or samplehand how to do something. She learned a great deal from the many designers, the difference, too, between a good and bad design room. Her experience was growing.

She stayed put in the popular-priced junior dress firm that hired her after she broke her ankle. Promotion to assistant designer came in a few months. She considered this a big step. As assistant designer, she supervised the workroom and also cut, draped, and made patterns. She learned to plan and organize the work of others, not just her own. The year and a half as assistant was invaluable. She learned to run an efficient design room.

Then the designer left, and M.K. got the job. Behind her were six years of specialized schooling, experience as samplehand and assistant designer. She felt well prepared for this next step. She enjoyed designing, liked her workroom, and for the next year and a half stayed on as designer.

But there were disadvantages. She felt underlying tensions, with one person played off against another. She knew her work was satisfactory but didn't feel recognized. Her boss introduced her to buyers as his sketcher, not as his designer. "If something went wrong, it was my fault. But he took credit for the good things. He was all. I was nothing." His partner, the production man, was leaving to set up his own business in the same line. He asked M.K. to come along as his designer. She knew she was taking a chance but she was challenged. Most important, she liked and respected this man, felt she would enjoy working for him.

A year later she's convinced she made the right move. Sometimes it's hectic, with lots of pressure, but she doesn't mind it. No underlying tensions here. People work together. This new firm is one of the many small producers in the industry. A staff of twenty includes those in the showroom, in the design room, in the cutting room. They sell mainly through central buying and resident buying offices to specialty and department stores throughout the country. A contractor gets the cut goods and the patterns and sews the garments.

The owner works closely with everyone. The atmosphere is casual and friendly but M.K. is "Miss K." The boss thought that degree of formality added dignity to her job. She likes it. She is, and feels like, a designer.

Her design room produces about five hundred sample garments a year. If a number doesn't sell well, it's withdrawn and another substituted. The firm emphasizes cottons, averaging ten samples a week. A spring line starts with sixty-five or seventy dresses, although there are additions and substitutions. In preparation, M.K. and her boss look at fabrics in

July. She starts her samples in August, and buyers see them in October. She shops the stores carefully, reads *Women's Wear Daily* and fashion magazines, keeps a file of dress ads sent by a clipping service, attends fashion shows. Frequently she gets ideas from a better-price line. But the finished garment is her own. Never does she take a "rub off" (make an exact copy).

M.K. sketches her ideas and sometimes drapes on the figure to clarify what she wants. Her assistant takes the sketches, and drapes, cuts, makes the muslin patterns, and gives the garments to the three samplehands for sewing. The assistant had been a good samplehand, but it took a while for M.K. to train her to keep the flow of work going for the design room. M.K. welcomes ideas from her assistant, talks over all her designs with her.

If the boss likes the dress and decides to put it in production, M.K. works with the patternmaker to be sure the fit is right before the factory pattern is sent to the contractor.

Experience has taught her many of the production problems. Now she can figure approximately the number of garments that can be made from 1,500 yards of fabric. Sometimes a design must be changed or discarded if there is too much wastage when the material is laid out for the cutters. This happens frequently with plaids and stripes. When she can anticipate this, she may save one of her designs. Adding a seam may save material because of the way the pattern will be placed. Although her boss takes care of costing, she has a working knowledge of it.

Sometimes it's hard to please everyone: salesman, buyer, patternmaker. A low moment is when a buyer points patronizingly at a dress: "That's nice, but something's wrong, I don't know what." She's not really a pusher, but sometimes she has to push, tactfully, to get her ideas across. Her boss used to pop into the design room, discourage her from finishing a dress if he didn't like it. She had to convince him that she should complete a shirtwaist dress that later became one of their best sellers.

One of the joys is seeing her dresses being worn. She enjoys the freedom of her job, the respect and recognition her boss gives her, and the satisfaction of having achieved her goal. If business is good, she thinks she may get a bonus too. Her hopes lie with the future of the firm. She expects to grow with it.

She's twenty-seven, lives at home with her mother. She hopes to marry, would work until she had children. Then, with a well-organized workroom, her knowledge of the line and an understanding boss, she

Designing

might be able to work out a part-time or free-lance arrangement. That sounds like a well-rounded life to her.

N.W. / Designer of Children's Coats and Snowsuits

N.W. was bounced on his honeymoon. A letter of dismissal, no explanation. (The firm was going out of business.) Two years later the memory still hurts. But he thinks it speeded up his climb to designer.

Once he wanted to be a doctor. But at the Bronx High School of Science his interest flagged—and so did his marks. Sketching women's clothes, just a hobby, became more important. He heard stories of Seventh Avenue from his mother, a sewing machine operator, and from his cousin, a dress manufacturer. A fashion designer's job and salary sounded glamorous. Why not for him? He couldn't sew nor was he sure his sketches were good, but perhaps he could learn.

After graduation he was accepted at the Fashion Institute of Technology as a major in apparel design. He studied art, sketching, figure proportions, garment design and construction, patternmaking, draping, sewing, history of civilization, fabric identification, psychology, sociology, English, and attended regular classes at the Costume Institute of the Metropolitan Museum of Art. He enjoyed those two years, had a satisfactory but not outstanding record, when he graduated.

Then came nine months of one temporary job after another. He was a hand cutter on ladies' robes, a trainee embroidery designer, assistant designer (he did cutting and draping) in a custom house, designer of infants' coats, assistant patternmaker on children's sportswear.

It was a period of learning, worry, self-doubts.

Next came a job as grader on children's dresses. The factory patternmaker was his boss. N.W. worked out the master patterns in all the sizes needed. He'd had a little grading in college, and an additional evening course. He liked this job, learned from the patternmaker and began to make some patterns himself. Gradually his salary was increased in the two years before the fatal letter reached him on his honeymoon.

Three weeks of unemployment ended when he answered a *Women's Wear Daily* ad for children's coat designer and was hired. He made the first pattern from the sketch-designer's sketch. Frequently he adapted the sketches, incorporating changes through the pattern that improved the fit without losing the spirit of the design. He considered himself a patternmaker because he did not originate the idea for the design. But he could see why the boss called him designer. The fit, flair, detail of the coat, so essential to the styling, depends on the pattern. This is the basis of design in men's tailored clothing too.

The first six weeks the head cutter helped him become acquainted with the large file of master patterns of this forty-year-old firm. Where a sleeve or collar pattern could be used again, it saved the patternmaker's and grader's time and the boss's money. His skill, confidence, salary mounted. He'd asked for a reasonable salary to start. The boss shocked him by paying twenty dollars a week more than he had requested.

When he left at the end of a year and nine months he had a contract with a much higher salary. When a sketch-designer who made her own patterns was hired, N.W. became a grader. His salary was the same, but he felt it was a step down the ladder, so he left after working out an amicable contract settlement with the boss.

"Young designer—children's coats" was his ad in *Women's Wear Daily*. A children's coat and snowsuit manufacturer answered it, gave him a three-month trial designing snowsuits. The trial period was successful. He has a new six-month contract, with a sizable increase in salary. Here he is the designer, responsible for the idea, the sketch, the pattern, the sample garment.

When he graduated from college he knew he wanted to be a designer but didn't care about any one field. Now, four and a half years after graduation, he expects to stay in the coat industry because he likes it, and because he has developed patternmaking skill, so important in coats, and thinks it will pay off. He'd expect to compromise on salary if he tried another branch. He likes his present job, hopes that this is "it" for a long time to come.

A staff of six maintains the New York office, showroom, and design room. A seventy-machine factory in Pennsylvania produces the medium-priced children's coats and snowsuits. They sell to stores throughout the country, from style-conscious Lord & Taylor in New York to I. Magnin in San Francisco.

N.W. starts his designs almost a year before they'll be in the stores. Regularly he reads *Women's Wear Daily, Harper's Bazaar, Vogue*, an ad clipping service. The line of a woman's dress, or the trimming on a blouse, may suggest ideas that can be adapted to a child's snowsuit or coat. He buys trimmings. His boss buys fabrics and works out total production costs. They discuss N.W.'s sketch; then N.W. makes the pattern, drapes the muslin on the dummy, fits and adjusts the pattern. He cuts the garment, and the samplemaker sews it for N.W. to fit on

Designing

the figure. When four or five samples are finished, he shows them to his boss, who selects the one he likes and perhaps wants one style made up in other fabrics and color combinations. He makes up these samples, adds new ones, turns out five or six sample coats a week. All his experience and training has helped. The embroidery experience has been a source of ideas for trimming the snowsuits and coats. He buys embroidery from his former employer. Most important has been the patternmaking.

"No, it's not glamorous; it's work—but my kind of work, I like it." He feels creative, he's achieved something he was working towards. He likes the friendly relationship with his boss, he likes his salary and his air-conditioned workroom. The tough times are when his ideas seem to dry up. It's almost as hard when the ideas come too fast and he has to sift them. Always there's the strain of wondering if his designs will catch on.

It's a strain, yes, but he finds it challenging. For the future he wants most to be recognized in the field as a good designer. He says this can come only through hard work and consistent acceptance of his lines. Perhaps some day he will have his own firm. He's twenty-four years old. There's time. The present needs his full attention. This six months is critical. Will his line sell?

E.D. / Designer of Children's Dresses

E.D.'s family took her to their native Sweden when she was a baby, returned to this country when she was eleven. She was growing by leaps and bounds—five feet ten inches when she was twelve. Nothing fit her. She says she *had* to make her own clothes. And she liked it. Her aunt, a village seamstress in Sweden, had taught her to sew when she was seven, and E.D. had a naturally good color sense.

She picked the high school where her best friend was going. Subject matter was frankly secondary. But she liked her major in costume design, learned sketching, draping, patternmaking. A teacher steered her toward further training at the Fashion Institute of Technology. Her two-year college major in apparel design convinced her that she wanted to be a designer, although her interest was not pinpointed to any branch. She won a prize in a children's wear contest, and spent a required college work period at a children's dress manufacturer. After graduation, she went right back to the same job and has been there ever since.

She can think of no better future than remaining here for as long as

IS THE FASHION BUSINESS YOUR BUSINESS?

she works. Yes, she likes designing children's dresses, but even more important are her thoughtful, considerate bosses, the encouragement and good training the head designer gave her from the start. "I was lucky to find a job I liked at the beginning." Lots of times there are pressures, deadlines to meet, fabrics not delivered when she needs them, but they're easily absorbed because the people are nice, atmosphere relaxed. Difficulties seem minor, satisfactions high. She is proud of the strides made by this progressive firm in the five years she has been there. Instead of one designer there are now four with a total of twenty-eight in the design rooms, making five separate lines. Spacious, colorful offices, showrooms and workrooms are the last word in modern comfort and elegance. Factories outside of New York produce dresses that sell in the stores for $1.98, $2.98, $3.98.

She was twenty when she started as an assistant to the designer. Her designer respected and complied with E.D.'s request to start off at the sewing machine, assembling the sample garment. Although she had learned the steps in college, she felt she lacked the practical knowledge of industry's standards. This she could get best by doing.

Still on her work period from college she started to design dresses under the designer's excellent guidance. She sketched, made the pattern, cut the garment, gave it to the samplehand for sewing. Two years later the firm introduced a new line, size 7-14 dresses, with E.D. as designer. Soon came her own samplehand and an assistant.

The three of them work together in a pleasant design room. E.D. doesn't feel like a boss, although she takes her responsibility seriously. She talks everything over with her assistant, who designs as much as E.D. does. She starts planning nine months to a year before the garments will be in the stores. She reads *Women's Wear Daily, Infants' and Children's Review, Tot 'n' Teen,* fashion magazines; she shops the stores to see what's being shown for children, for teen-agers and adults.

E.D. and her assistant work out rough plans for fabrics, styles, number of dresses in each price line. Then she and her boss, the president of the company, go over the plans, with frequent suggestions for style and fabric coming from him. Fabric shopping is next. Salesmen come to her, and she goes to converters—sometimes alone, or with the boss and head designer whom she used to assist. She can decide herself on a sample cut (a five-yard piece she makes into a sample garment). She may see designs on paper even before they are made into the fabric. If she wants a design "confined" (made up just for her firm) she discusses this with her boss and perhaps with the stylist who works with all departments.

Designing

Then she's back in her workroom. First comes her sketch, then the pattern. She works with the "sloper," the firm's master cardboard pattern that meets government standard sizes. Slopers are used for standard armholes and shoulder lines. For any variations, like a dropped shoulder or raised waistline, or full skirt, she makes her own patterns. She cuts the fabric, sometimes drapes on a figure, has the samplehand sew it.

Costing comes next. She takes her sketch showing construction details, along with her fabric and trimming swatches, to the cost clerk. He figures whether this style with these operations, this price fabric and trim, can be made for the price line she wants. When this system was introduced, E.D. secretly resented it. But now she's used to it, finds it practical. Sometimes it's frustrating to have to give up her design because it costs too much, but surprisingly often she makes changes to reduce the cost.

After a week she shows some finished samples to the boss and stylist. The stylist may suggest pushing certain colors or fabrics. E.D. prefers this early selection to waiting until all her samples are finished. As selections are made, she plans the rest of her line with more organization. Does she need more plaids, more for the $3.98 line? A duplicate room on the premises makes up three duplicate garments of each sample accepted in a second color combination, sometimes a third.

Exclusive of fabric selection, it takes eight weeks to complete the line. But she's busy designing all the time, adding to the line. She's responsible for four lines—fall, holiday, spring, summer. Approximately forty dresses are in each line although she makes up many more. Although she hears of the good and bad sellers, she's not too close to the buying and selling.

Now twenty-five, her five years on the same job find her comfortable, relaxed, secure. "This isn't just a job; it's fun," she says. Her starting salary is now three and a half times larger. It means much to her that she never had to ask for a raise. Perhaps she could get more money at another job. Some of her friends earn more. "But I'm not money-mad; this is a decent salary and the main thing is I like it here."

Recently E.D. married an aeronautical engineer. It took a while to get used to combining housekeeping and a job (they have a four-and-a-half-room apartment). She gets up at 5:45 a.m., because her husband must be at work at 8. Her job is from 9:30 to 5. Now she manages to keep both jobs rolling with considerable help from her husband and the miracle of frozen foods.

E.J. / Model and Sketcher

E.J. got the job on her birthday. Does that make it special? Or is it the smallness of the place, the chance to make her own job, the variety of her duties? Perhaps it's because the owners make her feel part of everything, ask her opinion, let her sit in on conferences about design, fabric, promotion. Or maybe it's the chance to work next to the well-known French designer who designs the firm's line in Paris but comes to New York twice a year for final fittings. All of it has underlined her interest in fashion, pointed her goal to staying with this firm, learning more about high fashion. That's a specific enough aim, she says.

As a little girl she liked copying pictures from magazines and newspapers. Later on she enjoyed the fashion magazines and was interested in clothes, although she never sewed. In high school she took art along with her academic subjects, learned something about illustrating and interior decorating. At Fashion Institute of Technology she did well in art, fairly well in draping, patternmaking, and construction; and she loved the visits to the Costume Institute of the Metropolitan Museum of Art.

During her college work-in-industry period she worked for a housecoat manufacturer. She sketched, draped, made the pattern, cut. Enthusiastically she worked up many sketches for new designs. To her great disappointment few were accepted. They used only standard styles—straight lines, peter pan collars. The firm's designer resented her, tried to hold her down. She was discouraged but more aware of the facts of life in industry. Came graduation, a summer vacation, then the call on her birthday to see her present employer about a job.

The firm makes women's coats, suits, and ensembles that sell in exclusive stores throughout the country for $100–$300. The staff of eighteen includes office and showroom personnel and ten highly skilled workers in the "inside" shop adjoining the showroom where the garments are made. She was hired as model and sketcher and to help out on other things. Finding and developing "other things" has been one of the main parts of the job. She likes to be busy. The only time the work becomes monotonous for her is when it's slow and there aren't enough "other things" to do.

Within a few days she was helping the bookkeeper who soon decided she had a new assistant. E.J. wanted to stay friends with the bookkeeper but began to look around for other fill-in jobs. She found that she could

Designing

be useful keeping records of incoming orders, making out cutting tickets in the factory. To her surprise she liked this, found that she was becoming familiar with style numbers, fabric sources, customers. The factory boss was pleased, managed to keep her busy in her spare time there, instead of bookkeeping.

She has learned much about garment construction from the highly skilled factory workers, has learned selling and office procedures from others. She respects the other workers, was careful to get this attitude over, and thinks it eliminated resentment they might have felt. "I'm the youngest, least experienced here. They can teach me." Perhaps it's helped to make her part of everything that goes on.

She keeps a sketch book with sketch, style number, fabric of each style for permanent reference. It takes about a month to sketch the completed line, spending about two hours a day on it.

E.J. models throughout the year. (She's 5′10″ without shoes, weighs 135 pounds, wears size 10.) Those who say to her, "You're a model, how glamorous," don't know the hard work during their showings. The first week of June and the first week of December are hectic. She models steadily from 9 to 4:30. Someone helps her to pull garments off and on, then she rushes back to the showroom, constantly on her feet. She states the style number and price of each garment as she models it. She adds fabric style number too, because she knows this from her factory records.

Sometimes during the showings she stays with a buyer to model again the clothes the buyer's most interested in. It's hard for her to say when modeling ends and selling begins. Frequently now buyers ask for her when they return, call her directly for reorders. Gradually she has taken over selling buyers of some of the smaller shops.

Everyone in the place is fashion-conscious, reads and talks women's wear, the French magazines, costume exhibits, fabrics. She feels part of high fashion.

She likes it best when the designer comes from Paris in April and November. Each time he stays a month. He designs in Paris to the measurements of the two New York models (E.J. is proud that this much of her has been to Paris). Sample fabrics are sent to him from England, France, Italy, and the U.S.A. He sends his sketches to the New York office, later ships his sample garments. For the fall line there were forty-two pieces: nine dresses, thirteen coats, four blouses, three short coats. His New York visits are for final fittings. He wants his garments to appeal to American women in style and fit, eagerly listens to

E.J.'s opinions. She finds a difference in fit. French clothes are less comfortable, with very high armholes, shoulder line at least half an inch further in than ours. He fits the garments with these differences in mind. One operator is assigned to work on the adjustments. Several refittings in muslin and fabric are tiring, require lots of patience. But she learns from him every minute, because he encourages her to ask any questions she wants.

Her beginning salary has increased in the two years she has been here. She thinks it is relatively low, but feels well paid because of the considerable value of the clothes her bosses give her from the line. Living at home with her family means low expenses. She saves money.

Her boss has given her the chance to show him sketches, work up designs. She feels she needs more patternmaking, may take a course this year. Last year she took more sketching. She's not sure she wants to concentrate on designing. She's learned much here about garment construction and fabrics that would help. But she likes selling too, the all-roundness of what she's doing. Instead of feeling limited by the smallness, she thinks it gives her the chance to grow, to be part of all phases of the business.

J.C. / Designer of Bags

She had always wanted to "be someone—not the fifth house in a row of sixteen all looking alike, but the big house on the mountain." Born in Strasbourg, Alsace-Lorraine, J.C. lived with her family in France, came to this country when she was thirteen. She liked color, to draw and paint, so majored in art in high school. Perhaps she might be an illustrator of books.

But her teacher suggested fashion design. J.C. had no special interest in fashion, didn't apply her good color sense to her own clothes. Never had she touched a sewing machine. But she respected her teacher, applied to enter the Fashion Institute of Technology, and was accepted. She enjoyed the art and academic subjects; sewing, draping, patternmaking were chores. Hard work earned her a good record. Her interest in fashion grew. Her own clothes reflected it.

In her second year at college she took an elective course in handbag design. She did well, found she preferred construction of a bag to construction of a dress. For her college work period she worked for a well-known manufacturer of medium-price handbags, learned the factory

Designing

operations, pasting by hand and machine, sewing, framing, clicking (stapling cardboard to lining). She looks back on this as invaluable. "It's easier to tell someone to do something if you can do it yourself."

When she graduated, she was hired by a large rubber-goods company to design nursery bags. A very experienced designer did the beach bag line. Soon the two were working together, although the bosses had deliberately kept the departments separate to avoid friction between "temperamental women." They got along well, found they benefited by combining forces to avoid overlapping. J.C. learned much from her experienced colleague and welcomed the chance to design beach bags as well as nursery bags.

She works at the factory four days out of five, goes to the New York office and the market once a week. Despite the hour-and-a-half trip each way to the factory, her job, she says, has to be done there, close to production problems. Much that she's learned at the factory is as pertinent to her designs as the research she does at the museums, the ideas she gets shopping, from fashion magazines and trade publications. She had to learn that if you want rubber dyed pink for a solid-color pink bag, this can't be done with reprocessed rubber. If fabric for the bag is heavy, the rubber backing can be thinner. Fabrics are rubberized at the factory. It's her job to decide the kind and thickness of rubber. She herself found a way to get on-the-job training, in a hurry, by visiting the rubber department after work or during lunch hour.

Her design schedule starts a year before the finished bags will be on the store's counters. She consults with fabric houses to learn what colors and design motifs they think will be strong. Then she goes to the bathing-suit firms to hear their style plans so she can coordinate the beach bags. Back at the plant, she sketches her ideas, makes a paper pattern, then the "dummy," the actual shape and design of the bag in muslin. She goes to the market again for trimmings—handles, clips, rings, seashells—and for sample cuts from the fabric houses. (Lots of comparison shopping first: if in doubt, takes swatches rather than the five-yard sample cuts.)

On these New York visits she shops the stores, eager for customer reactions at the bag counters. She picks up and examines competitors' bags, perhaps buys a high-priced bag that she might adapt (not copy) for her $1.98-to-$6.98 line. Once she was suspected of shoplifting. Since then, in the larger stores, she tells the department manager who she is and what she's doing. In New York she's Miss C., not J. as she is in the factory. In New York she may be invited to lunch at Longchamps; the next day, send for a sandwich to eat at her desk in the factory.

As soon as the sample cuts are delivered to the factory, she selects fabric for each dummy. She cuts, the samplehand sews the bag. They work closely together. Yes, the samplehand is the expert sewer and has taught J.C. many shortcuts. In a pinch J.C. does it herself. What's more she sits down at the machine to show the samplehand what she wants if the samplehand thinks it can't be done.

She faces the fact of costing. If she shortens or skips a factory operation, it reduces the cost of the bag. Maybe it means that one of her best bags can be produced. Only in "prestige" numbers made for publicity or to add tone to the line is price no object. The prestige numbers are her dessert; she saves them for the very last.

A production man, liaison for her department, the factory, and the New York office, goes over all the factory operations the sample calls for. The one thousand factory employees include six hundred sewing machine operators. Can it be made in the factory? "If you don't get along with the production man," says J.C., "you might as well quit."

Then she goes into a huddle with her production sheet to prepare for final costing. She lists the cost of all fabrics and trimmings, the number of cut pieces and yardage for each bag, breakdown of operations. The factory manager goes over the production sheet and samples. Perhaps he can combine two operations. Corrections made on the dummy are repeated on the paper pattern.

Then the cost department gets the production sheets and the samples. This is the nervewracking part for J.C. Some bags, of course, go through at the factory cost set for each price line. But others figure above this limit. Back it comes. If she wants it included in the line, it's up to her to get the price down. Otherwise it's out. Sometimes it's a matter of pennies, cutting down on thread, omitting some trimming, changing an operation. If she makes the change, she sends it for recosting.

Finally she sends her styles to the merchandise manager in New York. He usually accepts them, gives her freedom and leeway to include what she wants. This gives her an added sense of responsibility. Offsetting the pennypinching is the satisfaction she gets when she sees her bags displayed in a Fifth Avenue department store window. The bags look so much better on display, and they're *hers*. "I could stand there looking for hours."

"The most important part of the job," says J.C., "is getting along with everyone. I don't make the sewing machine operators feel I'm better

Designing

because I'm not. We need each other." Sometimes she finds it a tough job to sell the bags to their own salesmen. Sometimes she works with the publicity department on prestige numbers. She has to coordinate with the bathing-cap division.

"I don't consider myself really a designer yet. Too much still to learn," she says. She thinks that her school training helped her absorb more quickly all that must be learned on the job, not at school. Her starting salary was raised in six months, and she's due for another increase at the end of a year. She thinks it is a good salary for her stage of experience.

In a few months she will be married to a man who has recently gone into business in California. It is hard for her to leave a job she enjoys so much. There may be a spot for her in the firm's California merchandising office. Even though it is not designing, merchandising is so closely related that she thinks she will learn a great deal. Besides, she wants to stay with this company. But when she has children, she will stay home with them, at least while they're young. At twenty-one, she still has the dream to be the "big house on the mountain." Now it includes a husband, children, and somehow a chance to keep on designing.

E.L. / Stylist of Fabrics

For E.L. it was always art. As a small boy he copied illustrations, painted. He sought a specialized high school where he could study art, and spent four happy years at the High School of Music and Art in New York. He enjoyed his fine arts studies, but he found that his strengths centered around design and color. To develop them further he took textile design in his last year. While his interest in fine arts and painting continued, he was convinced that his career lay in commercial or industrial art.

Textile design seemed to combine both the esthetic and practical approach, so he decided to pursue this training at the Fashion Institute of Technology. He was an excellent student, managed to take extra art in his two-year program in textile design. While he had some academic courses at college, he wishes there had been time for even more: a broad cultural and esthetic background is as important for those who want to get to the top, he thinks, as the practical training. (He now studies oil painting, sketching, and etching at night.)

He became interested in leather and jewelry design on an assignment as an information and education officer in the Army. Evenings he spent at the arts-and-crafts hobby shop, oil painting, learning leather and jewelry design. (This was his second assignment. In his first he applied his art training by painting barracks.)

The civilian director of the hobby shop liked E.L.'s work and hired him as assistant for every evening when he was finished with his Army duty. E.L. learned a great deal about designing during this period and has sustained the new interests he developed then. "The principles of good design are basic, no matter what the medium," he says. Now his off-the-job designs in jewelry and leather, or ideas he gets in oil painting, frequently influence his fabric designs.

When he graduated from the Fashion Institute of Technology, his first job was textile artist for a high-style silk converter noted for the quality of its designs and fabrics. E.L. assisted the stylist, feels he "started at the top" because almost from the beginning he was given a chance to originate designs as well as to do colorings and repeats. The art department was small and he had a chance to see all that was going on. The firm made high-styled fabrics, almost custom, for exclusive women's fashions. He had the satisfaction of seeing some of his own designs made up in fabrics used by well-known dress designers. Although he was hired for a six-week temporary job, he stayed a year and a half until he was drafted. During this period his low beginning salary almost doubled.

During his two years in the Army, the firm's art department was liquidated so, to his regret, he could not return. After he was discharged, a few months of looking convinced him that he couldn't find a job just like the one he'd had and that he'd have to compromise. He was hired by one of the largest textile firms for its plastic design department.

E.L. had to learn the limitations and possibilities of plastic in designing shower and bathroom curtains, kitchen curtains, draperies. It was a challenge to harness the technical end. He learned, too, how a large converting firm works. His technique necessarily became "tighter" (neater); this was helpful, as he tended to work "freely" (loosely). Although much of his work was in the studio—originating, doing colorings and repeats—he was outside, too, visiting wallpaper and drapery firms, kitchen and bathroom equipment manufacturers, decorators. He learned the importance of making contacts and discovered the polite, businesslike way of "spying" to get advance information.

All in all it was two years of practical business experience. The firm seemed satisfied with him, but he wasn't satisfied with himself. He wasn't giving himself to the job completely. He didn't like the type of

Designing

designs he was doing. He felt a lack of individuality in this large organization. At the end of two years he left for his present job.

On his new job he's assistant stylist, with the opportunity to learn all phases of styling. His salary jumped appreciably over his old one. His new firm is small, with twenty employees in New York and a mill in Massachusetts. It's a style leader in medium-priced fabrics for men's and women's wear.

In the few months he's been there E.L. feels he's learned lots, has a chance to develop his own ideas, is deep in the duties of a styling job, and can see his way at last towards his goal of stylist. The head stylist, one of the two owners, has been in Europe for the last month and left E.L. pretty much on his own. He hired E.L. with this in mind, to develop him into a stylist.

E.L. stresses his color sense above all else. Here he spends much less time painting and hopes eventually to do even less. He recognizes that some textile designers don't want to give up their brush work. He doesn't miss it, does lots of painting as a hobby at home. Although he thinks his ability to paint is helpful, he has met successful stylists with excellent color sense, good taste, and fashion knowledge who cannot paint. His firm has no studio, but perhaps in the future he may want a colorist to assist him.

He selects designs from textile design studios, perhaps ten or fifteen from a hundred, discusses them with his firm's owners before the final selection. Soon he expects to make these decisions on his own. Sometimes he paints special designs—ones that are to be kept secret and therefore are not given to a studio.

When a lingerie designer wanted an Indian sari pattern, E.L. worked directly with her. He did research in the library to be sure that the pattern was authentic, then had the design roller-printed in a roller plant (roller-printing is used for certain designs because it's more exact than screen-printing). He rushed a sample cut to the designer so she could make it into a negligee to be displayed in Lord & Taylor's window. This was a fast, individual job, taking only six weeks from the time the designer suggested the idea until it appeared in the Fifth Avenue window. (The normal span would be six months to a year.)

E.L. goes to the firm's Massachusetts screen-printing mill at least once a month. Much of the styling is done right in the heart of the mill. Before the screen actually goes on the fabric, it prints the design on a "blotter" to see how it takes and also for reference. Five blotters are made for each pattern. On his last visit to the mill, E.L. styled about eighty patterns from the blotters, combining patterns, changing color combinations. The same pattern in different colors can give an entirely different effect. The "strike off" is the first sample cut (from five to fifteen yards) to be run off in the fabric. Is the strike off an exact replica of the design? Are the colors true? There's always pressure to get the strike offs done and rushed back to New York. The mill closes down for two weeks in July after the busy New York showings in June and July.

He doesn't have much to do with costing, but he does correlate designs and color with price lines. Although this house isn't as high-styled as the one he started with, he doesn't feel he's compromising his ideas. He insists that his firm emphasizes good taste, tries to make less expensive fabrics look high-priced.

He enjoyed reference work at the libraries and museums in college, has done only a limited amount in his few months on this job, but hopes to do more. He talks to piece-goods buyers and salesmen in the showroom to get their ideas, and to find out what the customers want. He works directly with the owners, getting their ideas for design and for merchandising the fabric.

He has no regular schedule or regimentation except what he imposes on himself. He works hard from 9 to 5:30 or 6 because he likes it ("but make no mistake, it's a business—no glamor job") and because he knows it's entirely up to him to prove his value to the firm. At twenty-four, he thinks he's making satisfactory progress towards his goal of being a recognized stylist, or even perhaps to be in his own business. But that's a long way off.

He doesn't advise frequent job-hopping, because there are things you can learn if you stick long enough; besides, there comes a point when employers are afraid to hire you because of your unstable record. But it's important to set a goal for yourself and if you're not heading toward it, to do something about it. Sometimes that means changing jobs. He finds that the young stylist or designer can't afford to be temperamental. Defying tradition, he claims that salesmen display more temperament than artists!

Chapter 4

Merchandising

MERCHANDISING is figuring out the kind of goods that will sell, finding it, buying it, getting it sold. R. Duffy Lewis, a prominent merchandiser and retail executive, defined merchandising as "the buying, selling, and control of merchandise in a manner that insures a good profit, sales increase, and goodwill for the company." A store may be described simply as an organization that *buys* goods in order to *sell* them to the consumer. In large organizations there are merchandising departments, or merchandisers, to plan and coordinate this function. In small setups the buyer is the merchandiser too. In any setup the buyer is a key figure.

Merchandising has three main aspects: buying, planning, and control of stocks; planning of sales-promotional events; and selling. All of these are closely related. Since the ultimate purpose of a store is to sell its merchandise, all buying is done with this question uppermost: Will it sell?

The buyer is a merchant. Like any store owner, he must make a profit. He must find or even develop the kind of merchandise that represents current fashion trends and will meet his customers' demands. The merchandise must sell. This is true whether he buys for a department store or specialty store, for a wholesale house, or for a central buying office. The need for these central offices has increased with the growth of chain management, and with the establishment of branches by the large department stores.

New York is the mecca for buyers. At least twice a year, in January and again in May or early June, buyers descend on New York. Some couture houses show fall collections in April and their fall-holiday lines early in June, while an equally prestigious group shows one fall collection in May. For buyers who must cover these houses, it can mean three trips to New York within a few weeks, and in between a visit to California to cover the important West Coast showings. Many make up to ten trips a year. Some buyers travel all over the world on buying trips. Most buying jobs have always been specialized, but today, with the growth of new departments, they are still more so. Teen-age and junior sportswear departments, off-shoots of the regular junior department, mean *more* buying jobs. As in designing, it's wise for the beginner to be receptive to all opportunities, to consider a wide range of departments rather than be limited to one initial interest.

The good buyer has fashion knowledge, good taste, and awareness of the quality and value of the merchandise he buys. He thoroughly understands his consumer market. Is he buying for the customer who wants high-fashion, expensive merchandise, or for the one seeking good value at low price? He has to know not only what to buy but how much; he works closely with past and current sales figures, estimates future demand. Unquestionably he is decisive. He has ideas, the courage and drive to try them. And he can plan and organize his own time, adjusting to quick changes in pace and pressure.

The buyer with good style sense can capitalize on it in selecting merchandise. But it's not enough. Unless he understands construction of the garment, quality of workmanship, the fabric itself—how it wears, launders, dry cleans—he's headed for trouble. One fashion expert who has worked hard to learn this part of the business recently complained to a manufacturer that the shantung in a sample dress should be of better grade for the price level of the dress. The manufacturer agreed. "But," says he, "the fabric you suggest is twenty-five cents a yard more. You're the only one of all the buyers who has noticed it. Why should I invest the difference if the buyers don't know?" True, the manufacturer had a responsibility here, but it's up to the buyer to hold him to it.

His job varies according to the type of organization—store, buying office, or wholesale firm—and the size of his department. He studies fashion trends, shops the market, establishes good contacts with his resources, the manufacturers. He buys for each season and is alert to new items and new ideas when it's off season, too. He trains and supervises his staff, getting customer reaction from them in a store or market information in a buying office. He follows up on deliveries, maintains

Merchandising

complete records on his orders and sales. He goes to fashion shows, sometimes gives them. He works with the promotion and display departments, selecting the merchandise he wants promoted.

It is universally accepted that a buyer must have done some selling. The final test is whether the customer will buy the goods. At some point in his career the future buyer needs the direct customer contact that comes through selling. As a buyer he may still manage to talk to customers or, at the very least, he gets reactions from those who do sell.

Yet, no matter how beautiful, functional, or in demand an item is, its actual sale depends on good promotion (advertising, publicity, display, special sales, and merchandise showings) and a trained sales staff. Merchandising departments work with the various promotion departments to push the merchandise. The selection, training, informing, and supervision of the sales staff is one of their major responsibilities.

The control of stock is the function of merchandising that underlines and relates all the others. Stock is the store of merchandise on hand in the retail establishment or its warehouses. Filling it is the buyer's function; emptying it is the function of promotion and the sales force. Therefore a good retail establishment must plan and control its stock operations in order to control its buying and selling operations. This is done by the use of some form of record or system, based on dollars (dollar stock control) and physical units (unit control).

Records of past sales partially determine the forecast for future sales. From this forecast the retailer or buyer estimates the amount of mer-

chandise he should carry at a particular time and, from this, how much he needs to buy. Dollar control records provide information on how much merchandise, in terms of dollars, should be bought. However, the merchandiser must know how to allocate this money in order to have a stock well adjusted to customer demands. This information is provided

IS THE FASHION BUSINESS YOUR BUSINESS?

by unit control records, which show the types, sizes, styles, price lines, and colors of merchandise which have been selling well and can thus be expected to sell again.

The following lists the range of buyer functions.

Functions of the Buyer

DEVELOP RESOURCES FOR BUYING:

Find manufacturers whose merchandise will appeal to his customers.

Establish good contacts with them. Exchange ideas, sometimes try out style in store for manufacturer; sometimes suggest style changes and new ideas to manufacturer.

Evaluate style, construction, fabric, value.

BUY:

May order small trial runs, then larger orders and later reorders.

Sometimes order in quantity in advance of season to ensure early delivery or to benefit from lower price.

STUDY THE CONSUMER MARKET:

Know type, quality, price level of merchandise sold throughout the firm, and firm's policies affecting consumer.

Study his customer's reaction to merchandise in his department by direct observation and through staff's comments.

STUDY FASHION TRENDS:

Watch for trends in color, silhouette, fabric.

Shop stores for ideas and to see what's selling.

Read fashion magazines such as *Vogue, Harper's Bazaar, Glamour, Mademoiselle, Seventeen.*

Read trade publications such as *Women's Wear Daily, Daily News Record, Home Furnishings Daily;* specialized trade magazines such as *Boot and Shoe Recorder, Infants' and Children's Wear Review.*

Read fashion bulletins from fashion services and central buying offices.

Attend fashion shows.

WORK WITH OTHER DEPARTMENTS:

Select merchandise for promotion or advertising.

Check copy and pictures.

Push merchandise for promotion, publicity, display.

PLAN AND CONDUCT FASHION SHOWS:

For customers, for demonstrating merchandise to sales staff, for special programs outside of organization.

MAINTAIN STOCK:

See that adequate stock is on hand.

Maintain it neatly—labeled and easy to get at for quick service to customer.

Merchandising

MAINTAIN RECORDS:
Keep complete records on amount of merchandise bought and sold, stock on hand, style numbers, price, etc. These are used to forecast sales, set department goals, and to plan amount of buying and reordering.
Check delivery dates of orders and handle correspondence.
PREPARE WRITTEN MATERIAL:
Write market reports.
Write fashion show commentary.
ORGANIZE AND MANAGE THE DEPARTMENT:
Select staff.
Train and supervise assistant buyer, head of stock, clerical assistants, and salespeople, through meetings and individual conferences.
Maintain good housekeeping—the department looking smart, merchandise displayed attractively.

REQUIREMENTS FOR ENTERING THE FASHION MERCHANDISING FIELD

What does it take to succeed in fashion merchandising? These are some of the desirable personal attributes: executive potential, drive, interest in merchandising and fashion, pleasant personality, ability as a "trader."

A high school diploma is the minimum educational requisite. College training is advisable, and carries weight with managements when they are considering potential executive material. Courses in communications (public speaking, English), psychology, sociology, economics are helpful. Specialized training in fashion and merchandising is considered an asset by many firms. Specifically helpful are courses in color and silhouette, fashion history and trends, apparel design and construction, fabric identification and use, merchandising and retailing principles.

Should a student who will enter the merchandising field go to a liberal arts college or to a college specializing in fashion, merchandising, and retailing? Both types of training are acceptable. It depends on the individual.

If he is so interested in fashion and merchandising that he wants to take such courses before he gets into the field, he will probably prefer a specialized school. A college with this specialty will include some liberal arts subjects, too. There are junior colleges as well as four-year colleges giving these programs. This training is highly respected. The retail business management department of one school recently estimated

IS THE FASHION BUSINESS YOUR BUSINESS?

that two-thirds of retail personnel executives prefer the specialized training programs. Many organizations consider it an advantage because the graduates have an appreciation of the scope of the field as well as some practical understanding of operations that helps them immediately on the job. The specialization, too, is concrete evidence of their interest in the field. On the other hand, if a student prefers to spend his college years acquiring as broad a cultural background as possible, he will want a liberal arts college. This includes, too, the student whose vocational interest is far from clear when he enters college. If he has the executive potential and personality that merchandising executives seek and he develops interest in the field, he will find opportunities. A sizable number of organizations feel that the liberal arts graduate can get his specialized training on the job. Spare-time courses in fashion trends, fabrics, color, apparel design, and construction are valuable supplements to his daily work experience.

Career opportunities are there, too, for the high school graduate with the personal qualities sought. He, too, will gain from specialized courses in addition to his work experience.

The beginner looks towards buying as a goal, never starts at it. If he's in a store he may start at sales and over the years be promoted to assistant head of stock, head of stock, assistant buyer, and then buyer. Perhaps modeling or comparison shopping or clerical assistant to a buyer is the start. Stores' "flying squads" and executive training programs take primarily college graduates or those with at least some college or specialized training beyond high school. Sometimes store employees who are considered promotable will be transferred to one of these programs.

If the beginner starts in a central buying office, he may be a clerical assistant who takes and follows up the orders for merchandise or he may be an assistant buyer or market assistant, and finally work up to buyer.

In the wholesale field he may start as stock boy or inventory clerk, assistant to the piece-goods' buyer, salesman's assistant, or showroom assistant. He can work towards the goal either of buyer or of salesman.

RETAIL

Retailing is the second largest industry in the United States. Some 2 million stores had total retail sales of more than $338 billion in 1968, an 8 percent increase over 1967. A review of results in women's and children's clothing by the research department of the International

Merchandising

Ladies' Garment Workers Union showed a volume of $21.5 billion in retail sales in those products alone for 1968. With figures like these it isn't hard to understand that there are rapidly increasing opportunities in the retail field.

G. Fox and Company, a well-known department store in Hartford, Connecticut, presents an encouraging picture of retailing opportunities. The following is from the company's recruiting literature:

> More persons can and do progress to executive positions than in practically any other career field. The fact that over 40 percent of retail executives are women illustrates the opportunities for women in retailing.
>
> Retailing proportionately has a larger ratio of executives to total force than most other businesses. Executive and supervisory personnel account for 12 percent of a department store's total staff.
>
> Pay for top executives is equalled by few industries. College graduates who have achieved middle management assignments, usually about four or five years after graduation, receive yearly salaries ranging from $8,000 to $16,000. The following will give you a general idea of how executives are paid in stores doing a volume of 20 million dollars or more annually:
>
> > buyers may earn between $8,000 and $30,000
> > sales promotion managers, $13,500–$60,000
> > merchandise managers, $16,000–$80,000
> > personnel directors, $8,000–$40,000
> > branch store managers, $9,600–$50,000
>
> Retailing is no different from other industries in which top executives must be willing to give extra hours to their jobs.

At G. Fox everyone works a five-day week with the benefits of a two-day weekend, as the store is closed on Mondays except during the Christmas season.

There are many types of retail establishments, from small specialty stores and boutiques to enormous stores with every conceivable type of goods and a variety of consumer services, such as interior decorating.

Probably the best-known type of store is the department store. A department store is an establishment employing twenty-five people or more and engaged in selling some items in each of the following lines of merchandise: furniture, home furnishings, appliances; a general line of apparel for the family; household linens and dry goods. Merchandise lines are normally arranged in separate sections with accounting on a departmentalized basis, but departments and functions are integrated under a single management and ownership. Some department stores have become discount operators as well, and occasionally set up both discount and traditional stores in the same city.

Women's and girls' and men's and boys' specialty stores are the other two main types of clothing stores. These can be independently owned and operated or can be part of a chain store organization. Independent stores are separate units, generally specialize in one line of clothing, and are not very departmentalized. A chain store organization is composed of multi-unit stores. Under central management and ownership, all of its stores carry similar merchandise, and the buying of merchandise for its stores is performed by a central buying office. Individual chain stores are generally much larger than independent stores and thus offer more job opportunities. And since each chain store is part of a larger chain organization demanding executives in charge of units composed of more than one store, opportunities for advancement in management and merchandising positions are more numerous here than in independent stores.

Retail buyers do all their own buying, or get partial or complete service from a central buying office. Either way, they buy with one question in mind: "Will it sell?" Or rather, "Will it be sold?" Their selection of merchandise may be good—i.e., salable; but "will it be sold" means there must be good promotion, advertising, and display, and a trained sales staff who will go all-out to sell it. Oddly enough, this "selling" is part of the buyer's job.

Has the buyer "sold" the salesgirl on the merchandise, explained the advantage of new fabrics, helped her to know something of the new silhouette and color trend? It's not enough for the salesgirl to have a pleasing personality. She needs to know what she's selling. The buyer who can stimulate her and train her for this will sell more goods.

The buyer's assistant probably takes on most of the figure work. The head of stock, with perhaps an assistant and a stock boy or girl, maintains stock inventory. But the buyer is still responsible for the department.

Will the buyer be daring enough to try new merchandise that differs from tried and true sellers? It takes courage to make these buying decisions, but if buyers are too conservative they'll find themselves behind the times.

As large retailers have expanded, adding stores in suburban areas, shopping centers and even other cities, some have changed the buyer's function, separating it from management responsibilities. In this setup the buyer concentrates entirely on the buying of merchandise without

Merchandising

responsibility for sales and department management. The department manager supervises the sales staff and is responsible for the management of the department.

The specialization in the fashion industry is reflected within the stores. Actually the stores themselves, often pushed by buyers with imagination and knowledge of customers' needs, have developed and encouraged this specialization. Over the years new departments have been added—the subteen, preteen, the special boutiques for accessories, for rainwear—and on and on. Not every department has its own buyer, but frequently that's the next step if there is increased volume.

In large stores there are many departments to help buyers: personnel, in selecting and training staff, promotion and publicity, in advertising and display. There may be specialists in fashion coordination, and in accounting, to advise and even do some of the work. These people help the buyers—but do not exempt them from responsibility.

The black figures on white paper are as important to the buyer as the new silhouette. How much should be bought? Figures on past sales, current sales, and amount of stock on hand help the buyer to plan. He analyzes sales figures on styles, sizes, colors, price. And the buyer must forecast what he expects to sell. After he has figured stock on hand, the buyer estimates the "open-to-buy": the amount of goods needed to meet the sales forecast by the end of the month.

The buyer knows for each day the amount the department should sell. He must at least "make his day" (equal last year's sales figures). The "markup" is the difference between the wholesale price paid to the manufacturer and the retail price charged the customer, usually about 40 percent. When there is a sale or the garment hasn't sold, the buyer reduces it to make it move. The "markdown" is the difference between the original retail price and the reduced price finally charged. In large stores the merchandise manager also is responsible for sales forecasts and "open-to-buy" figures, but the buyer helps him reach decisions.

A buyer spends at least 20 to 30 percent of his time in the market traveling to New York and other markets. He surveys the market first, comparing values, and the next time around he may buy, selectively. Good relations with manufacturers pay off in special courtesies, such as extra-fast delivery, or substitute colors—sometimes, even style changes. If the buyer is a shrewd trader, he'll know when to order in quantity and perhaps save money, or give an order before production starts so that the manufacturer will give him a special price.

The buyer's degree of specialization depends on the size of the store.

In a small one the buyer may buy all women's wear, in a large one just corsets and brassieres, or women's underwear, or better dresses.

The retail buyer works hard and long. Sometimes in a small office on the sales floor near the department, sometimes out on the sales floor, in the stock room, in the merchandise manager's office, in the market. Almost always the buyer is on his feet. Happily, required working hours have been cut considerably, so that the forty-hour week, in contrast to forty-eight hours or more in the past, is quite usual. But the buyer's responsibility may drive him to work beyond that, especially during heavy market periods. The buying trips are hectic, rushing to cover as many showings as possible, to find special items. He's treated royally by the manufacturers, with lunches, dinners, theatre tickets. The buyer is an important person in this business.

Length of time to arrive at a buyer's job depends on the individual's ability, store policy, and breaks. It may take from two to ten years. One personnel director, who was emphasizing the opportunities for promotion within his store, said that 29 percent of their buyers fell in the age range of twenty-four to thirty years.

Practically all large stores have training programs and promotion-from-within policies. As many have a ratio of one executive to every eight employees, their need for training and promoting is constant. Executive training programs aim to develop carefully selected trainees for junior executive assignments, such as assistant buyer, in training periods ranging from four months to a year. Programs vary in formality in different stores, but their aims are essentially the same.

Recently I attended "commencement exercises" held by a store for its executive trainees. This store "graduates" about eighty executive trainees a year after a "curriculum" that is taught over a two-year period by key executives, including the president, the vice-president and general merchandise manager, the vice president of sales promotion, and the vice president for personnel. Seventy of these executive trainees came directly from college, ten from the ranks. All those originally hired as executive trainees are immediately assigned to junior executive assignments as assistants to more experienced department managers. The promotional steps are assistant department manager, branch store, to department manager, branch store; to assistant buyer, parent store; then buyer for five stores; with divisional merchandise manager, branch assistant general manager and branch general manager as the steps above to top management status. This retail organization has one parent store with four branch units. The regular staff comprises about 3,000 asso-

Merchandising

ciates, rising up over 4,000 at Christmas time. There is an annual need of from 65 to 75 new executive trainees to insure the strength and prepare for the growth and expansion of this organization.

R. H. Macy & Co., a pioneer in employee training, gears its programs to develop good merchandisers and managers. The Herald Square store in New York City, with employees ranging from 8,000 to 10,000, is the largest store in the world. In addition there are fifty-seven other stores in suburban areas, shopping centers, and several cities. The Macy New York division has 110 buyers. Under them are about 200 assistant buyers. Large departments have several assistant buyers. In 1963 a new form of organization was established, separating the merchandising and management functions. With the increase in the number of stores, the buying responsibility became heavier and the buyers were relieved of the supervision of the sales force. That function is now done by a sales manager (department manager). Over the buyers are twelve merchandise vice presidents who have three senior vice presidents of merchandising over them.

Although Macy's executive training has always been an on-the-job training program supplemented by classroom training, the major change has been to shorten the training period with emphasis on getting the trainee into actual assignments as soon as possible. The trainee has three weeks of classroom training followed by a period of five to eight weeks, on the average, of rotated job assignments in store administration and merchandising functions. Completing this in five weeks is rare, just as occasionally but infrequently a trainee may stay on the program for six months. Within this training period he will have two or possibly three assignments under a sales manager and a buyer. After this he gets a regular assignment as sales manager. From that, the next step will probably be to assistant buyer, then to group manager (supervising a group of sales managers). Although the individual's ability as well as job openings available are variables affecting the length of time, this progression might occur within a year. Throughout the first year the trainee attends a weekly series given by top management on broad store policies. For the first two years there are semiannual performance reviews, then annual reviews. Six months after each promotion he is evaluated. It usually takes four to five years to become a buyer.

Macy's actively seeks graduates of two-year and four-year colleges and of graduate schools for its executive training program. Even with the number of college graduates hired, most of its executives come from the ranks of employees who do not start as executive trainees. If a salesclerk or stock clerk shows executive potential after being carefully reviewed, he can be recommended for junior executive placement. At peak times, such as the Christmas shopping period, the store needs temporary executives. The personnel department looks for possibilities in the permanent staff, and interviews with this in mind. It is an opportunity for the salesclerk to get experience as a junior executive and also to prove he can do the job if a permanent opening comes along.

In 1969 starting salaries for executive trainees ranged from $5,720 ($110 a week) to $7,800 ($150 a week), depending on the individual's maturity, educational background, and experience. The average salary was $7,020 ($135 a week). Salaries for assistant buyers were $7,500 to $9,500; for group managers, $8,000 to $12,000; for buyers, $12,000 to $30,000 or higher.

Not only has the executive training program been shortened but so have hours for executives. It wasn't too long ago that a Saturday off was a phenomenon. Now a group manager works only one Saturday a month; and within a four-week period he works only one six-day week. A sales manager works only one Saturday a month and throughout works only a five-day week.

A smaller department store, known, too, for its good training program, individualizes its training for each potential executive hired. Thus an executive trainee may be hired at any time of the year. The individual is assigned to jobs to give him experience and to test and develop his abilities as future merchandiser. The personnel department arranges for some in-service training courses, and suggests outside training, too, if that seems advisable.

Most of the executive trainees are college graduates, although it is not an absolute requirement. One advantage of college, says the employment manager, is that the graduate has had extra time for just plain maturing. At the regular six-month job review, each employee has a chance for promotion. The high school graduate who has not been spotted as an executive trainee at the beginning may reach the same goal in a little longer time.

This employment manager emphasizes the value of summer and Saturday work for those interested in this field. She hires about twenty-five extra salesgirls for the college shop to work from the end of July until they return to college late in September. Each girl, on the basis of her own college experience, can advise the young shopper or worried mother about the right thing to wear on the campus. Frequently the

Merchandising

store spots some of these girls as good possibilities for executive training after graduation from college.

There are many other areas within the stores besides merchandising. Personnel and training departments, research, finance are some. The scope of this book permits no more than the acknowledgment of their existence and importance.

Branches of the large department and specialty stores have grown in number and importance. Stores have struggled to find the proper nomenclature for them. Does "branch" of the parent store sound less important than its due? Macy's solved it with SOTH, i.e., Store Other Than Herald Square. Once I'd heard that, "branch" sounded fine, and I use it throughout the book as a designation of approval!

The growth of branch stores means more opportunities in merchandising and management. The buyers in the parent store buy for the branches. Branches are responsible for getting goods sold, for giving customer reaction and local preferences to the central buyer, and determining the quantity of merchandise needed. These are essential merchandise functions.

The manager of the branch is a merchant, at some point has been a buyer. Depending on the size of the store he may have one, two, or three assistants, one or two of them in merchandising. Under the merchandising managers are sales managers, probably forty or fifty in a large branch with a thousand employees. Executive jobs within the branch may be filled from within the store or by transfer from the main store. Many stores try to fill branch jobs, even executive spots, from local personnel in the community. Here's a chance for the woman buyer who has retired to have a family, and wants to return to the field when her children are older. If the period of retirement hasn't been too long, if she has kept abreast of retail and fashion trends, she might even start as department manager or work up to it in a suburban branch not far from her home.

The chain store operation, like the branch structure of department stores, has many job opportunities, in stores throughout the country, that include merchandising functions. The chain store organization frequently spots promotable material in the distributors' department. Here its buying office centralizes and controls the flow of goods, all sales and stock information. This department has the answers to who bought what and when, where and how much was shipped. A good distributor or assistant may advance into a junior executive job in the central buying office.

IS THE FASHION BUSINESS YOUR BUSINESS?

J. C. Penney Co., Inc., a leading chain store organization, has approximately 1,650 stores in every state except Rhode Island. Although the number of stores is the same as fifteen years ago, by 1969 the stores themselves were much larger. The average new store opened now is as much as two and a half times larger than those opened five or six years ago. Stores opened since 1962 have all been full-line department stores, with few exceptions. The following changes made since 1963 point up not only growth but expansion of services:

Movement to shopping centers; larger stores in major metropolitan markets.

Growth into hard lines: by 1969, 190 automotive centers with more planned; building materials; paint and hardware; carpeting; furniture; sporting goods; appliances. Almost all of these products are manufactured for Penney's and bear the Penney label.

Direct sell: direct services to customers in their homes: carpets, drapes, home improvements such as plumbing and heating.

Chain of drug stores.

Mail order.

Insurance: sells accident and health insurance.

About 300 buyers in New York City buy for all the stores, sending the store managers illustrations and complete descriptions of style, price, color, and fabric. The buyer buys goods in the market but also has items specially styled to definite specifications just for Penney stores. Knowledge of fabrics and garment construction is a definite asset here. The store manager, in consultation with the store's department managers, selects, determines quantity, requests other merchandise if his local situation demands it, and sends his orders to the central office.

With this necessary feedback from the stores to the buying offices in New York, there is obviously opportunity for merchandising as well as management in the stores. Electronic data-processing expedites the flow of information to New York, but there is considerable direct contact between people in the stores and in the New York offices. Stores get groups of catalogues—for women's wear alone there may be ten or more. Department managers and their assistants select their assortment from the catalogues. They work with open-to-buy as any buyer. Except for going into the markets, they have active merchandising as well as management responsibilities. They are involved with advertising, promotions, display. Some are company-wide services, emanating from the headquarters offices in New York, but most are done locally. New York

Merchandising

has central services in advertising, promotion, and window and interior display, available to the stores if they want them. A department manager or store manager may have an idea for a promotion or special ad and ask the central services for aid in presentation.

Penney's promotion-from-within program pays off in low turnover of executive staff. They recruit actively to fill openings on their training programs. Best known are their programs for developing buyers and store managers. In addition there are training programs in: financial management; systems (data-processing), real estate (leasing and site development, store layout and design); engineering (quality control, warehousing, and distribution).

For the buyer-training program they seek mature candidates with strong educational background, usually college graduates. There is a buyer-assistant program for candidates who are younger or are not college graduates; after a year to a year and a half on this program they may be eligible for the buyer-training program or be promoted directly to an assistant buyer assignment. All of the buyer training is in New York City. The store management training is in stores throughout the country where candidates will usually start as management trainees.

In the field of merchandising, retailing offers the most career opportunities and the future looks still better. We have concentrated on the occupations of buyers and store managers as career goals; now follow some of the jobs that lead towards these goals.

STOCK BOY (OR GIRL)

The stockroom maintains reserve merchandise. The stock boy's duty is to keep merchandise properly arranged, receive and store incoming goods from the receiving room, and make disbursements to the selling departments. A stock boy is in an excellent position to learn about the total operation of merchandising, since the stockroom is in contact with manufacturers, with merchandise, and with the sales floor and force. In such a position the stock boy can reach out to other functions, such as assisting the salespeople.

The position is open to both sexes. Whether a boy or a girl is accepted in a particular position often depends on the type of merchandise in the stockroom.

The stock boy can be promoted to selling, or to assistant head of stock and then head of stock.

HEAD OF STOCK

The head of stock, a junior executive, is responsible for keeping a complete assortment of merchandise in stock for a selling department, in an orderly arrangement. Depending on the size of the department, he or she will supervise an assistant and stock boys or girls. He also fills special orders, retickets returned merchandise, and calls the buyer's attention to slow-selling goods. He sometimes sells, also.

Perhaps his most important duty is keeping stock records. By keeping these he familiarizes himself with the records so important to all of merchandising.

It can lead to higher merchandising junior executive positions, such as assistant buyer.

UNIT CONTROL CLERK

This is a highly specialized job generally available only in large stores; in smaller stores the same functions are performed by the stock boy, assistant buyer, or buyer. The unit control clerk is under the direct supervision of the merchandise manager, buyer, or unit control department. He operates a piece control system, recording unit sales, receipts, stocks, returns, and orders, etc. He, like the head of stock, is in a good position for learning all about merchandising records.

Open to both sexes.

Leads to junior executive positions, such as head of stock.

MERCHANDISE CLERICAL

A direct assistant to the buyer, or merchandise manager, he keeps records and handles correspondence. Though this work he familiarizes himself with some of the buyer's work and is thus in a good learning and promotional position.

Open to both sexes.

Can lead to junior executive positions such as head of stock or assistant buyer.

Merchandising

SALESPERSON

The salesperson is in contact with the consumer, the product, and the customer's reaction to the product. Experience gained in selling is useful in all phases of the fashion field. All retail training programs include some selling—one indication of the importance of sales experience.

The salesperson's duties vary with the organization. In a small store he has duties other than selling, which include stock and record keeping. As the store enlarges, his functions are more specialized, although they are never limited only to selling.

Besides actual selling the salesperson keeps sales records and records customer requests. He maintains his own counter and stock. In smaller stores he has some responsibility for display. He (she) can participate in fashion shows. He should interpret and communicate customer reactions to his superior.

Direct promotion possibilities: clerical work assisting the buyer, head of stock, section manager, and comparison shopper.

COMPARISON SHOPPER

The comparison shopper goes out to other stores to shop for and compare specific items of merchandise with merchandise sold by her store. She evaluates the quality and price of the merchandise and determines if the item is similar or exactly the same as the merchandise sold by her store. Sometimes she buys the item in question for further comparison with the one in her store. Her observations are listed in reports.

She follows up ads placed by her store's competitors; she follows up complaints by customers who claim they have seen the same merchandise at lower prices elsewhere. She compares methods of display and of salesmanship.

Knowledge of fashion, fabric, and construction stands the comparison shopper in good stead. It is an excellent opportunity to learn about merchandise and methods of operations in several stores. Most comparison shoppers are women although certainly men can qualify.

This job can lead to advancement in the comparison shopping department and to junior executive openings in other departments of the store.

ASSISTANT BUYER

Usually the assistant buyer is delegated the responsibility of keeping the buyer's records. This means work with the head of stock (who makes up stock records) and supervision of him. It means placing reorders and following up on new merchandise ordered. It also means supervising the merchandising clerical worker.

Usually the assistant buyer's duties have more to do with sales supervision than with actual selection of the merchandise, which is still the buyer's job. However, he may assist the buyer in ordering new goods.

The assistant buyer works with the advertising and display departments, taking care of details as well as furnishing promotional ideas. Often he is liaison between the buyer and the sales force, informing sales personnel about merchandise and receiving customer reactions from them to transmit to the buyer.

This is not a position for the beginner to walk into. It demands some experience and training; the next step up is full-fledged buying.

BUYING OFFICES

The buyer in the central buying office has the same goal as the retail buyer. "Will it sell?" But he hasn't the store buyer's responsibility of getting it sold. He has no sales staff to train and supervise, he has no direct customer reaction, he has no stock and inventories to maintain.

There are several kinds of buying services. Resident buying offices serve independent stores that pay for this service. Buyers from these stores can use the service exclusively, to supplement their own resources, or not at all. Chain stores and mail-order houses centralize all buying for their member stores, which work only through this office. Some very large stores located outside of New York City maintain their own buying offices there. The cooperative buying office is formed by large independent stores, which share the expense of centralized fashion information and other buying services. Bulk buying on staple items reduces cost for each store.

A representative New York buying office is a firm that specializes in serving medium-size, independent department stores. It represents one store in a city, serving a total of 160 stores (125 main and 35 branches). A staff of 258 including 120 resident buyers in New York, along with smaller offices in Chicago and Los Angeles, give complete market cover-

Merchandising

age, buying service, fashion leadership, and advice. A laboratory service tests the merchandise they buy for fabric content, shrinkage, fading. Visiting store buyers have the use of separate offices where they can see manufacturers' representatives and salesmen with their samples. Merchandise manager and buyers follow the organizational pattern of a department store. All that's missing is the customers and the stock!

There's a basement department with buyers for lower-priced garments, a men's wear department with a buyer of men's furnishings, another for men's coats, in women's wear a buyer for better-priced dresses, one for children's wear, etc.

The buyers spend most of their time out in the market, scouting for merchandise, lining up sample garments, finding good resources for the store buyers when they come to town. There are scheduled hours for buyers to see salesmen with their samples in the buying office. Some assistant buyers or "follow up" girls write up orders, check on deliveries, maintain files and records. Other assistant buyers, or market assistants as they are sometimes called, shop the market for their buyers, getting detailed information about items carried by specific manufacturers.

The buyer may arrange for a staple item, such as men's white shirts, to be manufactured in large quantities under special labels, maintaining good quality at reduced cost. This is aimed at the customer who is not brand-conscious. The same buyer buys brand-name shirts for the customer who wants only well-known brands.

For at least six weeks before the heavy buying periods the resident buyer scouts the market to line up merchandise he hopes to buy for the next season. Months in advance he visits manufacturers' showrooms for staple items that go into production before the market periods. November, January, and June, the market months when buyers descend on New York, find him at his busiest. He may spend one hour or two days with the store buyer, taking him to manufacturers' showrooms, showing him samples in the buying office, noting his preferences for the future, writing orders.

The resident buyer's job is to inspire confidence in his service, because the store buyer does not HAVE to work through him. But once he's sold himself, the store buyer will give him leeway and money authorization to buy "hot" items whenever he sees them. He reorders, follows up deliveries and complaints. Essentially the resident buyer does not have direct responsibility for the final test of the buyer's job—did it sell? But indirectly his success is based entirely on store sales figures. In an effort to find out customer needs, he occasionally may visit the individual stores, but he depends mainly on the store buyer's comments. This is true of other buying services owned cooperatively or by individual stores.

In some organizations, mainly chain stores and mail-order houses, the central buyer controls the buying in his specialty for all member stores. Besides selecting merchandise, he may decide on quantity for each store. In that case all figures on sales and inventories are forwarded from each store to the central office. In other organizations the local store lets the central office know how much of each item it wants. As in all buying offices, the central buyer must know customer reaction, and the needs of different localities.

All buying offices welcome store experience. Nothing substitutes for direct contact with the customer. The beginner in a buying office may start as a clerical worker or "follow up" boy or girl, writing up orders, checking on deliveries by telephone and mail. In some offices this is part of the assistant's job. Often he is expected to know typing. He may start as, or be promoted to, assistant buyer or market assistant, helping the buyer to get market information. He spends much of his time out in the market. From buyer, the line of advancement is similar to that in stores, although titles may differ.

WHOLESALE

"Will it sell" dominates the wholesale buyer and merchandiser as well as the retailer. The fabric that will be made into the finished garment is a major factor in merchandising, styling, and selling. Buying is a key function. The phenomenal changes in textiles have made the wholesale buyer's job challenging and demanding. New synthetic fibers, new blends of natural fibers and new uses of all fabrics keep him hopping. Wool frequently looks like silk, cotton like wool. Denim, once used solely for work clothes, turns up in a cocktail dress. The Dacron blouse or skirt, washed before one retires, is worn without ironing the next morning.

The good buyer uses taste and knowledge of fashion trends in selecting fabrics, imagination in considering new uses of established fabrics and in introducing new fabrics. His technical background enables him to identify fabrics, to know grades and weights, the value and effect of the finishing processes, and to understand how the fabric will react in the cutting, sewing, and pressing operations of the manufacturing processes. His function is closely related to the designing, producing, merchandising, and selling of the product.

Merchandising

The piece-goods buyer buys fabrics six months to a year before they show up in the store in a dress, suit, or coat ready for the consumer. First he selects swatches or sample cuts to show to his merchandise manager and to the design staff. The designers too will be looking for fabrics on their own and will select samples to try out before they ask him to buy in quantity. Like the retail and central buyer he is concerned with knowing his buying sources, always shopping the market to be aware of the fabrics being developed and styled. He's a shrewd trader, too, shopping for price and good delivery arrangements. His figures are important, analyzing last year's sales returns and amount of fabric used, predicting the amount to be needed in the future. Records of orders and deliveries, and of sales orders in relation to goods sent to the factory for production, may well be part of his responsibility. And, like all buyers, he keeps careful inventory records. When there is an unexpected run on one style, will he be able to get additional quantities of the same fabric? If not, is he resourceful enough to find a substitute to please the designer, the production manager, the store buyer, and finally the consumer?

Buying trimmings, thread, buttons, zippers, all the supplies that go into the garment, is obviously important. Here, too, the buyer explores market sources, works closely with the design and production departments, keeps records of suppliers, of quantity needed, delivery dates. Frequently the braid or the embroidery to trim the coat or dress may sell the garment. Novelty felt animals add zest to children's wear. While the designer seeks these touches, the resourceful buyer can do much to bring them to her attention.

All of this is an integral part of merchandising: determining what will sell, finding it, buying it, pricing it. It's so closely tied up with selling that often the merchandise and sales departments are combined. The small manufacturer may do his own buying, or perhaps will have a piece-goods and trimmings buyer. The piece-goods buyer may have an assistant who will keep records and perhaps do some buying of trimmings. The large organization will have a merchandising department.

Styling is a significant part of merchandising. Knowing customer needs and reactions, understanding when to introduce new styles and designs, are major functions of the merchandising department.

In one very large shirt company the merchandise manager is out in the market a great deal, confers with the retail buyers and salespeople, with magazine editors and with merchandisers in other fields. Although there is a separate promotion and publicity department, he develops ideas for them to execute. This large firm even includes textile artists in its merchandising department to develop designs for fabric produced in textile mills. Piece-goods and trimmings buying are, of course, major functions of the department. A merchandise manager of this department usually has had some sales experience, often in the organization itself, and has worked up to merchandise management. The assistants in the department keep style books, assign style numbers, and keep records on sources of supplies.

The merchandise manager of a well-known manufacturer of medium-priced men's coats and suits defines his department's functions as buying the piece goods, pricing it, styling it, promoting it. He must understand consumers' buying habits and sell ideas to the retailer so that new colors, even new styles, can be introduced to the consumer. Especially in men's clothing, he says, the wholesale merchandiser is the one to break through traditional habits and patterns so that color, gaiety, comfort, and style can be in men's clothes as well as women's. He attempts to get retailers interested in long-range ordering rather than last-minute commitments. He works out packaged promotion kits with the advertising and promotion departments that retailers throughout the country can use for his products. He has two piece-goods buyers in the department. Each has two assistants and additional clerical help. But the merchandise manager shares in the major buying decisions. The buyer and merchandiser must foresee trends in color and fabric development. In this company they buy fabrics a year in advance, plan in September for the fall clothes of the following year.

Wholesale merchandising and wholesale selling are closely allied. Large textile and clothing firms seek executive trainees whose goals are merchandising or selling. Some prefer college graduates, although all agree that the individual's personal qualities, personality, and interest in the field are the primary qualifications.

Wholesale selling may involve selling in the showroom, to buying offices, and to stores in the same city where the sales or headquarters office is located. Many jobs involve traveling or relocating to cover a territory. The traveling salesman of the past traveled much more, with extended periods away from home. Now he may relocate to cover a territory where he can travel and be home the same night or be away only one or two nights at a time.

With merchandising as a goal, a beginner can start as stock boy or inventory clerk or even as assistant piece-goods buyer for an apparel firm. His records will be important to the sales and production departments

Merchandising

as well as to piece goods. He knows when no more fabric is left for a certain style and whether his buyer can reorder. From assistant piece-goods buyer he can go to buyer, although this is not a quick step, especially in large organizations where the buyer has major responsibility. In a textile firm beginners frequently start as assistants in the sample department, preparing swatch cards of all the fabrics for the salesmen.

The beginner who can start as salesman in a store will find it harder to do so in the wholesale field. The wholesale salesman has broader responsibility, selling in quantity rather than by individual item. His customer is the retail buyer who represents thousands of individual customers. Sometimes he may start as salesman in the showroom and work towards having his own district or own accounts. He may be a salesman's helper, carrying the salesman's sample case, perhaps modeling the jacket of a man's suit and keeping sales records. He should be able to travel, willing ultimately to relocate.

In one large shirt company a trainee starts in the sales office, takes telephone orders and follows through on them, learns the setup of a sales sample room so that when he is on the road he'll be able to set one up for himself. Next he will go out on the road with an experienced salesman, lugging the sample case in and out of the car. He will take some staple orders, gradually handle small accounts on his own. The next step is to be given his own territory. If he wants additional responsibility, he can work towards district sales manager with seven to ten salesmen to supervise.

A large men's clothing firm, with six regional offices besides its New York headquarters, looks for trainees whose interest in clothes is reflected in their appearance, who can talk well, have initiative and energy, and want a career in this field. College graduates are preferred as executive trainees. The non-college graduate is considered and, if not accepted as executive trainee, may start as assistant in the piece-goods department or sales clerical in the sales department and work toward the same goal. The executive trainee may help in the showroom, prepare swatch cards, and work on promotional material. He will be sent to the factory for a month to learn about the production of the garment. He is encouraged to get as much technical information as possible about fabrics. He may work in customer relations, handling customer complaints and special orders by telephone and mail. He may then become house (showroom) salesman, then road salesman, then assistant sales manager or account executive. He may work towards piece-goods buying, too, although there are fewer openings.

EARNINGS

Earnings spread through many income brackets, from $4,000 to $40,000 a year and sometimes higher. This range includes the trainees as well as the retail buyers, department managers, merchandisers, branch and chain store managers, wholesale salesmen, buyers, and merchandisers. In 1969 trainee salaries ranged from about $4,000 to $9,000 a year. The lower end was in the smaller buying offices, where salaries are lower than in central buying offices of chain stores, in buying offices representing groups of large stores, or in stores and wholesale companies. Salaries for retail executive trainees range from $5,000 to $9,000, the top bracket usually going to strong candidates with master's degrees from well-known graduate schools of business. The median range is $5,700 to $7,000. Salaries for trainees in the wholesale field approximate those for retail trainees, with experienced salesmen, piece-goods buyers, and merchandisers moving rapidly to higher brackets.

JOB TURNOVER

"There is no buyer but a successful one—not for long," said *Mademoiselle* magazine in an article several years ago on "The Young Buyer." It is as true today. Results can be measured clearly, coldly in dollars and cents. When there are too many minuses, the boss finds a new buyer.

There is turnover, but not alarmingly. An increase in training programs, promotion from within, and help from other departments assist the buyer in keeping the job. As there are buyer and store management jobs throughout the country, job mobility is a natural accompaniment. Those

Merchandising

who are open to moving when they need or want to change jobs will have more job opportunities and greater job security.

M.L. / Branch Store Executive

An argument with his father propelled him into the retail business. Two weeks before he was to start his senior year at college he asked for more spending money. "Go work for it," was his father's response. Aside from summer camp counselor jobs, he'd never worked. Besides, a bout with rheumatic fever had kept him in bed for a year. Looking back, he admits he was getting a liberal allowance. But then he was furious with his father, determined to show him he could earn the money.

He took the first job he could find—contingent stock boy in the women's dress and suit department of a New York department store at a low hourly wage. His buyer spotted him as "promotable." At the end of the first day she made him acting head of stock to fill that vacancy. He clicked with the buyer and assistant buyer, both fashion-conscious, capable women. By the end of the two weeks he agreed to come back Thursday nights and Saturdays while attending college.

Although he'd had to give up his original plan to go away to college because of illness, he liked Long Island University where he majored in economics and minored in psychology. The courses were not particularly stimulating to him, but he had a good scholastic record and a very good time. Three months after he graduated with a B.A. degree at age twenty-two, he returned to his store job as head of stock, with a good salary increase. He was liaison between the department, the stockroom, and the buyer's office. He took care of unit control records for the department in three branch stores. In addition to gaining practical knowledge of stock maintenance and inventory, he was close to the buying and liked it.

His two bosses, the buyer and her assistant, gave him excellent training, included him in many of their conferences, developed his interest and knowledge of fashion. Before coming to the store he had never thought about the field, had had only an average interest in clothes even for himself. But he was eager to learn more about it. After one month on this assignment, the assistant buyer left. His buyer showed her confidence in him by giving him the job. A small immediate raise without his asking for it meant more to him than any he's had since.

He was assistant buyer AND head of stock, with a competent stock boy to help him. As he was responsible for keeping the branch stores supplied with merchandise, he studied their weekly sales and stock reports to maintain a minimum of each style unit at all times, and to find out the styles that were most successful for each store. His buyer kept him informed of all she was doing, gave him a chance to try his wings at everything. He went into the market frequently to check buying sources and gradually did some buying himself. Sometimes he went with the buyer, trying to absorb some of her fashion knowledge, merchandising ability, and creative buying. She worked closely with manufacturers, giving them ideas for designs for clothes she wanted to buy. Her taste and fashion sense were excellent and backed by years of experience.

M.L. conferred with her on items to be advertised and followed through with the advertising department. He helped plan department budgets with the buyer and her merchandise manager. He learned to set up displays for the department and to choose merchandise for the large Fifth Avenue windows. He was on the floor a great deal to get customer reaction. Although he could not take customers into the fitting room, he helped them select merchandise and turned them over to the salesgirls to try on the garments. He exercised some supervision over the sales staff.

Much of his time went into department records. He became thoroughly familiar with unit control, the system that records for each style number the sizes, colors, and quantities bought and sold. The buyer relies on this to determine stock needed and to check customer response to each style. M.L. maintained the system, introduced some constructive changes.

He was assistant buyer for two years. He thoroughly enjoyed it, even the hectic pressure periods and the constant need for maintaining figures. But eight months before the end of the two years his buyer retired. Her successor felt that he still had allegiance to the old buyer, and did everything she could to encourage him to develop his abilities—elsewhere! He tried hard to work for her but finally decided to make a change. There wasn't any other department in the store that interested him as much as this one, so he thought the change should be to another store. His salary and experience had grown in these two years; he was ready for the next step.

He was hired by a large New York department store as dress department sales manager of one of its Long Island stores with 600 employees. He was eager to become associated with this well-known store, but disappointed to be sent to a branch. He knew he liked buying, merchan-

Merchandising

dising. Wouldn't this assignment take him away from it? He wished the opening had been in the main store.

But very soon he discovered that a suburban store sales manager has considerable merchandising responsibility even though he doesn't buy. He was completely responsible for getting the merchandise sold. He supervised twelve salespeople and one stock clerk. He worked with seven buyers from the main store, to find out about their merchandise and to let them know buying needs for his department.

Most important was selling each item of merchandise to his sales staff. Several times a week he met with his staff to discuss selling problems, to highlight the fashion points of new items. He set high standards and found that they respected them.

He saw the importance of working with other departments for the good of the store as a whole. When customers came to buy maternity dresses, he suggested that the layette and infants' furniture department put them on their mailing list for special promotion, with good results. He had responsibility with no one to lean on and liked it. It was a challenge to figure out the right time to mark down merchandise to clear out the stock and yet make a profit for the department. In the year he was there he felt he developed as a merchant. He was pleased, too, that his earnings were increasing.

Then he was drafted into the Army. After a brief three months he was discharged because of the recurrence of an old ailment. Another two months in bed at home and he was eager to get back to work. His department had grown, required two sales managers. When the store administrators knew he could return soon, they held an opening for him. He and the other sales manager worked out a plan for the department as a whole, rather than split it in two with inevitable overlapping. M.L. assumed the merchandising functions, the other man took over management. This continued for three months.

He had been rated "outstanding and promotable" on his six-month job reviews. He was eligible for promotion, had a chance to be interviewed for another job along with several other candidates. As a result, after a year, he became assistant buyer of women's large size and maternity dresses in the main store.

He had been warned by many who knew her that the buyer was a "battle-ax," and would "push him around," although she knew her business. None of it was exaggerated. He was miserable for six months. She yelled, blew her top at him consistently. Despite this, he knew she was an excellent buyer with a low markdown record and good profit picture for the department. Finally he learned to "take it," realizing her ranting wasn't personal. She did it to everyone! To his surprise she gave him an outstanding job review at the end of six months.

Most important, she gave him a chance to learn. He was responsible for two branch stores and had two junior assistant buyers to supervise. He bought some categories himself—cocktail and evening dresses, special sales items. He made every effort to "style up" the department. He was out in the market a great deal.

This period of one and a half years was one of intensive learning. He knew that his buyer liked and respected him. Yet her type of supervision had sometimes interfered with his creative drive, his urge to try new methods. At times he felt beaten. He was ready for a change when he had a chance to try for group sales manager in a suburban store. His salary had mounted steadily.

He started his present assignment as group sales manager in the company's Westchester store at $10,000 a year, and he is responsible for the departments that sell women's sportswear, dresses, shoes, coats, suits, furs, junior wear, accessories, cosmetics. He supervises five sales managers and through them fifty salesclerks and five stock clerks. His job, he says, is to stimulate and help those he supervises to the best performance possible. "My effectiveness must be judged through the people who work for me."

He sets standards, coordinates activities of the various departments, initiates ideas for promotion and display, and goes into the New York store once or twice a week to meet with buyers and merchandise administrators to learn their buying plans and to give them a picture of the needs of his store. He must figure the amount of space allotted each department, even each counter, in terms of returns brought in. Can he afford to give a prominent counter on the main floor to a new cosmetic, or should it go to the glove department? His boss, the store manager, gives him leeway to handle his department as he sees fit.

He likes the responsibility. He works five days a week except for one week when he is at the store six days, including one Saturday a month. At times he sets no limits, staying longer than expected of him. Added to that is an hour-and-a-half trip each way from his apartment in New York City, in a car pool with other young executives. He thinks perhaps he'd be earning more money in other fields. But now he knows this business is for him and he plans to stay with it.

Whenever there's a choice, he takes the opportunity for more responsibility, where he can try his own ideas, new methods. The satisfactions

Merchandising

he gets outweigh the worries that come with extra responsibility. His goal used to be buying. He still likes it, but the future is open. He likes the tremendous size of his organization. There's room to stretch and grow. "You have to trust the people you work for, or else don't work for them." Besides, he has great faith in the store organization, considers it the focal point of merchandising. He thinks the future will reflect it in increased job opportunities, increased earnings.

K.B. / Department Store Buyer

Are buyers frustrated designers? K.B. wanted to be a fashion designer, but was discouraged by a high school counselor who pointed out her weaknesses in sketching and drawing. Now, as buyer, she insists she does some designing as part of her job, and is anything but frustrated.

She sold hosiery and handbags in a local store in New Jersey, after school and Saturdays, while attending high school. Extra earnings went for clothes. Clothes, fashion were strong interests. She had ideas for designs, but perhaps her teacher was right—if she couldn't sketch well, she couldn't be a designer! After graduation from the academic high school program, she went on to Montclair State Teachers College, where she majored in science. She continued to sell in local stores after school and Saturdays, worked one summer in the credit department of a New York department store.

In her junior year she switched from Saturday work in a local store, where she had to work until 10 p.m., to a New York store where she finished at 5. Her social life looked up. Besides, she loved her assignment in the brand-new teen shop serving the high school crowd. She worked there that summer, too. In her senior year she was back again Saturdays.

The service manager who was responsible for personnel in that department found her an enthusiastic, effective salesperson. He encouraged her to consider merchandising as a career, arranged for her to discuss this with the personnel department. She weighed her genuine interest in store work and fashion and told the personnel department (which liked her store record) she'd like to come back permanently if she could be trained for a store career in buying. With amusement she recalls her surprise at the question "How tall are you?" Did it mean that her five feet four inches was too small for an executive trainee? No—it was just right for a spot in a department soon to be opened for women of that size and smaller.

After graduating from college with a B.A. degree, she started full-time in the store. She sold bathing suits five days a week, until the new five-four shop opened in July. She worked closely with the buyer in setting up the department: display, stock, promotion—she was part of everything because the department was new and small. She was the right size, too, to try on the clothes. She and the buyer got along famously. Three months later, in October, she was assigned as assistant service manager on the first floor. This was part of her training program, to be tried out at various executive jobs. For two months she was relief assistant, in a different department each day, handling customer adjustments, arranging schedules and assignments for the floor personnel. In December she was assigned to one department, assistant service manager in handkerchiefs, a temporary opening for the hectic Christmas rush.

While she was on this job, the buyer of the small women's shop asked for her as head of stock. K. was eager to get the experience and to work again for the buyer she liked so much. K. learned plenty during that year as head of stock.

Two months before Easter, the assistant buyer left. K. took on many of her duties. The buyer told her frankly that she was interviewing candidates for the job, but that if K. showed she could handle it, it was hers. K.B. absorbed more of the assistant buyer duties, continued to handle her head-of-stock responsibilities. The buyer threw everything at her. It was hard work. She liked it. Result—she got the assistant buyer job.

For fifteen months she continued here in an assignment that was varied and interesting. So often, she thinks, a buyer knows her work but can't train her assistant. K. appreciated her buyer, who could do both. She liked the intimacy of the department, the quality of the merchandise. She felt she was in the heart of fashion. As assistant, she took care of five branch stores, visited them, selected their merchandise, took care of their returns and all the records. She handled their advertising and promotion through the main store. In the New York store there was plenty of record work and selling, too. She was in the market, checking buying sources for her buyer, and doing some of the buying.

She remembers one manufacturer who made coats and suits exclusively for the store. Sometimes she helped him select fabrics, suggested designs suitable for the customer requirements she learned firsthand from her own selling and from the salesgirls' reports. Once in a while she was

Merchandising

offered outside jobs at higher salaries, but she liked her job, was appreciative of the time and effort the store had put into her training. She felt too that these job offers were largely due to the store's prestige. She wanted to continue to have this prestige by remaining.

Because her buyer had recommended her as promotable material in her six-month job reviews, soon she was to be moved to round out her experience. She was crushed when she heard that she was to go as assistant buyer to the budget coat department, far removed, she felt, from the fashion spot where she was happy. The disadvantages of being "promotable"! But her buyer and merchandise manager assured her that the experience in a volume department was grist to the mill of becoming a buyer. She was in budget coats for a year. For three months, when the buyer was on maternity leave, she took over. It was good experience, all of it, even though the satisfactions weren't as great as in the previous assignment. She asked the personnel department for a chance to work as assistant buyer in the college shop when she heard there might be an opening. She was assigned there and spent seven busy months helping to select sportswear for college students, again keeping the buyer's records, supervising the head of stock, and during the summer keeping an experienced eye on twenty-five temporary college salesgirls.

Then the president of the store called her in to offer her the job of buyer for the teen shop. K. was so excited that she thought she was just one of the candidates being considered. No, the job was hers, in the department where she had started six years before as a Saturday extra. She was twenty-six, looked scarcely older than the teen-agers for whom she would buy. The department was being reorganized and was moving to another floor. It was almost like starting from scratch. She loved the challenge, was delighted to work with teen-agers whose needs and desires she thought she understood.

Two years on the job have underlined her enthusiasm. Merchandise includes coats, suits, dresses (tailored to evening), rainwear, ski-wear, bathing suits, play clothes, millinery—eighteen different classifications to buy. Her staff includes one assistant, two clericals (one handles records for all branch store transactions) and a sales force that ranges from three in slow periods to ten at peak, averaging five or six.

Once a week she meets with the merchandise manager, who is her boss. With him she goes over her six-month budget plan, in which she predicts the amount of sales she expects each month, analyzes stock on hand, figures her "open-to-buy," the amount of stock she'll have to buy to meet her forecast. A solid week of figuring sometimes goes into these plans, into sales analyses of the past two or three years, in interpreting current needs. The figures are broken down for the main store and each of the five branches. Her figures better be accurate!

Yet she feels she has plenty of leeway, makes her own decisions. During a big year for "shrugs," when not one appeared in the teen shop her merchandise manager urged her to get some because customers had asked for them. "You can't buy for your personal taste," he said. Not entirely, but she knows her personal taste enters in and does consider it! She didn't like shrugs for these teen-agers, thought they belonged on older people. She compromised with the merchandise manager, bought a small quantity until she could find a substitute item. She'd been scouting the market for a short sweater that served the same purpose but looked smarter on these young figures. Finally she found it. Her customers bought them up fast, leaving the "shrugs" on the shelves. A buyer, she says, must individualize the needs of her department.

Usually she's out in the market two full days a week. In May, when she's buying for back-to-school, she spends three full weeks in the market. She has four main buying periods. At the end of January she shops for summer merchandise, in October for the spring, in May for the big back-to-school period in early fall, and in August and September for the holiday season. During these peak market periods she ends up with her records at home, studies style numbers, descriptions, colors to make her buying plans. If she's sure of her merchandise, she may place large orders immediately. With some items she places small orders, plans for reorders after she tests the trial run.

She likes simple lines, combs the market to find them. Because her store is well-known as a fashion leader, she finds manufacturers eager to listen to her ideas. Teen-agers need their own kind of clothes, in keeping with the general fashion trend but related to their special needs and desires. Frequently this means creating a new type of dress, a new sportswear item. She may go with the manufacturer to the fabric houses to select the fabric she wants, work with him on the actual design of the garment. She wishes now that she'd had some design training in her background. Knowledge of patternmaking and construction would be helpful.

But on the whole she's satisfied with her preparation. Her teacher training has been most helpful in training her staff, in understanding the needs of the teen-age customer. Once she considered specialized retail courses at night but her bosses thought it wasn't necessary. She was getting what she needed on the job. She's not sorry that she didn't go to

Merchandising

a school for merchandising. She had a good enough background in math to handle the figuring and planning necessary. On-the-job training has given her the practical knowledge of store operations.

Her assistant does some market scouting for her, even some of the buying, helps a great deal in maintaining records, is responsible for stock. Once a year her assistant is changed because of the store's program of moving promotable people around. K.B. needs this type of person, would rather train a new one each year than have a less imaginative person permanently.

Her sales staff represents a major part of her job. If the salespeople are sold on the merchandise, if they are alert to customer reaction, the merchandise will move. She meets with her staff at least two or three times a week, almost every day when new merchandise is coming in, from 9:15 to 9:30 in the morning before the store opens. She discusses new fashion points, why particular items are selling, why others aren't. Together they analyze problems of stock maintenance. When samples come in, she models them, asks for salespeople's reactions. She learns from each one of them. The best saleswoman in the department has been in the store fifteen years, another thirty years. Both of them take personal pride in helping her. Sometimes her staff doesn't like something she buys. If she's convinced it has value, she gives her reasons, asks them to try it. Frequently they'll come back to her saying she's right. She feels equally comfortable about admitting she's wrong. She had to urge her staff to consider the short sweaters (substitutes for the "shrugs") to be worn with full skirts. But they got behind them for her sake, finally convinced themselves that here was a good buy.

She truly believes that success of the department depends on all of them working together. She started as buyer telling them she relied on each one for help and guidance. The department works as a team. But still she's responsible, must check carefully when a suggestion is made before she adopts it. One girl, reporting that a dickey in a dress didn't fit, recommended return of all these dresses to the manufacturer. K.B. discovered that the salesgirl had tried one dress on two or three customers. This was not enough of a test. Checking further, K.B. found that the dickey in this dress did not fit well but all the others were fine. Another girl urged her to reorder a wool dress because customers were so enthusiastic about it. Check of the sales records showed only one dress had been sold, but the salesgirl's memory of its warm reception had multiplied the figures.

Even during buying periods when she's out in the market all day, she manages to be back in the store by five o'clock to discuss sales tallies with the staff, to look over the individual records as well as totals for the day. Did you have a good day? Did we "make the day" (equal or better last year's sales figures)?

It's most important that she sell too. During the busy season she sells every Saturday afternoon, other times manages to be on the floor as frequently as possible. Or she can be easily reached in her small office behind the department. Her salespeople enjoy introducing her to special customers, the out-of-towner who comes in regularly to buy a complete wardrobe. Sometimes a customer asks to meet the buyer. Are such extremely short shorts really being worn by teen-agers or is this just her daughter's whim? What does the buyer think of a clothing allowance for a fourteen-year-old?

She visits the branch stores to keep department managers informed about her department, to talk to the salespeople, to find out special needs of their customers. She finds slight differences in buying for these stores, differences that increase with distance from the city—more sportswear, less dressy clothes, more price-conscious. When the teen-age department was opened in a new branch she spent a week there training the sales staff.

Promoting her department, inside and outside the store, is high on her lists of duties. Because teen-age shops and manufacturing for teen-agers are relatively new, she feels like a pioneer. To wangle a full-page ad for her department from the store's advertising department is a major achievement. She works closely with *Seventeen* magazine to promote teen-age business. She must be an initiator. The older departments can get promotion and publicity more easily. She suggested the idea of fashion shows for her customers, had notices in the newspapers, signs in the store to bring them to her department. Now she holds them regularly—twice a year in the main store, arranges them, too, for the branch stores. She selects the clothes, the publicity department gets the models, she fits the clothes on them. She manages adroitly to get others to give the commentary (although she prepares it) because, she admits frankly, she doesn't like that job.

Her job is truly satisfying. She likes working for and with teen-agers. It's a joy to start with an idea for an item, find it or develop it in the market, and finally have it in the store, see it successfully sold. Sometimes her enthusiasm is dimmed by the welter of figures she must live with. An average of a day a week goes into them. Her assistant is a big help but K.B. can't stay far away from them. Even this she accepts be-

Merchandising

cause she knows she can't run her department without them. It takes stamina and pep to take the long hours when she works at home, too, and commutes from New Jersey (two and a half hours daily travel time).

It's within her discretion to work five or six days a week. During busy seasons she's there six days, at times she tries to alternate Saturdays off with her assistant. Her usual hours are 9:15 to 6. Peak times find her in at 8:30 and working straight through to midnight on her records at home. As buyer her salary increased substantially, plus a bonus based on percentage of net sales. The bonus puts no limit on her earning potential.

Soon she will marry a petroleum engineer who will whisk her off to Venezuela to live. At first it was hard for her to think of giving up her job. But she knows she's going into a full life. Fashion will always be part of it. She can't predict now whether she'll work in Venezuela or how long they'll live there. But she looks forward to learning about fashion in this new country, with emphasis, of course, on teen-agers. She plans to keep abreast of the world fashion picture, even if she's not actively working in it. Naturally she looks forward to having a family. But in the future there may be a possibility that she will return to work in the fashion field. She will be ready.

B.S. / Resident Buyer of Junior Sportswear

Even as a child she loved to shop. Not just for clothes for herself, but for anyone in the family who would take her along. She gobbled up fashion magazines, frequently visited her aunt, a dressmaker, who let her play around with fabrics. When she was a little older, a special treat was a trip to the shoe market in New York with her father to buy shoes for his suburban shoe store. She felt she had interest, taste, and a flair for fashion.

At seventeen, a graduate of the academic course of a New York City high school, her ambition was to be a fashion coordinator. Now she realizes she had a vague, glorified idea of this job with no awareness of the experience and background behind it. She wanted college and at the same time training for the fashion field, so she selected C.C.N.Y. (City College of New York) where she could combine both. She majored in retailing and fashion, minored in psychology. Her major courses, started when she was an upper sophomore, opened her eyes to the scope and breadth of the fashion industry. She studied the history of fashion, fashion cycles. Her fashion courses included an over-all picture of textiles, jewelry, furs, and accessories, as well as coats, suits, and dresses in relation to the fashion world. She dreaded figures, so left the required economics and statistics course till her last semester. She earned an "A" through sheer determination and hard work. But she admits now that a tally full of facts and figures from one of the stores she works with makes sense to her largely because of the dreaded course.

Other courses have proved their worth to her, especially psychology and public speaking. She is enthusiastic about the value of her extra-curricular activities. Through the Retailing Society she heard speakers from all branches of the fashion industry, and she took part in the club's annual fashion shows. For one year she was president of the society, and actually ran a fashion show; she claims this experience was largely responsible for the promotion to her present job.

Summers she had occasionally worked in the garment district as a coat and suit model (size 12, height 5'6½", weight 122). She managed to work Thursday nights and Saturdays throughout college selling girls' and women's sportswear in a well-known Fifth Avenue department store. She was under no financial pressure, but wanted the experience, and enjoyed too the independence of earning her own money. In her last year she was accepted for the college work-study program. For four months she attended college classes mornings, worked afternoons in the same department store where she'd been a Thursday-Saturday extra. She worked all over the store as fill-in salesgirl wherever needed. If she had chosen the alternate work period—shorter but full-time—as some of the students did, she might have had a chance at a junior executive job. She wanted an executive job, leaned towards buying as a goal, thought she might reach it faster in a buying office than in a store.

Her second four-month work period she again spent mornings at school and afternoons working for a large resident buying firm that served department stores throughout the country. She was assigned as clerical worker to follow up orders in all the departments of women's ready-to-wear. The junior dress buyer, who had an opening for an assistant, liked B.S. and the way she worked, decided to try her as assistant even though she'd been there just a week. In addition to keeping records and following up orders with manufacturers, B.S. was soon writing market reports for the buyer, who would bring in a dress and ask her to write a description. Actually it was a full-time job. She worked very hard, frequently took work home nights, but was glad to gain the experience, appreciated the training her buyer gave her. When she worked full-time during her spring vacation week, she was thrilled with

Merchandising

the chance to get into the market. She visited manufacturers' showrooms, evaluated junior dress sources for her buyer. When her work period ended she knew she wanted to return to the same job.

Commencement in June rounded out four years she had enjoyed thoroughly. Besides her B.B.A. degree, she made the highest average in the retailing class, got an award for having contributed the most to extra-curricular activities, was a member of Beta Gamma Sigma, honorary business fraternity. Immediately afterwards she was back at work in the midst of a busy buying period. She began to buy for some of the smaller stores.

Three weeks after B.S. returned, her buyer was going on vacation, leaving the responsibility for a fashion show in her assistant's lap. The bosses questioned the buyer's judgment, B.S. herself wondered if she could justify the buyer's faith. The buyer selected the merchandise and, with B.S., planned the show. B.S. wrote the commentary, selected the models, and when the time came read the commentary herself. It was a success, and it won her recognition from her bosses and the store buyers for whom the show was given. They all talked about it. The practical knowledge she gained in college fashion shows helped her through this. Six months later she read the commentary for the fashion shows of all the dress departments. Many buyers don't like to do this; she does.

Two months after that, when a new department of junior sportswear was set up, separate from women's sportswear, she was made buyer. At twenty-two she was the youngest buyer in the firm, with only eight months full-time and four months part-time experience behind her. She knows she moved fast, is grateful to the buyer who gave her every chance to grow on the job. A year and a half later, she and junior sportswear are a good team. She does everything herself, but hopes that her growing volume of business will bring an assistant.

Most of the time she's out in the market, visiting manufacturers who make junior sportswear, always alert for a good line or a good number. She looks for good workmanship in the garment as well as smart style. Are there clean seams? Is the fabric allowance skimpy? She tries on garments herself for fit and general feel from the wearer's point of view. In her preliminary surveys, she does no buying, but lines up sources for her visiting buyers when they come to New York.

The peak buying periods are January and June, when buyers descend on New York from all over the country. B.S. prepares for each peak with six weeks of intensive market scouting. Throughout the year she visits specialty and department stores to see what's selling. She reads *Women's*

IS THE FASHION BUSINESS YOUR BUSINESS?

Wear Daily, Vogue, and other fashion magazines. *Seventeen* is her bible. She goes to magazine luncheons to see showings and also attends fashion shows given by manufacturers of popular- and medium-priced sportswear. Gradually she has met buyers in her own field, some in retail. They discuss trends at lunch, sometimes help each other in checking on a manufacturer's enthusiasm for a "sensational" number that "such and such buyer bought in quantities." From 9 to 9:30, two mornings a week, she sees manufacturers' salesmen at her office.

When June or January is upon her, she's ready for the influx of 75 to 100 buyers who may want her services. She has prepared, too, for the fashion show that the buying firm gives each market period in one of the large hotels for the visiting buyers. She has selected merchandise, arranged with manufacturers for samples, selected models. She sometimes models herself; she writes and reads the commentary. After the show, buyers make appointments to see the garments in her office. She may line up six or seven buyers at her desk to examine the garments carefully.

To give individual attention to each buyer who wants her help requires careful planning and organizing of her time. She visits the market with many buyers, one at a time. One may need two hours of her time, another two days. Other appointments are made at her office. This hectic period lasts three or four weeks. During this time the major buying decisions are made. Buyers may place large orders, frequently smaller ones on trial with plans for reorders. Heavy reorder months are March and April after the January market period, August and September after the June influx. February and July are the only slow months.

She telephones manufacturers to follow up on orders, to check on late deliveries, to track down complaints of the wrong style number received by a buyer. She reels off style numbers, sizes, complete reorder information into the dictaphone. Frequently she types her own correspondence to the stores when the central correspondence unit is swamped.

On the whole, paper work isn't a burden. Most comes during reorder weeks, when she estimates two hours a day for it. During busy market periods, with the buyers in town, she works three or four hours a week at night, at home, on records that she herself needs (the office does not require them). It's the only way she can keep up to date. Her complete record shows the orders for each store, by buyer. It has many uses in planning, in getting a picture of buyers' preferences. A review of these figures before the buyer's next visit points up the buyer's needs, gives B.S. a solid base to start from. She finds it a great help in gaining their confidence. Buyers don't have to use her services at all. It's up to her to

Merchandising

develop a good relationship with them. Some lean on her completely, others use her sources to supplement their own.

A sign of confidence is for a buyer to leave an open order backed by money for B.S. to buy new items according to her own judgment. Her records are helpful, too, in spotting good numbers that have been reordered. One season she picked a jumper that had 100 percent "check out" (reorder). Every buyer reordered, one store eight times. She suggested that the manufacturer include a similar number in his next line; he did, with good results. Most of the buying is done three months before it appears in the stores, six months for sweaters and special items.

Four times a year she prepares market reports and, in between, reports on individual items. These are write-ups for buyers in member stores, showing current trends and good items in the junior sportswear field. These reports go to the fashion department for illustrations to be added, and to be sure that they fit in with the total fashion picture established for this firm.

Twice a year she attends meetings held by the fashion department with all the buyers and merchandise managers, to discuss current trends in color, line, and style. Sometimes each buyer finds appropriate merchandise for an over-all promotion or display program that the fashion director plans around a theme. It may center on a color, for instance "spice brown," or a time of the year, such as Easter, or back-to-school.

B.S. worked with her boss, a merchandise manager, on a back-to-school promotion. She selected merchandise for it, saw the copy and layout proposed by the advertising agency, made suggestions for changes that were included in the final ad.

Sometimes a store will ask her help in selecting merchandise for a window display. Sometimes she suggests holding a fashion show in a nearby store, plans it, commentates, even models in it. These occasional visits to stores bring her a little closer to customer reaction which the resident buyer gets only indirectly. She tries to remedy this by talking to the store buyers, listening in on young people's "clothes talk." She's taken to eavesdropping. She had a fine time with the high school advisory board of one of the stores, took them to lunch, and then to manufacturers' showrooms to get their reactions to the clothes shown.

It's not all roses, but she's enthusiastic about her work. She likes the freedom to make her own decisions, even though it means assuming responsibility. She likes the mobility of her job; not being tied to a desk. But like the postman, she's out in all kinds of weather, a real disadvantage in the winter when she suffers from the cold. She works hard, frequently under pressure, from 9 to 5:30 five days a week. But she glories in her free Saturdays, to her an advantage of resident buying over retail buying. She accepts the importance of figures but still doesn't like them, knows she has much less to do with them than her counterpart in a store. Nor does she regard figures as a threat to her security. She is indirectly affected, of course, by final sales figures in the stores. But even if her selection of merchandise has been good, it's up to the store buyer to cope with the many other factors that enter into the selling of the merchandise.

She thinks the salary is low for the responsibility she carries, and lower than if she were a store buyer. She manages well because she lives at home. There's cash value, too, in buying her clothes wholesale and in being taken to lunch frequently by manufacturers and store buyers.

And the satisfactions are high. She's treated regally in the market. She glowed when a store buyer recently wrote her of the big increase in her department's sales due largely to B.S.'s selection of merchandise. She likes to split her two-week vacation, recently took her winter week in Mexico, her summer week on Long Island in a beach apartment shared with three other girls (this took care of summer weekends, too).

She manages time and some money, too, for her photography and record collection hobbies. She looks forward to a time when her earnings will be considerably higher, probably in a few years here, sooner if she moved. But she likes it where she is, gets along well with the people, appreciates the confidence they've shown in her. She's been offered buyer jobs in out-of-town stores, although she doubts if she could start at that level in a New York department store. She's enthusiastic about junior sportswear, expects it to grow in importance. At twenty-three, with a year and a half of buying experience behind her, she finds herself in a challenging, satisfying field.

Chapter 5

Planning and Promotion

Fashion planning and promotion have grown in importance, paralleling the growth of the industry into big business. As a senior vice president and fashion director of a prominent advertising agency said to me, "Now that Wall Street recognizes the importance of the fashion business, we fashion people have become respectable, significant parts of the business, not just silly women playing around with color charts."

Fashion planning and fashion promotion are closely related, but they can be analyzed separately. Fashion planning and coordination has grown into a function on its own, although it had its origin in promotional needs and is still closely related. Often the same person combines both functions. Here we head into problems of job titles. The solution is to look behind the classification to find out what the individual does. The title of stylist, fashion coordinator, fashion director, fashion consultant, and promotion director are frequently interchangeable tags. They point generally to some responsibility for fashion planning or promotion or both.

FASHION PLANNING

If beige is an important color for the coming season, shoe, handbag, belt, millinery, dress, and coat manufacturers are all affected. If acces-

IS THE FASHION BUSINESS YOUR BUSINESS?

sory manufacturers don't have merchandise to coordinate with dresses and coats, the retailers' business as well as their own will slump.

Predicting fashion trends, outlining a fashion picture for color, silhouette, and fabrics is basic to plans for the manufacturer, wholesaler,

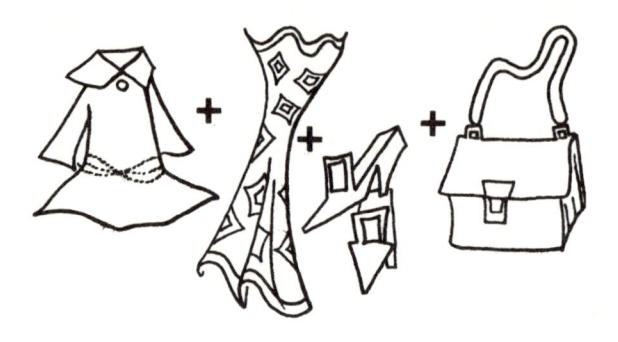

retailer and buying office. Fashion coordination follows logically. It requires a professional approach with the exchange of information and ideas among all branches of this competitive industry.

The extension of fashion to volume merchandise as well as high-priced brackets, and the introduction of new and diversified products have contributed to the growth of the fashion industry. Growth has brought complexities. There are new business opportunities, but also new pitfalls. Money investments are greater and possibilities of losses serious. To meet this, the fashion industry, like others, looks towards specialization and professional knowledge to protect and to forward its growth.

How is it done? Is it all guesswork, intuition, a sixth sense that dictates trends? No. Careful study of fashion cycles, observations of straws in the wind placed by key designers and merchandisers to test consumers' reactions, awareness of needs due to changes in living conditions, are down-to-earth methods used by fashion experts. Predictions, as in any field, will not be completely accurate. But they can be helpful guides. Always there will be the final test of consumer acceptance, of the human element that frequently defies the most scientific predictions. Nor can the expert spot in advance the "hot" number or new item that unexpectedly catches the public's fancy and becomes a best seller for that season. The fashion planner must work more broadly to ascertain trends in silhouette, color, fabric texture, finish, and design.

Does fashion planning bring dullness and uniformity? No, but it may reduce trial-and-error methods. Planning and guidance can result in

Planning and Promotion

promoting the right merchandise at the most productive time, rather than wasteful expenditures to push a waning fashion. The designer will find it helpful to know the silhouette that will probably be in vogue for the coming seasons. This will direct her thinking, but not limit her originality. Designs are projected for many types of figures, and stores and their customers have a wide choice of styles. When a whole market gets working on an idea with all the different methods of approach possible, there's more chance for the fashion to have a long life.

The fashion planner will steep himself in fashion knowledge by seeing and reading about all phases of the fashion industry and by exchanging ideas with people in every facet of fashion work. Wherever possible, he will attend functions where high-fashion clothes are worn, sports events where he can observe spectator attire. He will observe the clothes people wear at work as well as at play. He will study the effect of the trek to suburbia on clothes for the housewife, her husband, and their child. He will study the consumers his firm tries to reach, to understand their living habits and fashion needs. He scouts the fashion markets, shops the stores, travels, if possible, to fashion markets throughout the country and even all over the world.

Once he's ready with his fashion picture, his job is twofold. He has to get his story over to his firm and to the employees who design, buy, and sell merchandise. When the fashion theme is established for the firm, then it must be presented to the public. He will plan, and even give, fashion training programs and arrange fashion clinics and fashion shows for buyers and sales staff. His written market reports and forecasts will help get fashion information to them. He consults with buyers and merchandisers who seek his advice on their buying problems. If merchandise doesn't move, he may help analyze the reasons. His eagle eye sees that the over-all fashion program is followed throughout the organization. If oranges and yellows are dominant colors, his vigilance may prop up a buyer who has stocked too few items in those shades. Where there are many departments or a range of products, coordination is a major responsibility. Are the silhouettes of the corset and lingerie departments coordinated with dresses?

Functions Performed in Fashion Planning

STUDY FASHION TRENDS:
    Analyze trends in color, silhouette, fabric.
    Scout the market—apparel, accessory, fabric manufacturers.

IS THE FASHION BUSINESS YOUR BUSINESS?

Shop the stores.
Read fashion magazines of all countries; trade publications.
Read fashion bulletins from fashion services.
Travel to fashion centers all over the world.

STUDY THE CONSUMER MARKET:

See fashion as it's worn at theatres, concerts, resorts, fashion and sports events.

Analyze consumer market served by firm—its fashion needs in relation to living habits.

DEVELOP SOURCES OF FASHION INFORMATION:

Keep in touch with key fashion people in all branches of the industry—retail, wholesale, on magazines and trade publications—to exchange ideas.

MAKE FASHION FORECASTS:

Prepare written market reports and fashion predictions.

ESTABLISH A FASHION PICTURE AND
COORDINATE A FASHION PROGRAM:

Arrive at fashion decisions about color, silhouette, fabric, for the firm.
See that themes are generally followed in all departments.
Suggest possibilities for coordinating merchandise of groups of departments.
Give fashion information and specific material to other departments: design, buying and merchandising, sales, promotion, advertising, and display.

SPOT NEW ITEMS, SIGNIFICANT SOURCES,
IDEAS FOR DESIGN:

Select strong fashion items.
Scout the market to find good manufacturing sources.
Suggest ideas for design in line with fashion theme.

GIVE FASHION TRAINING AND CONSULTATION:

Prepare written training material.
Conduct training sessions for buyers and sales staff.
Give fashion advice to firm executives, staff, customers.

PLAN AND CONDUCT FASHION SHOWS:

Select items.
Write fashion commentary, sometimes give it.
Conduct shows for staff and customers.

PREPARE PROMOTIONAL MATERIAL:

Suggest and select items for promotion, advertising, and display.
Prepare written and illustrative material.

ORGANIZE AND MANAGE THE DEPARTMENT:

Select, train, supervise staff in the department.

Planning and Promotion

REQUIREMENTS FOR ENTERING THE FIELD OF FASHION PLANNING

Personal requisites for entering the fashion field: a strong interest in fashion; ability to express ideas clearly—both orally and in writing; imagination; initiative; decisiveness; analytical approach.

Sound fashion experience in sales, merchandise, design, promotion, publicity, or publication, or a combination of two or more of these, can prepare an individual for fashion planning. Specific knowledge of color, fashion history, fabrics, garment design and construction is essential. Courses in these subjects are valuable preparation, and a broad educational background provides a sound base.

Fashion planning is a function that cuts across many jobs. In a small organization the designer, the buyer, or the head of the firm does it. The need is there even if it isn't isolated and given a job title. The term stylist or fashion coordinator indicates that the individual has some responsibility for that function. No one is called a fashion planner, but it's part of the job of any good designer, merchandiser, or promoter. It is a distinct function that is gaining greater recognition as an essential part of the industry. It's still in its early stages of development. Does the firm have a fashion theme that represents current trends and yet tells an individual fashion story about *this* line of clothes or *this* specialty shop? Lots of people in the firm contribute to the fashion picture. In a large organization the story must be coordinated. In a small one, coordination is simpler, but there is the same need to plan and develop the firm's fashion program. The important thing, then, is not who does it and what his job is called, but is the job being done? The professionals in the business can answer yes. The future will mean expansion of this approach.

The beginner who is interested in this end of the business can look towards it as a goal. Fashion experience in any branch of the industry is good background. With this goal in mind, she can use her jobs and perhaps supplement them with training to gain the knowledge she needs —to learn trends, fabric analysis, and garment construction, to develop her color sense and awareness of consumer reaction. This comes gradually. There are many routes. The salesgirl, assistant designer, showroom girl, model, assistant buyer, fashion illustrator, and fashion reporter are all gaining experience useful to the fashion planner. Those in the top planning jobs have been drawn from all branches of the industry. Frequently the job itself has been created by an individual with varied fashion experience, initiative, and an urge to coordinate her firm's fashion program. Although tailored to the individual, the job generally requires knowledge of merchandising, design and style, and promotion. It demands, too, ability to organize, plan, and follow through, as well as practical knowledge of pricing and timing in the business.

THE FIELD IN PRACTICE

The fashion director of one resident buying office in New York does the fashion planning and coordinating, initiates ideas based on the fashion picture. She reports directly to the president, works with the firm's merchandise managers and resident buyers. For the member firms using the buying service she consults with store owners, merchandise managers, buyers, and salespeople. She exchanges ideas regularly with fashion people on magazines and trade publications, in fabric and apparel firms, in stores. She covers all aspects of the apparel and fabric market down to the $12.75 dress, analyzing trends in color, silhouette, and fabric. Years of experience have developed a sound knowledge of fabric and garment construction to aid her in evaluating quality of finish and wearability as well as style.

For fall merchandise she scouts the fabric market in February, the ready-to-wear market in April. In May she holds a fashion meeting for the firm's merchandise managers and 112 resident buyers to set the over-all fashion picture. In June she holds similar meetings or "clinics" for member stores' merchandise managers and buyers visiting New York on their buying trips. She's fashion consultant to stores on all fashion matters—display, promotion, advertising, or why specific merchandise doesn't sell. She travels to the stores, meets with salespeople to give them the fashion picture. She stimulates their interest by telling them the story behind the dress—about the fashion designer, the fabric, the new silhouette. She prepares training material. Store owners consult her on merchandise policy affected by fashion trends. Her advice has encouraged them to create teen-age departments, placing them close to junior wear instead of in children's departments.

Her department consists of two market assistants, a secretary, and three artists. She will consider beginners for any of these jobs. What does she look for? First, she seeks initiative, imagination, interest in fashion, and good work habits. No amount of training or experience

Planning and Promotion

substitutes for these personal qualities. In the art department she requires some art training. For market coverage, training related to fashion design, color, or merchandising is helpful.

The beginning artist learns to lay out copy and illustrations for promotional booklets, for display material. He makes figure drawings and sketches of garments and accessories.

The beginning market assistant goes out into the market with the director to learn what to look for and how to write up market reports. The next step will be to go into the market herself. She maintains a fabric swatch book, writes a résumé on fabrics after each day she's in the market. She prepares material for fashion clinics, writes commentary, and helps to select merchandise for fashion shows the stores want to give. She learns to understand the retail buyer's problems, finds out how to figure "open to buy" even though she won't have to do it in her work.

Sometimes the assistant does research. When the director met with store owners to discuss setting up teen-age departments, her assistant's research gave her facts and figures on buying habits of consumers, on population and income changes.

There are fashion *consulting services,* organized to give information and advice, similar to the department described above. Most frequent opportunities for beginners are as secretaries or typists, clerical assistants, and "paste-up" girls in the art layout department.

Ready-to-wear and fabric *manufacturers* often have stylists to coordinate their fashion programs. They work closely with the firm's designers, buyers, and salesmen, and keep in touch with other fashion people. The stylist may have been a designer, a buyer, or have had promotion or fashion magazine experience.

Fashion coordination is important in the *retail business.* Sometimes a fashion coordinator assists a merchandise manager to coordinate color and fabric themes for several departments, such as accessories. She may give fashion advice to customers. In one well-known New York store no one has the title of fashion coordinator but it's part of each merchandise manager's responsibility. Emphasis on this from the president on down has brought real fashion coordination to the store. Any of the beginning jobs in retailing will be good preparation for this work.

Fashion planning has grown up. It's influence touches every phase of the industry.

IS THE FASHION BUSINESS YOUR BUSINESS?

FASHION PROMOTION

Promotion can spark the whole business. It makes an unglamorous item exciting. It creates a demand where none existed. Whether glittering and fanciful or high-pressure and mundane, relentlessly it strives to sell more goods.

Promotion is done for all parts of the business, for the manufacturer, the retailer, the pattern company, the mail-order house. It's done, too, for a whole industry. Size and attitude of the company determine the setup. One small company does no promotion. Another of the same size is promotion-minded, and uses an advertising agency to prepare leaflets and ads. A large manufacturer has his own department or supplements a small department with an outside advertising and publicity agency. Large retailers have their own departments that include advertising, window display, and publicity. Newspapers and magazines have their own copywriters, and artists work up ads for smaller stores that don't have promotion departments. Central buying offices prepare material for their member stores, to supplement the work of the store's promotion departments.

Functions Performed in Promotion

DEVELOP A PROGRAM AND PLAN THEMES:
Study over-all need for promotion.
Determine style of material, individual approach for firm.
Select outlets for promotional material.
Select advertising media: newspapers, radio, television, magazines, direct-mail program.
Select fashion items or trends to be promoted.
Plan specific themes for Christmas, Easter, back-to-school, and other needs.
Plan for window and interior display coordinated with whole fashion program.
Plan informational programs for outside agencies (schools, community organizations) that have publicity value.
PREPARE WRITTEN MATERIAL:
Write copy for ads, leaflets, brochures, posters.
Write publicity releases.
PREPARE ART AND DISPLAY MATERIAL:
Sketch garments and figures.

Planning and Promotion

Make rough and finished drawings and colorings for ads, leaflets, brochures, pattern booklets, posters, catalogs.
Photograph fashion models in studio and on location.
Plan layout, select printing type.
Work with printing department.
Prepare window and display material.
INTRODUCE THE LINE TO BUYERS:
Travel with line of fabrics or garments to show to buyers and merchandisers throughout the country and get their reactions.
Arrange showings in showrooms or hotels for each seasonal line.
PLAN AND CONDUCT FASHION SHOWS:
Write commentary, select models, conduct fashion shows.
WORK WITH THE MERCHANDISE, DESIGN, SALES, FASHION DEPARTMENTS:
Get information from these departments.
Discuss promotion plans.
Analyze special promotion needs for individual departments.
Coordinate promotion plans of all departments.
Have the departments select items to be promoted, check material for accuracy.
DEVELOP CONTACTS FOR PUBLICITY:
Meet fashion people in all branches to develop and improve publicity for the firm and product.
Develop good working contacts with magazine and newspaper editors. Invite them to showings. Send them releases. Try to get editorial credits.
Develop publicity outlets on radio and television.
ESTIMATE COSTS:
Figure costs of color reproduction, paper stock, printing, display material.
Figure cost of advertising media—newspaper, radio, television, etc.
ANALYZE AND EVALUATE THE RESULTS OF PROMOTION:
Check sales returns to determine effect of promotion.
Check editorial credits received.
Evaluate various methods used.
Use evaluation in making plans for future programs.

REQUIREMENTS FOR ENTERING THE FASHION PROMOTION FIELD

A high school diploma is the minimum educational requirement for this field, and a broad educational background is desirable. *For art work,* specialized training is required. Recommended courses are life drawing, color, anatomy, fine arts, lettering and illustration, layout and typography, display. In addition, courses in fashion history, trends, and design are helpful. *For general promotion work,* courses in English composition, public speaking, journalism, advertising copywriting, layout, and printing can be helpful. In addition, courses in fashion history, trends, and design.

THE FIELD IN PRACTICE

Broadly, the functions of promotion are planning and initiating ideas, and carrying them out through the media of writing, art, display, photography, film, and demonstrations. Good promotion gives a clear fashion picture to the firm's customers. It aims to get the firm and its merchandise well known, and to sell more goods as a result. It is promotion that establishes brand names.

Promotion plans and programs have the same goal but may use different angles. Perhaps the approach is to build glamor into an item that is primarily utilitarian. The promotion director of a corset manufacturing firm insists that corsets can be glamorous and exciting. They can be linked to high fashion, with profit to both retailer and manufacturer. Her "let's keep in touch" campaign is aimed to supply stores with concise, usable promotional material at regular intervals, and to let buyers know that the manufacturer is truly interested in working closely with them on their promotional problems. Presentations are mailed to publicity directors, display chiefs, fashion coordinators, merchandise managers, and ad men, in addition to buyers. The material stresses the fashion level of the merchandise rather than sheer utility.

Typical presentations include these items: (1) a suggested newspaper ad layout geared to the current fashion theme; (2) suggested window display to coordinate with the fashion theme of the ad; (3) newspaper mats; (4) tear sheets (extra printed copies), when available, of successful newspaper ads on the product, together with detailed results. One recent window display suggestion was used by several leading stores. The centerpiece is a surrealistic tree figure in black velvet with magenta leaves against a soft gray background. Gleaming jewels and girdles in light colors are draped on the branches. On the back wall, shadows of three important silhouettes are painted—the bell, the Empire and the sheath.

Planning and Promotion

Another program gives the customer skills or knowledge that encourage her to buy the product. Fabric departments or specialty fabric shops hold sewing classes as good promotion for their fabrics. Often there are tie-ins with related firms. An example is a New York department store's fall fabric promotion featuring back-to-school goods. A fashion show based on *Seventeen* magazine's editorial featuring Simplicity patterns was given twice daily during a three-day event at a large New York store. Sewing machine demonstrations by Singer, Necchi, Pfaff, and Elna were held before and after each show. Tiny mannequin displays of the garments used in the show, posters and fabric drapes throughout the main counters, contributed a festive air in the department. Teen-agers were especially numerous in the audience. Youthful subscribers to the magazine had been notified of the event by postcard. An editor of the magazine welcomed the audience. The pattern company stylist was commentator of the fashion show. The store played up the event in three Fifth Avenue windows. The promotion departments of the store, the magazine, and the pattern companies worked closely together. It is likely, too, that the sewing machine companies and fabric houses assisted in the planning of the program. The department store's fabric buyer worked closely with all of them.

There may be a tie-in promotion with another product, centered about one theme. A men's shirt company has added a line of sports shirts coordinated with a well-known sports car, and will participate in a joint promotion of both in stores and auto showrooms during the week that the new car is introduced to the public. The shirts have car motifs in printed and embroidered fabrics. The promotion will be backed by advertising and publicity.

Some programs are geared to promote a whole industry rather than one firm. A promotion for "National Slacks Week" was organized by the Trouser Institute of America, an employer association, to promote the industry as a whole. Individual firms could supplement with their own program, gaining extra impact from the industry-wide promotion.

Special occasions or holidays, like Mother's Day, Christmas, or Easter, prompt extensive promotional campaigns that use all media. These regular events permit long-range planning. Work starts during the summer on a department store's big Christmas catalogue.

Often a program will center around a character made prominent through popular interest. If the interest stems from children, all the better. Nothing beats the promotional impact of the combined power of children and radio, children and television. Promotion directors know that small fry are a big factor in merchandising. Air waves are filled with straight commercials aimed specifically at the children, who promptly respond with, "Mommy, buy me that."

Developments in packaging and new methods of display have affected merchandising methods. Now the supermarket customer buys a packaged blouse along with a can of beans.

All of this requires planning. Main responsibility for this goes to a promotion director, whether for a manufacturer, retailer, or agency. Plans start three to six months before the program is launched. Budgets are set for large campaigns, and for the ads, leaflets, and displays that are regular promotion outlets.

The promotion department introduces the merchandise to the public. Fashion shows and demonstrations are effective means, frequently used. When a manufacturer is ready to show his line of dresses, the promotion department arranges the announcements, seating, pads and pencils with firm name for convenience of buyers, perhaps small souvenirs for them to take away. It will write commentary and hire models. There may be as many as four or five in the department or only one. Some manufacturers have no special person assigned to this. The head of the showroom or the manufacturer himself may take care of it. The young person assisting in the showroom, or sketching and modeling for the designer, has a chance to gain experience in promotion by helping plan the showings and by participating in them. It is a good beginning.

Stores, too, have fashion shows for their customers, and often give them as entertainment for outside organizations. A woman's club, for example, might have a fashion show for one of its programs. A store will gladly arrange this for the publicity value gained. A beginner in the department may work with the buyers to get their selections of merchandise, may dress the models, and perhaps model herself. She will take care of all the details of collecting and returning the merchandise.

The girl who can travel will find this an asset. If she has good fashion training, knowledge of dressmaking, and perhaps a little experience, she may find opportunities as traveling representative or stylist for a pattern company. She visits stores throughout the country, to put on fashion shows featuring new patterns and to answer customers' dressmaking and fashion questions. Sewing machine companies have similar job openings, to demonstrate how to use the machine and to put on fashion shows.

Writing the material is of course a major part of promotion. The

Planning and Promotion

copywriter's job is to use words that will make the customer want to buy the merchandise. Often new descriptions will bring new interest to a dress or coat that isn't very different from last year's. The words must be appealing, sometimes exciting, yet geared to the product so that the customer will be stimulated to see it but not disappointed because it doesn't look like the description.

ART

The artist's role in promoting fashion is an important one. A good illustration brings the merchandise to life. A startling color catches the consumer's eye, a subdued shade sets the mood for the delicacy of the item advertised. An effective layout of illustrations and copy demands attention.

Many a beginner is discouraged when the large department store or advertising agency says "experience only" for their art departments. How is he to get it? Art training is essential. Smaller stores are more receptive to beginners than the large ones. Pattern companies offer opportunities to trained beginners as assistants in the layout and coloring department. Buying offices have opportunities, too.

The illustrator must know how to draw both figures and garments in pencil, pen-and-ink, and in color. The figures he sketches are not only to be attractive but must show the correct anatomical structure. The illustrations of garments will emphasize fit, silhouette, even texture of the fabric. He may go to the manufacturer or store to make his rough sketch or croquis directly from the merchandise. He does the finished illustration in the studio. After years of experience some artists develop a reputation, skill, and unique style as illustrators that permit them to do exceedingly well on a free-lance basis. Many art departments employ some of these artists to supplement their full-time staff. This is highly individual and something for the beginner to work towards, never start at.

Good training along with evident ability is enough for some fashion sketching jobs. When a manufacturer has completed his line for the season, he may want it sketched for his future reference or for rough or finished illustrations to be used for promotion. A beginner sometimes starts here. A good letterer finds his skill helpful in getting into the art department.

Some illustrations are photographs. One of the country's largest department stores now uses photographs almost entirely for its ads and leaflets. The fashion photographer of course must know how to handle a camera. He may take his pictures in the studio, or "on location" in a place that gives the desired setting. He knows how to pose the model, understands the effect of different lighting methods, uses the background to highlight the dress or bag or texture of the fabric. After he takes several shots in different poses, he submits proofs. Then the photograph is selected from the proofs. Perhaps the line of the dress isn't sharp enough, or a slight shadow darkens the model's face. It's the retoucher who paints the print, or etches the negative with a sharp instrument to make the corrections for the finished print. Sometimes a beginner interested in photography can get started in the retouching department. The photostylist gets the clothes and accessories ready for the models, pins and fits them when necessary, makes minor alterations, works with the hair stylist and make-up man when required and is generally a resource person to insure that all is ready for the photographer. Beginners with some background in fashion and an interest in photography will get a chance here. It is excellent experience, too, for getting into other areas of fashion as well as photography.

The layout artist plays an important role. He places the illustration in relation to the copy, determines the proper balance of blank space with the material. Good illustrations and good copy can be ineffective if the layout is poor. Often the layout artist makes the layout first and gives it to the illustrator, who then does the sketch and coloring. The beginner who is willing to do paste-ups and work on rough layouts will gradually get more difficult assignments. He will find it helpful to know something about printing type and printing reproduction methods.

The head of the art department of one well-known pattern company, where beginners are hired, makes preliminary selections from portfolios sent to her by the personnel department. She expects to find some

Planning and Promotion

fashion illustrations or sketches, if the individual seeks a job in the fashion industry. She looks for style sense. Is the current silhouette there in the drawings? Are the accessories in keeping with the dress or coat? The portfolio may show strengths in layout. The color may be good even if the illustration itself is weak. She will see the person if she thinks there are possibilities for placing her in the department. The catalogue department, with thirty in the studio, does the art work for the pattern catalogue and the individual pattern folders. The art promotion department has three or four artists. All but two of all these jobs require art training and ability. The two are production expediters and schedulers who see that the work gets done on time.

The beginner may start as "paste-up" girl in the catalogue layout department, pasting up illustrations and copy from a rough layout planned by someone else. The next step is for her to make her own layout. She will start with a relatively simple assignment. Meanwhile she has a chance to see all the styles that go through the department, to study color and silhouette. Often the beginner paints at home or during her lunch hour. Someone will notice if she does good figure sketching or has a flair for color. She may be given some coloring to do. A beginner sometimes starts as colorist. The colorist paints the sketch after a stylist has selected the color, fabric, and style that will be illustrated. Perhaps, instead of colorist, she will be assigned as correction artist to make changes on the illustration from the original design, or to correct mistakes found in checking against the approved sketch. This is exacting work requiring a high degree of accuracy. She may do some figure sketching, small illustrations for a pattern folder, and gradually get more difficult tasks, more high-styled illustrations. If she's interested in the smaller departments that do promotion through leaflets, brochures, posters, and ads, she may be transferred after she's gained some experience.

DISPLAY

Display is a vital part of promotion. A leader in the field aptly calls it visual merchandising. Primarily it calls attention to specific merchandise. It can also be a mood setter, or be startling, exciting, and beautiful enough to have great publicity value.

More and more manufacturers find that effective displays in their showrooms have real value. One manufacturer, who devotes considerable attention to display, says it adds interest and excitement to merchandise. It also guides and stimulates the promotional thinking of retail merchandisers and buyers. He is stressing the Italian influence, and this is strongly reflected in the firm's showroom display. Visitors' attention is immediately attracted by a mechanical display in the vestibule, showing a gondolier bobbing up and down on a canal in Venice. Inside, the walls are decorated with rhinestone-trimmed Italian travel posters, and Italian and American flags.

Of all the branches of the industry, stores put most emphasis on display. The display department works with buyers and merchandisers, fashion planners and coordinators. Display is most effective when it represents the coordinated plans of the merchandise and promotion staff. Good display is built around a theme or idea. The ideas must fit the store and its customers. Each store has its own look. Display presents it to the public.

The display department and the buyer must work together. Effective display helps to sell more merchandise. Window space is carefully allocated and budgeted to each buyer, who selects the merchandise she wants displayed. Store windows frequently show great ingenuity and imagination and months of planning. Backgrounds for setting off the garments are of obvious importance. Winter sportswear shown against a snow-covered hill uses a direct background. Other types are indirect—historical scenes, or color themes imaginatively used. The display person needs knowledge of fashion trends and costume history in his use of color, in buying and designing display props and mannequins. Knowledge of lighting and stage setting helps him, too. In some large department stores, display is planned centrally for all its branches; in others, the branch store handles its own display, occasionally supplemented by ideas and suggestions from the central store. In large stores windows are changed about once a week or every two weeks.

Interior display is a prime example of point-of-sales display—an exhibit right at the spot where the merchandise will be sold. The mannequins in a department, effectively draped in gowns the buyer wants featured, can set the tone of the whole store. Coordination is often emphasized in these displays. Each gown may be complete with accessories. Perhaps the same dress will be shown on several mannequins, each with different, challenging accessories. This is an exceedingly important phase of display. The assistant buyer or salesperson interested in this may have a chance to suggest ideas for display in her department. Sometimes she will find the display person glad to let her assist him. A "stylist" from the display department may work just on selecting merchandise and

Planning and Promotion

dressing the mannequins inside the store. He or she must know the merchandise that is in stock and what is coming in, so that she can plan in advance.

Posters and placards noting practical items such as price, size, and department are made by the display department for both window and interior display. The tremendous growth of self-service in stores has given interior display added importance.

Jobs in the display department include sketching the plan of the display; lettering cards and placards; making posters; selecting and buying dummies; designing new mannequins; selecting, buying, and designing props; dressing mannequins for interior display; setting up the display; and dressing the windows. Window dressers often work late at night. More men than women are in window display, although some women have established themselves here. Both are found in interior display.

The beginner faces a frequent "experience only," especially from the large stores. Often the small store that does not have a specialized department will be more receptive to the trained beginner who can do display along with selling or other duties. Sometimes the beginner who is a good letterer can start as card writer or letterer in the display department. These cards give price or other identifying information, such as department or floor where the merchandise can be bought. An alert salesperson or assistant buyer has a chance to use her ideas for display in her own department, and thus gain experience. A secretary in a display department may find this a practical way to break into the work. A showroom assistant, working for a manufacturer, can use his initiative in introducing suggestions for display.

ADVERTISING

Advertising is done directly by manufacturers and stores and by advertising agencies that serve them. Printed ads appear in newspapers, magazines, and in direct-mail leaflets. The other media are radio and, more and more, television. Stores are doing much more with television advertising, both closed circuit (within the store) and on open television. On the whole, the larger the advertising budget, the greater percentage will be for television. A mammoth textile firm with a huge advertising budget may allot as much as 80 percent of the total to television advertising.

COPYWRITING

The copywriter looks for significant features in the merchandise, confers with the buyer or designer to learn more about its fashion points. In addition to glowing words he must include practical information on sizes and colors. He works within the limits of space of the brochure, ad, or leaflet, and he meets deadlines.

A college graduate with writing ability may get a chance as junior copywriter in an advertising department or agency, but those opportunities are limited and the competition keen. Courses in fashion, journalism, copywriting, and advertising are assets to the junior copywriter. Stenography and typing, or at least typing, is a good entering wedge into a promotion department or advertising or publicity agency. (Typing is an indispensable tool even to the established copywriter.) In a large agency the job as secretary may be an end in itself, rather than a step toward copywriting. One can explore the opportunity, however, frankly indicating one's interest in copywriting.

Practical fashion experience, especially in the retail field, is a sound background for the future copywriter. The assistant buyer or salesperson has firsthand knowledge of the customer, a real asset for the copywriter. This may help her, along with writing ability, to break into the field. The beginner gets and returns merchandise needed by the copywriter, takes proofs of ads to buyers for approval, sometimes keeps a scrapbook of the firm's advertising. He may stuff envelopes, and check on sales returns. Perhaps he will check copy proofs. Gradually he may get small writing assignments for leaflets or cards to be sent to customers. A junior copywriter will start with these smaller writing assignments. Smaller stores, mail-order houses, pattern companies generally require less experience than the larger department stores and manufacturers. Fashion copywriting is done best when the writer has fashion knowledge as well as writing ability.

STYLING

The positions of fashion stylists in advertising agencies have increased. There are plenty of applicants, hence lots of competition to get them. The stylist selects, buys, or borrows the clothes to appear in the ads from manufacturers. She shops the markets and stores, works with designers

Planning and Promotion

when a new or special outfit has to be made. She will be on location working with the photographer, the hair stylist, the make-up man, and the producer if it is being filmed. She has to be able to follow through on details and meet pressing deadlines.

The increase in use of television commercials by this industry has added to the duties of the stylist in the advertising agency. Where she does only television commercials for an agency or becomes an experienced free-lance stylist for television, she must become a union member by passing a test given by the United Scenic Artists. This requires knowledge of fashion and costumes and of television production. In 1969 the union minimum rate for stylist was $262.35 a week.

The stylist's job is demanding, with pressures of deadlines and sometimes irregular hours. Fashion training, experience as secretary on a fashion magazine, as photostylist, and in retailing are all good backgrounds. There are opportunities for trained beginners who can meet the demands. Opportunities for growth are to senior stylist and even to fashion director, creative director, and television producer.

PUBLICITY

Publicity is another phase of promotion that sometimes has its own department, or is integrated with the rest of promotion. The function of publicity is the same as promotion—to get good reaction to the firm and its merchandise, and ultimately to sell more goods. Publicity often travels devious paths and is less direct in its appeal. The primary difference is that publicity is never direct advertising. A sharp distinction is made between the paid ad that the newspaper carries, and the news item on its fashion page that describes the new silhouette and color of the same dress. The publicity item, just because it isn't paid for, has prestige value to the firm. Writing publicity releases to go to the newspapers and magazines is sometimes done in the copywriting department if there is no separate department. Preparing information for educational purposes, giving fashion shows for community organizations, comes within the scope of the publicity department. The publicist has a nose for news and an ability to spot its appeal to the buyer, editor, and consumer. Often he will come across a human-interest story—about an unusual customer, or a salesgirl's good deed. The local paper may gladly carry it for its news value, and the store welcomes the favorable publicity.

EARNINGS

Beginning salaries range from $4,000 to $6,500 a year. Prospects are good for those with experience to reach $8,000 to $15,000 a year. Top promotion directors, stylists, fashion directors, with years of diversified experience behind them, who carry full responsibility for the planning and promotion programs, command high salaries. Some reach $40,000 to $60,000.

JOB TURNOVER

Keen competition faces the beginner who wants to enter this field. Once he's in and has acquired experience and competence, he faces about the same turnover picture as in any of the fashion fields. There is mobility among top stylists, fashion directors, and promotion directors. They are drawn from all branches of the fashion field, notably merchandising and publications. Their diversified experience often opens up several opportunities for them. At the same time, the bosses seeking fashion and promotion directors recruit from all the branches of the fashion industries. As a result there is often more turnover and mobility among those in the top jobs than among their assistants.

E.U. / Children's Wear Stylist

Business school followed E.U.'s high school graduation. Then came seven years of secretarial jobs. Dreary work to E.U. But what else could she do? A blind date gave her the answer. He knew a turban manufacturer who was looking for an assistant to help him set up concessions in department stores. Was she interested in fashion? Yes, definitely. She liked clothes, had good taste, good color sense, and a flair for unusual color combinations. Was she willing to travel? Yes, if she could break away from secretarial work.

The manufacturer hired her on a three-week trial to set up a turban department in stores and to help select saleswomen-demonstrators. She discovered innumerable ways to drape the knitted turban on herself so that she could train the women she hired. She worked in department stores in New York and Brooklyn, in Rochester, Philadelphia, Newark,

Planning and Promotion

and even in Florida. She arranged the displays, trained the saleswomen, ordered stock, did some selling herself. She liked the pressure, change, and responsibility. The job lasted fourteen months until the turban fad wore itself out. The commissions she earned supplemented her salary satisfactorily. Most important, she had discovered that fashion work was for her.

A young firm making children's snowsuits hired her as showroom girl. She took care of the showroom, did some selling, all the secretarial work, and ran the office. (She didn't mind secretarial work when it was combined with her other duties.) The firm was small and she had a chance to learn all phases of the business. The two partners discussed designs (there was no designer), production problems, sales accounts with her, and welcomed her opinion. She enjoyed the job, but after five years thought she had reached the peak in salary and opportunity for advancement.

Her next job was showroom selling for a much larger children's wear firm, making five lines of children's dresses, boys' wear, snowsuits, and jackets. When her boss asked her if she was happy on the job, her only complaint was that she wanted more to do. Soon she found herself working with the firm's advertising agency, giving suggestions and following through on details in addition to showroom selling. She had ideas about garments in their lines, and found that her suggestions were greeted with respect. One of the owners told her later that she impressed him when she said "I don't like this number *because—*" never giving a flat statement of approval or disapproval without reasons to back up her opinions.

When she'd been on the job two years, her bosses decided they needed a stylist. Admittedly they weren't quite sure what a stylist did, but she should do it! Three years later, she can define her duties but knows the future means more responsibility, new functions.

She has a finger in every part of the pie. Essentially her job is to plan the lines, but it's not her responsibility alone. She works closely with the bosses, the piece-goods buyer, the designers, and all five factories. She shops the market before each season, searching for interesting fabrics, new items. A bright men's outfit for resort wear seen in a Madison Avenue window gave her an idea for a shirt, short, slack set for their boys' wear line. Regularly she reads fashion magazines, trade papers and journals, studying fashion trends, color, silhouette. She visits stores, sees buyers to get their ideas. What are their best sellers? After a conference with her boss, the piece-goods buyer, and the designers, she makes out a guide for the designers on color, fabric, number of garments in each line, and breakdown by price.

She handles the advertising and publicity. She selects items for the ads and clears all details with the advertising agency. She gives information to trade publications, such as *Women's Wear Daily* and *Daily News Record*. She hopes to do much more of this to get more publicity for the firm. During busy market periods she sells in the showroom. She enjoys it and finds it invaluable in getting buyers' opinions.

There are four designers, with a total staff of twenty-eight in the design rooms. E.U. screens trainee designers and samplehands for the firm's training program in the design department. Four times a year she costs the garments that go into the spring, summer, fall, and holiday lines. She figures cost of fabric and trimming, and estimates number of operations. Sometimes a ruffle has to be dropped or embroidery left off to bring the cost down. She developed a uniform card for exchanging information about the sample garment with the factories (all outside of New York).

A professional-looking camera in her office does not represent a hobby. She takes pictures of each sample garment sent to the factory. A picture attached to the cost sheet helps her in checking the duplicate sample when it comes from the factory. And if it's not right, back it goes until the duplicate is satisfactory, and then production can go ahead. Often she's on the phone cajoling a production manager to rush the duplicate or to make corrections. Frankly, she's not keen on all the detail work, but it's part of the job. "If nothing else," she says, "it's taught me that I can't afford to be temperamental." Some day she hopes to have someone relieve her of much of the detail and follow-up in the costing function.

All in all she loves her job. Most satisfying is to see some of her ideas worked out in the line and then have them turn into good sellers. There are dark days, too, when no one seems to cooperate and details bog her down. She's had to develop her job, overcome resentment, gain respect for her judgment. Her goal is to broaden her scope, increase her responsibility for fashion planning. She has just applied for membership in the Fashion Group, Inc., an organization of women in fashion work. She thinks courses in fabrics and sketching would be helpful, and will try to take them at night. At thirty-seven she looks forward to growing, learning, staying in the fashion world.

Planning and Promotion

L.O. / Textile Promotion Director

She majored in journalism at the University of Wisconsin. But history of art and advertising courses interested her more than those in writing. By the time she graduated she'd decided on promotion and advertising as her field. The only hitch was that she couldn't get a job. She settled for stenography and typing courses.

Before she could use her new skills as an entering wedge into the field she sought, she was selling novelty scarf-hats in New York's Lord & Taylor. The turban manufacturer, a friend, thought she'd be a good salesperson and had urged her to sell in his concession in the department store. Soon she was topping the department's sales. She moved fast, wanted to be busy, had lots of energy. The pace suited her. She spent two years working for the manufacturer, travelling throughout the country to set up his departments in stores, hiring and training saleswomen.

Merchandising became more and more challenging to her. She wanted to learn more about it. Retailing seemed the answer. She had been earning a good salary plus a bonus, but accepted a salary cut when a large New York department store hired her as "accessory fashion coordinator." L.O. was too embarrassed to ask what it meant. It turned out to be a brand-new job. She had to define her duties herself with the help of her boss, the merchandise manager of the first floor. He encouraged her to learn all she could and to use her initiative.

She worked with fourteen departments that sold accessories, and with the advertising and display departments. She went to meetings of the store's merchandise staff, to keep abreast of fashion trends and plans for all departments. She had to learn about the accessories themselves—their styles, price ranges, seasonal factors. Sometimes she visited the market for first-hand knowledge of manufacturers' products.

Under the merchandise manager's supervision she planned themes and promotion programs for groups of accessories. She still remembers a successful promotion built around a beautiful shade of aqua. There was an aqua aura over the whole floor. Each accessory department featured aqua merchandise, large promotion placards were in aqua, and a prominent window devoted its display to aqua. To do this she had to work closely with the buyers and with the advertising, window, and interior display departments. Sometimes she had to sell the program to a buyer, or suggest another item for display because it was not the exact shade of color in the promotion.

IS THE FASHION BUSINESS YOUR BUSINESS?

There were bound to be pressures, sometimes personality clashes. It was a stimulating two years, a chance to learn much about merchandising, promotion, color, and coordination. Her job was a steppingstone to other store jobs, such as assistant buyer. But a course given by The Fashion Group, Inc., had opened her eyes to the breadth of the fashion field. Retailing was important, but so were the other branches. When a textile converter offered her a job, she was ready to leave retailing.

The firm was small. (Seven years later, its staff of 30 has grown to 150, with an additional West Coast office.) They wanted to start a line of draperies. Could she find out what they should make? It was hardly an outline of duties, but she was ready to try. Two weeks later she was in tears. There wasn't enough to do. Once again she realized she had to build the job herself. Soon she was doing some selling. Even now she takes care of some of her first accounts, enjoys the chance to sell and get direct reactions from buyers.

Her original assignment became just one part of the duties that emerged. Right from the beginning she reported directly to the president, was considered an executive even when no one was quite sure what she was to do. "Promotion Director" became her title when she had to have cards printed. Gradually she has built up a job that is a recognized function in the firm—one of fashion planning, styling, promotion. Now she has a secretary and an assistant, a department humming with activity. At the beginning of the year she confers with the other executives to develop over-all plans for styling, merchandising, and promoting their fabrics.

She is responsible for the firm's advertising, promotion, and publicity. She works with an advertising agency, suggests some of the ideas, selects fabrics to be advertised, checks all the copy and illustrations for accuracy and color. She has learned a great deal about layout and printing. She prepares promotional booklets and flyers herself. When she was first there, she devised a format and trademark for stationery, still keeps a keen public relations eye on all printed forms and labels that represent the firm. She works closely with editors on fashion magazines and trade papers, frequently gets editorial credits for the firm.

The trickiest and most interesting part of her job is styling and merchandising and the planning that precedes it. While there are eight stylists and six merchandisers working hard at their jobs, she sees herself as coordinator, liaison between the firm and the fashion world. She must find out in advance what the fashion trends will be in color, silhouette, fabric texture, and finish. This scouting supplements the work of the

Planning and Promotion

stylist-designers and merchandisers, develops a unified fashion picture for the firm as a whole. Once the theme is established, it's her job to get the firm's story over to the manufacturer, the buyer, the editor, and finally the customer. She insists there's neither intuition nor guesswork in fashion planning. Instead, making fashion predictions is plain hard work with no short cuts. It means being aware of current trends, judging when the public will tire of a texture or color, and then introducing something that, although new, still fits in with the prevailing way of life. Such knowledge comes gradually with the experience of actively working in the fashion business.

A year before the fabrics appear, she starts thinking and planning for the line. She shops the stores, reads American and foreign fashion mazazines, trade papers, fashion pages. She keeps in close touch with fashion editors, buyers, and merchandisers, exchanging ideas and discussing opinions on trends. As a member of the Fashion Group, she knows women working in all phases of fashion. She attends many fashion shows.

Once she's established her color predictions, she has the studio paint them for reference. The print designs prepared by the stylists and designers are coordinated with these solid colors. She advises on new cloths and finishes. She's worked hard on the job and visited the company mills to gain the highly essential technical knowledge of fabrics.

Timing, she finds, is of the utmost importance. And this comes only with experience. It's best, of course, to be first with an important style. But if you can't be first, at least get there! She remembers her great responsibility when she pushed a satin finish until it was accepted in the line. Its success was satisfying; equally important was prestige gained for the firm by being early with a new style.

Her firm deals in volume, medium-priced fabrics. Essentially she feels it requires the same planning as the high-priced lines. Quality and good taste have become important in all price lines. She works closely with store buyers, once the line is completed. If the ready-to-wear buyers like it, they can put pressure on manufacturers to buy the fabric. Sometimes she travels to merchandisers and buyers across the country to launch a new cloth and to get reactions to it.

L.O. loves fabric. To her it's the heart of fashion. She thrives on variety, pressure, and wide range of responsibility. Her energy and enthusiasm are a match for the heavy demands of her job. Her salary, she says, is "good," much, much higher than when she started seven years ago. It might be even higher if she moved to another firm. But there's no question of that. This job holds maximum satisfaction for her. At thirty-six she has a busy, well-rounded life, with a husband and six-months-old son playing leading roles.

M.N. / Fashion Publicity

M.N. has the job she wants to stay with for as long as her boss will have her. Fashion publicity combines people and fashion. It's for her. But when she finished college, she didn't see this as a goal—actually didn't have any goal. Ruefully she reflects on her unemployment periods. Lack of guidance, she thinks, made her path too hit-and-miss for comfort. But now her interests and all her jobs have meshed together to make a sound background for this one.

She'd always been interested in fashion. In occupational courses in junior high school and high school she chose "buyer" and "merchandising" for her assignments. She liked to hear about her father's shoe store and her uncle's dress shop. Sometimes her father took her to the shoe market in New York and let her help choose the styles. Her selections were usually popular the year after, so she thought she had fashion sense. At Syracuse University she and her friends read fashion magazines closely. School vacations and summers, she sold in Syracuse and New York department stores. She earned the B.B.A. degree from Syracuse as a business major.

She knew she was going to work. But where? In what field? Job hunting in New York was logical, as her home was in nearby Yonkers, but she felt lost. She answered an ad for assistant buyer, placed by a large chain store. The man who interviewed her said, "You're only a college graduate without experience; take a course at Tobé-Coburn or someplace and then you'll be ready for this." She remembered she'd seen an announcement in college about scholarships for the Tobé-Coburn School for Fashion Careers. She had vaguely thought of applying. This decided her. She applied and got a scholarship for a one-year program open to students who had completed two years or more of college. (It's a two-year program for those with less.) Knowledge of typing and some retail selling experience were part of the entrance requirements. Her courses included fashion trends and history, fabrics, buying and merchandising, fashion promotion and advertising and salesmanship.

She liked the school's work periods in industry. In one, she assisted a department store coat buyer during the hectic Christmas rush. For the

Planning and Promotion

other one, she did market analysis for a blanket company under the supervision of an outstanding fashion consultant. The year's main value was to confirm and develop her interest in fashion. And she learned to read *Women's Wear Daily* in twenty minutes flat!

Soon after she finished at Tobé-Coburn, she was hired on the executive training squad of a large Brooklyn department store. After eight weeks she was assigned as assistant buyer of home furnishings. Although she hadn't thought of this as part of fashion, she used her fashion knowledge. It broadened her outlook and she liked it. At the end of a year and a half she heard she was slated for a buyer's job in the near future. She'd learned a great deal here, but the thought of promotion to buyer crystallized her feeling that she really didn't want buying as a career. So she quit, even though her salary had risen considerably.

Job hunting . . . agencies . . . weeks and months of looking for something in fashion outside of department store work followed. Although she'd never had much confidence in her writing ability, she thought she might fit into the merchandising department of a fashion magazine. She says she looked hard but couldn't get to first base. If she'd known stenography, there were some possibilities of beginning jobs, but alas, she just knew typing. She wished she had taken seriously the opportunities in college to try out for *Mademoiselle's* College Board of Editors. Girls who placed high in that contest found it helped in looking for magazine jobs later.

Finally she hit a small magazine specializing in bridal wear. The assistant merchandising editor, who had just been made editor, was not planning to hire an assistant. But he liked her merchandising experience and her enthusiasm. Most of all, she thinks, he couldn't resist a bargain. She had expected to take a salary cut to start in another field, she was willing to work at a beginner's rate. He hired her as his assistant at that salary.

Her first assignment was to analyze manufacturers' sales after their ads had appeared in the magazine. When she discovered what it cost a manufacturer per dress for each increased sale resulting from his magazine ad, she worked up some promotional material on her own initiative that her editor used. This gave her more confidence in her writing ability.

She did more of this type of work in the next year. And she was learning, learning all the time. An advantage of a small organization, she found, was that just by listening she could learn about the other departments. She was so close to the advertising department that she became familiar with that operation. But after a year she felt stymied,

IS THE FASHION BUSINESS YOUR BUSINESS?

with no chance to learn more or to get a better job on the magazine. So once again she started her job-hunting rounds to agencies, to magazines. To her chagrin, one year's experience on a small magazine didn't mean enough. Again she was faced with "no stenography, no job." Besides, beginning jobs didn't pay too well, and she was tired of compromising on salary (she was still getting the same beginner's rate when she left the magazine).

When a small electrical appliance manufacturer in Westchester hired her through his newspaper ad to develop a mail-order advertising campaign, she plunged into a new field with no one to help her. She was the advertising department. She wrote copy, did layout, arranged for illustrations, typed, worked with printers and advertising departments of newspapers, planned the timing and placement of ads and direct-mail promotions. She had absorbed more than she realized in her year with the magazine. Her keen observation of its advertising department was valuable. Although she wondered often if her efforts would pay off, in the end the campaign was successful. She earned a better salary with the promise of a bonus for additional products sold. At the end of the year, when the boss reneged on the bonus, she left.

Once again she was on the hunt, now for fashion copywriting in an advertising agency or department store. Merchandising in a department store, magazine experience in merchandising and promotion, advertising for a small company gave her a well-rounded background. At least she thought so. But countless employment agencies made it clear that employers demanded specialists for the work she sought. She was living at home and could afford to hold out longer to try to get what she wanted.

At long last, the publicity director of an advertising agency got discouraged trying to find someone with five years' copywriting and three years' children's merchandising experience for a job in her department. She decided to try M.N. M.N. is sure her wandering is over. She does publicity mainly for fashion accounts, two very large and two smaller children's wear firms. Usually she has one or two small accounts in other fields, too (at present, an ice tray manufacturer). She visits her clients frequently to get first-hand knowledge of their merchandise. She works closely with the fashion director or the head designer or the head of the firm. When the line is ready to be shown each season, she has seen it in advance, and calls the magazine and newspaper editors who cover the children's field to take them individually to the showroom.

She must know the bias, preference, and policy of each magazine, so that she can select the numbers that will interest each editor. One likes

Planning and Promotion

frilly dresses, another prefers sport clothes. Her hope is that the editor will like the line, or perhaps one dress, well enough to give editorial credit or feature a picture. This is the essence of publicity, the placement of *unpaid* items about clients in publications. Advertisements, by contrast, are paid for. She reads the fashion magazines, fashion pages of newspapers, trade papers, and journals.

A major part of M.N.'s job is to plan a theme for a client, prepare material and send releases to publications throughout the country. Children photograph better "on location" than in the studio, so for a back-to-school theme she planned a set at the Museum of Modern Art, selected the dresses, dressed the models, met the photographer there. Hiring the models, arranging with the photographer, was her job, too. She picked the final pictures, wrote and typed the copy. After her director approved the material, it was sent to the production department, then returned for mailing to fashion publications and newspapers all over the country. She couldn't wait to see how many of her items were used, and eagerly perused the agency's clipping service to keep tabs on herself.

She works with fashion coordinators of television shows, to lend her clients' clothes for wear on the program in exchange for credits. On give-away programs she arranges to give merchandise in exchange for a plug mentioning the manufacturer's name. Sometimes the television fashion coordinator seeks the manufacturer, but where M.N. can see a spot for the merchandise, it's up to her to develop new contacts, new publicity ideas. Initiating new ideas is essential in all phases of her work.

The department works as a team, so frequently she helps with fashion shows for other clients, or last-minute "on location" assignments. No one waits to be asked. They pitch in to help each other. She plans her time herself, usually working from 9:30 to 5:30, and during hectic times even works nights, although this isn't frequent.

She's out in the market a great deal. Her expense account allows her to take editors and television people out for lunch and cocktails. She loves it. But she stuffs envelopes too, frequently gets out her own mailings, has to dress fashion models, stands on her feet until they HURT. There's the constant strain of knowing that the "customer" (the client and the magazine editor) is always right. She has to be able to take cancellation of plans, doing-over-again from the start, to adapt her pace to changing needs of the agency and of individual clients. For the person who wants to know what each day ahead will bring, she says, this is not the job. But she thrives on it. Her department-store experience has been invaluable in giving her direct knowledge of customers and merchandising problems. She would rather have it than additional years of copywriting experience. Advancement for her will mean more responsibility, more accounts, more money. Her good starting salary had increased satisfactorily and she expects it to grow much higher in a few years.

She has an apartment with another girl just six blocks from her Madison Avenue office. She enjoys doing her own cooking, manages to retain enough enthusiasm and energy for theatres, dates, and community activities. During the peak of a fund-raising campaign for her favorite charity, she worked four or five nights a week. As to work and marriage, it would depend on the man. Perhaps she would continue to work for a while, but definitely not after she had children. She considers her job too stimulating and engrossing to combine it with a full home life.

B.J. / Head of Art Promotion

A five-year detour in a bank was B.J.'s route to an art job. She'd always sketched and made her own clothes. In high school she majored in art. She kept up with her school work, but having fun with her friends was most important. A career wasn't a burning issue, although she knew she'd have to work. Stenography and typing courses helped land a bank job after graduation.

At first it was a challenge to develop the speed required on the International Business Machine key-punch cards. Her interest flagged once she'd set and maintained a good pace. When the boss found fashion sketches on B.J.'s cards, he decided the job lacked spark for her and transferred her to another department. Soon she was supervising a small unit and welcomed the responsibility. She liked the people, the atmosphere was pleasant, and her social life was fine. The work itself was less important. Gradually she felt herself growing stale. Perhaps it would be stimulating to follow up her art interest.

Four years after she'd started at the bank she enrolled in art school to study fashion illustration three nights a week. Night school was a tough grind after a full day at the bank, but she enjoyed the courses. A year later she applied to a well-known fashion publishing firm that owned a subsidiary pattern company and published a pattern magazine. She was offered a job as size 16 model for the pattern company, with a chance

Planning and Promotion

of doing some art work too. To break into the art field she accepted a small salary decrease.

Modeling the muslin garments for the design department was hard work. She stood for hours on her feet. The part she liked was coloring for the art department. For three years she combined the two jobs, gradually doing less and less modeling. She matched colors to the tones in the department's color books, and mixed her own colors. Later came pencil and ink corrections, and finished color sketches made from the rough drawings of the free-lance artist. A promotion to assistant to the head of the color department gave her more responsibility. She liked her two years in that spot, but thought further advancement there was unlikely.

When the grapevine alerted her to a possible opening in art promotion, she promptly applied to the art director. Night courses at the Art Students' League in fashion illustration and advertising design had supplemented her experience. She got the job. That was three years ago. There were two in the department; B.J. was the assistant. Six months later, when her boss left, B.J. was promoted to head the department. She's been there ever since and loves it.

The promotion department plans brochures, leaflets, ads, and displays for stores and fabric firms to send to their customers. Aim, of course, is to push the sales of patterns and fabrics. The art promotion department that B.J. heads is responsible for the illustrations, color, typography, and layout.

The plan for promotion may be initiated by the pattern company or by the store or fabric firm. The promotion director confers with the art promotion, copywriting, and styling staff to discuss ideas and plans. The stylist selects the pattern and fabric swatch, the copywriter prepares the copy. B.J. roughs in the fashion figures in pencil—the figures are her selection. She plans color and background. Sometimes the fabric is the background and the sketch and style in the forefront. Or it's reversed. She lays out the copy in relation to the illustration. The rough may include just a figure sketch and layout without the design of the dress. If the promotion director approves this step, a finished rough comes next. This includes design of the garment, actual size of type, paper stock, and colors.

B.J. works with a budget estimate and has had to learn costs in relation to her selections of color and paper. One color, for example, is cheaper than several. A solid color with tones of the same color may be effective and also less expensive than different colors combined. A shiny finished paper is more expensive than a dull finish. She uses a book of printing types to select the size and form of type that fits in with the over-all appearance of the brochure or ad. Evening courses at Columbia University in advertising design and layout, in printing methods and type, have helped her. Once the finished rough is complete, a cost estimate is made by the production department. Often it is given to the pattern company's salesmen who show it to buyers for their reactions. The salesmen estimate the number they want and suggest changes.

Then comes work on the finished piece. B.J. does the basic planning and layout with the help of her assistant. Usually she assigns figure drawing to an artist who specializes in it in the general art department. B.J. tells her what she wants and makes final decisions on its acceptability. To select the proper silhouette and know how to accessorize the figure—is a large hat appropriate with this gown?—B.J. has to be hep to fashion trends. Regular reading for her is *Women's Wear Daily*, fashion pages of newspapers, fashion magazines, and Paris reports.

Precision is vital in her layouts. The paste-ups for the "mechanicals" must be exact. The "mechanical" is the finished layout ready to be photostated and sent to the printer. She sets the dummy type in place for the copy, with the aid of a triangle, and lays out the art work. Good preparation was her earlier experience as correction artist and colorist for plaids and stripes. She thinks it's good background for textile design, too.

She handles leaflets and brochures that stores send out to their customers, often along with their bills. She sends out material for fashion show programs, an important phase of promotion in a pattern company. Layout and art work for newspaper ads for out-of-town newspapers come from her department.

B.J. works with promotion departments of magazines, stores and fabric firms; with the styling, copywriting, art, and to a great extent, the printing department of her own organization.

All this is for her. It's a creative job from the start, although full of detail and exactness of deadlines and pressure. It is most satisfying to see the completed piece in print and then to discover that the promotion has been successful.

There's frustration, too. Recently her promotion director was trying to get a fabric firm to send out fabric swatches with a pattern. He suggested an accordion-type brochure, representing a fashion show. This limited B.J., who prefers to develop her own ideas from scratch. She submitted a plan based on her knowledge of the fabric. The director held out for his own idea. It had to be large, elegant—and on a very low

Planning and Promotion

budget. Cost limited her to one color. Brown with beige tones finally gave the hoped-for background to set off the fabric effectively. Along with the brochure went suggestions for display and newspaper ads. Aside from the printing, it took two girls one complete week to do the art work and make all the changes necessary to meet the director's approval and the relentless budget. When B.J. couldn't bear to look at it any more, the final straw was a printer's error discovered too late to be corrected. In desperation she rearranged the swatch to cover the mistake. It was an improvement!

In her eight years with the company her low starting salary, of course, has grown considerably. Raises were five or ten dollars each, at first every six months, then annually. She considers this a little low compared to other fields, such as advertising agencies, for which her experience qualifies her. But she likes her job, the responsibility, and the people she works with. (The low proportion of men, however, is not an advantage.)

Hours are 9 to 5, five days a week. She has two weeks vacation with pay, and usually takes another week at her own expense. Weekends and holidays are active. An ardent sportswoman, she puts skiing first, but also ice skates, plays tennis, swims, and is a member of a rifle and pistol club. As much time and money as she can spare goes into fixing up and rebuilding a tiny cottage in the country she bought with her parents. Home is an apartment in the Bronx with her mother and father. Although she's completely absorbed in her work, once she's home she can forget about it and relax in an old pair of slacks.

A major regret is that she did not go to college. The summers at the beach were wonderful, but she wishes now that she'd worked instead. It might have eased the financial problem of college. She's managed to take enough technical training at night to meet professional qualifications, but she misses the broad educational background and cultural stimulation she thinks college would have given her. She is considering taking some English and fine arts courses.

At thirty-one, B.J. has achieved satisfaction and recognition in her work, and maintained her other interests as well.

Chapter 6

Publishing

The power of the press is enormous. To most people the printed story or picture means prestige and glory. It is not surprising, then, that an aura of respect and glamor surrounds publishing. There's hard work behind the glamor.

The fashion story is told directly to the customer through fashion magazines and fashion pages of newspapers. Trade newspapers and magazines are directed to those in the business, to the manufacturer, retailer, buyer, display and promotion people. All these publications report what goes on in the fashion business, analyze trends, and try to present a coordinated fashion picture. They make predictions. Sometimes they are deliberately provocative, trying to stimulate and lead the industry. Unquestionably it's a business; so, directly or indirectly, they attempt to further merchandising, promotion, and advertising. Many of the same functions described in the preceding chapter as part of fashion planning and promotion are equally important in publishing. It is a surprise to most people to discover how many assignments on a fashion magazine, for example, involve more footwork, merchandising, and promotion than writing. No matter what the assignment, whether on magazine or newspaper, it's essential to have knowledge of and interest in the fashion business. Publishing cuts across every branch of the industry.

Publishing

Functions Performed in Publishing

DEVELOP SOURCES OF FASHION INFORMATION:

Scout the apparel, accessory, fabric markets, stores, and buying offices.

Establish good relationships with key people in all branches, to get and check information relating to trends, new developments, new resources, news about people in the industry, consumer reaction.

REPORT FORECASTS AND FASHION TRENDS, CONSUMER REACTION, AND NEWS ABOUT THE INDUSTRY:

Cover fashion news and stories in fashion centers throughout the world.

Attend fashion shows, events where high fashion is worn.

Cover conventions and meetings of trade groups in the industry.

Write up stories and reports to include trends, styles, merchandising, and display.

Work with art department for illustrations and photographs.

SELECT FASHION ITEMS TO BE FEATURED:

Select individual items that represent current trends or unusual ones that will help to *start trends* of the future.

Work with individual manufacturers to develop items with color, fabric, silhouette that the editor "believes" in.

PERFORM MERCHANDISING FUNCTIONS:

Work out all details with manufacturers and retailers, to make sure that items featured in the magazine will be in the stores ready for the customer.

Check delivery dates, prices.

Arrange editorial credits.

DO PROMOTION AND ADVERTISING:

Prepare promotional letters, kits, leaflets, and display material for manufacturers and retailers to implement the merchandising of items featured.

Plan and conduct fashion shows. (Work with manufacturers and stores.)

Prepare promotional material about the publication, to increase circulation and advertising.

Write advertising copy.

Analyze results from promotion and advertising.

DO ART WORK FOR ALL DEPARTMENTS:

Make rough and finished sketches and merchandise to be featured.

Do fashion illustrations for cover and fashion pages.

Photograph fashion models and merchandise.

EDIT:

Decide on over-all theme for issue.

Coordinate material of all departments.

Select feature articles.
Select items to be featured.
Rewrite reporters' stories.
Copyread—check all material for accuracy; write captions and headlines.
Work with production department to get the issue to press on time and in the most attractive format.

REQUIREMENTS FOR ENTERING THE FASHION PUBLISHING FIELD

Broad educational background. Minimum of high school graduation. College graduation is often preferred. Development of writing ability through English courses. Journalism training may be helpful, but is not required. Specialized courses in typography, art, fashion history and trends, fabrics are all helpful. Knowledge of and interest in the fashion industry, along with an ability to express ideas clearly in writing, are prime requisites for employment on a fashion publication.

It's hardly necessary to dwell on the important role of the fashion magazines in this business. If anything, too much glamor, too much reverence is attached to it, especially by the young person seeking entrance. There's no question of its influence. An editor can do an enormous amount of good for an individual manufacturer, or a whole branch of the industry. She can stimulate ideas, push an unknown designer into a position of prominence, help spread fashion trends throughout the world.

Less known to the public, but of vital importance in the business, are the trade and industrial magazines and newspapers. Some are special-

Publishing

ized for retailers; others, for individual branches such as corsets and brassieres, accessories, shoes, furs, men's wear, children's wear.

In general a beginner doesn't walk into this field easily. Previous experience in the fashion business, or even in a particular branch, is often required. There are opportunities for beginners who are willing to face competition and to accept beginning jobs as part of an apprenticeship for developing in the field. On a paper a beginner can start as copy boy or girl, distributing and picking up copy from each department. Typing, or better still, typing and stenography, are essential for the beginner on a fashion magazine.

FASHION MAGAZINES

Most fashion magazines are published for women. *Harper's Bazaar, Vogue, Mademoiselle, Glamour, Seventeen, Ingenue,* and *Modern Bride,* to mention some, epitomize fashion to their many readers. Several specialize in men's fashions: *Gentlemen's Quarterly, Esquire, Playboy,* and *Men's Wear Magazine.*

Most of the jobs are non-writing. It still is a great surprise to me that sometimes two or three copywriters do all the writing for the fashion departments of national fashion magazines. The fashion editor's role is to know fashion, have excellent taste, know the fashion centers and markets throughout the world, understand merchandising and retailing trends. Once she's selected the merchandise, a copywriter writes its description for her.

On large magazines, several fashion editors with their assistants or associates cover the fashion market, specializing in branches as do designers and buyers. There will be an accessories editor, a fabrics editor, etc. The beginning secretary or typist assigned to a fashion department learns about trends in color, silhouette, and fabric. Often she goes with her editor to help with a photographic sitting. She will be responsible for collecting the merchandise the editor wants photographed, and for following through on details with the manufacturer and photographer. She will work with the other departments of the magazine, such as art and production, as part of her secretarial duties.

Fashion copywriters write descriptions of the merchandise selected and featured by the fashion editors. A flair for apt description, for vivid, arresting words is their forte. Along with their writing ability should go knowledge of fashion. The copywriters stay in the magazine's office.

Market coverage, selection of merchandise is not their responsibility. The fashion copy editor may have one, occasionally two, assistants or junior copywriters. Experience is usually required, but sometimes a well-qualified beginner gets a chance as junior copywriter. Here again, a secretary to the editor gains experience and perhaps a chance to write some copy.

The merchandise department sees that merchandise featured in the magazine is in the stores for its readers to buy. One magazine works regularly with 500 stores throughout the country. Once the fashion editors have selected merchandise for an issue, the merchandise department is busy checking with manufacturers and stores on delivery dates, quantity, color, sizes. The beginner who can work under pressure, who types, is good at detail, may be assigned many of the follow-up functions. Last-minute checking by telephone and telegram supplements correspondence. A file clerk is kept busy with files listing manufacturers, retailers, buyers. Then the editorial credits are carefully checked and rechecked. It must be the right manufacturer, the right store, the right price. The editor decides which manufacturers, which stores get the editorial mention. Editorial credit refers to merchandise selected and featured by the editor, not advertised merchandise. Some merchandise editors travel to stores to develop and maintain contacts, put on fashion shows and do related promotion.

Promotion is a major function of the merchandising department. Leaflets, suggestions for ads and displays, folders and inserts are sent to manufacturers and stores to help them sell the merchandise featured in the magazine. Both writing and art ability are helpful in promotion. This department analyzes and evaluates sales returns as a result of the merchandise program.

The magazine's beauty editor is aware of fashion trends and their relation to hair styles and color of make-up.

Some magazines include departments not specifically related to fashion but of interest to their readers. The job editor gives information about career opportunities in many fields of work. The feature editor selects articles or fiction for the enlightenment and entertainment of the readers. Fashion knowledge or experience is not required in these departments. Writing and research ability is stressed.

The art department is responsible for the appearance of the magazine, the illustrations, selection of type, and layout. The illustrators are experienced. Many come from other branches of the industry. Some have worked up from other jobs in the art department. Often illustrators work

Publishing

free-lance. The beginner may start in the layout department doing paste-ups and rough layouts.

The advertising department may get ads written by a firm's advertising department or agency, or will write and illustrate them itself. Copywriters and illustrators in this department are experienced. The beginner travels the same path as in any advertising department.

The production department gets the issue to press on time. Scheduling material, proofreading, even emergency rewriting are the responsibility of this department. A beginner can follow up many of the details and can learn to proofread. Four months before an issue appears on the newsstand, the editor-in-chief meets with her editors to plan themes and to make assignments. Ideas are weighed carefully. The number of color pages in relation to black-and-white, and space allotment among different departments are decided. Then schedules and deadlines are set. The production department moves into action until the final copy is off the press. Then on to the next issue.

There are three ways of getting started on a fashion magazine: as a secretary with stenography and typing, or at least as a typist; as a winner of a fashion magazine contest; or with merchandising, retailing, or promotion experience.

A buyer or stylist with specialized experience needed by the magazine might come in as shoe editor or fabrics editor. Her fashion merchandise knowledge and contacts will be as useful to the magazine as they were on her previous jobs.

The beginner who sets her goal early for magazine work is wise to acquire secretarial skills. Even the college graduate with broad educational background, interest in fashion, and a flair for writing, will need these tools in most of the jobs assisting editors and assistant editors. Maybe she will use her stenography only occasionally. This varies with the department. She will miss out on some opportunities if she is not prepared with secretarial skills.

The staff of the magazine is not large, so that a secretary in a fashion department, for example, will do much besides take dictation and type. If she shows promise, she may even have a chance to go out into the market with her editor. She will become familiar with the merchandise, with fashion trends and market sources. Whether advancement comes quickly or not, she is learning the fashion publishing business and overcoming the blight of "no experience." There are good opportunities for the beginner with fashion interest and taste and patience to last through an apprentice period. She may be advanced as secretarial assistant to an editor of a larger department, or she may become assistant editor in a smaller department. On a smaller magazine these steps are more rapid than on the larger ones, where competition for entering is keen.

Some fashion magazines provide opportunities through contests for young women who want fashion careers. For those interested in fashion writing, art, merchandising, promotion, or advertising, *Mademoiselle*, a Condé Nast publication, has a College Board contest that can open up many possibilities. It is an annual event open to men and women undergraduates enrolled in an accredited college (four-year or junior) and available for work in New York for the month of June. Contestants try out by choosing a question to answer in one of four categories—fashion and merchandising, art, writing, promotion and advertising. If the tryout is accepted, they become College Board members. (There are usually over 700 College Board members selected.) Then during the year they will do two assignments—the kind they would get as regular members of *Mademoiselle's* staff. Some assignments may win cash prizes, or may be published. Primarily, the College Board member becomes eligible for selection as one of the 20 Guest Editors who will be brought to New York for the month of June. During that month they will work on salary for *Mademoiselle's* editors, help write and illustrate the August college issue, visit advertising and publishing offices, meet manufacturers, attend fashion openings, the theatre, parties, visit the United Nations. They are considered for openings that develop on the magazine. (Write to College Department, *Mademoiselle,* 420 Lexington Avenue, New York, N.Y. 10017.)

Besides the tangible advantages of winning or placing high in this contest and the knowledge gained in the preparation of the material, these young people also have achieved recognition helpful in getting a job in the fashion field. This contest is highly regarded. Unquestionably the top contestants have a better chance of getting started on a fashion magazine than they would have without this label. It gives them an entree into other fashion fields as well.

Glamour magazine, also part of Condé Nast Publications, has an annual contest seeking the Top Ten College Girls. The winners are required to show leadership in fashion and grooming and also in some campus or community activity outside of fashion. Winners of this contest have their photographs taken by leading fashion photographers for the August issue of *Glamour*. In addition they have an all-expenses-paid trip to a foreign country where they will be the guests of *Glamour* at an outstanding festival or international exhibition. Those interested in a

Publishing

modeling career have found this contest helpful in getting them started, and contacts made through *Glamour* sometimes have resulted in winners getting other jobs in the field. (Write to College Editor, *Glamour* Magazine, 420 Lexington Avenue, New York, N.Y. 10017.)

Vogue's Prix de Paris, another well-known contest, was discontinued in 1969.

FASHION PAGES OF NEWSPAPERS AND MAGAZINES

Quite different from the fashion magazines is the daily column and daily news coverage that appears on the fashion page of a large metropolitan daily. The editor who covers the Paris openings rushes to cable her reports, so that they will appear in the next day's issue in this country. If the paper is very large, the editor will have two or perhaps three assistants, but on small or medium-sized publications she handles all the market coverage and writing herself. She must have knowledge of fashion, and writing ability. She has no responsibility for merchandising or promotion, as on the fashion magazine. There may be a Sunday supplement with space allotted for her to fill regularly. The big newspapers require experience for their fashion reporters and editors. Smaller newspapers and those outside metropolitan areas have lower experience requirements.

Many magazines include fashion coverage as part of their content. On women's magazines considerable space is allotted to the fashion editor. Even such well-known picture magazines as *Look* and *Life* have fashion editors. So do the "homey" magazines on sale in the supermarkets. On the large magazines the jobs tend to go to those with previous fashion and writing experience. Here again, the smaller publications are more receptive to the beginner with no previous magazine experience but with sound fashion knowledge and preferably some experience. Typing as a tool for the beginner is absolutely necessary.

TRADE PUBLICATIONS

Some newspapers and magazines direct their news coverage and articles to members of the industry. Such publications as *Infants' and Children's Review, American Furrier, Corset and Underwear Review,*

135

Department Store Economist, Stores, California Apparel News, Southern Garment Manufacturer, Western Apparel Industry, Daily News Record, to mention a few, are highly specialized.

Prominent in this field is Fairchild Publications, with seven publications, and with news offices in key cities in this country and Europe. *Women's Wear Daily,* a daily newspaper, is read by all branches of the women's fashion industry for complete news coverage on trends, showings, firms, and people.

A different type of publication is *Apparel Manufacturer,* an industrial magazine that goes primarily to men's clothing manufacturers. Its editor often commissions articles by professionals in the field on management and engineering problems, with suggested solutions.

One editor of such a magazine said to me, "We're not looking for young people whose sole interest is to write the Great American Novel. Yes, we need writing ability, but even more important is an interest and enthusiasm for the industry, a nose for news, an analytical sense, and an ability to get along with people." He went on to say that the specialized experience gained on a trade publication is primarily an asset in such other jobs as advertising and merchandising within the same industry, rather than in writing jobs outside of the field.

Experience in the industry is often stressed more than writing experience. The beginner who seeks an opening will find that summer jobs in retailing and skill in typing may help him get started. Along with this he must be able to express himself clearly in writing.

A large publisher of trade newspapers hires six or seven beginners a year who show promise, to start as copy boys or girls. College graduates are welcomed, although accepted, too, are non-graduates who usually are attending college at night. Specialized training related to the industry is an asset, as are courses in writing, journalism, business, and economics. The copy boy or girl is a messenger, taking copy to and from the departments. Sometimes he will take down a reporter's story on the telephone. He is encouraged to write up market reports, or stories on fashion based on visits to the stores, to show his potentialities for reporting. An editor will examine his work for power of observation, ability to evaluate fashion and to express himself clearly and effectively.

From copy boy he can advance to junior reporter, going out to cover minor markets. The next step would be reporter, with responsibility assigned for one or two specialized markets. Or he might go from copy boy to junior copyreader where he proofreads, rewrites copy, and writes some picture captions and headlines, with increased responsibility when

Publishing

he moves up to copyreader. Copy boys and girls start at a low salary, in 1969 between $60 and $75 a week, with recognition that advancement comes usually within six months. Junior reporters get $100 to $120 a week.

Secretary to an editor is another good route to junior reporter and a career with this publishing firm, as it is with other publications.

EARNINGS

Beginning salaries are in the range of $4,000 to $6,500. The girl on the fashion magazine may find that the aura of glamor the public attaches to her job is accompanied by slightly lower salaries than in the design, promotion, or merchandising field. Yet the salary of a top fashion magazine editor, like those of editors on other publications, can reach $25,000. By and large, good reporters and editors earn between $8,000 and $18,000 a year.

JOB TURNOVER

Movement and turnover here is similar to that in the fashion planning and promotion fields. Experience on a fashion publication opens up opportunities in merchandising, promotion, and advertising. Conversely, the latter experience is equally valuable to a publication. Hence there is movement of experienced people from one field to the other. The beginner gaining a foothold faces the same picture as in most of the industry branches. He can feel confident that the experience he gains is welcomed elsewhere, too.

N.J. / Assistant Accessories Editor

She defied tradition. Instead of coming to New York's famed Greenwich Village as a starry-eyed career girl, N.J. was born there and promptly moved away. Her father's hotel work took them to Michigan, Illinois, Minnesota. Much of the time she was at boarding school. Her last two high school years were spent at the local school in the small New Jersey town where her father owned a farm. She loved the small-town life.

IS THE FASHION BUSINESS YOUR BUSINESS?

She'd always liked writing and illustrating, hated math. She was art editor of the high school magazine. She landed a job as cub reporter for the local weekly newspaper when she took the junior prom programs to be printed. Working after school, weekends, and right through the summer, she covered the police docket, fires, obituaries, and small features. Still vivid are her interviews with parents of boys killed in military service. She was seventeen. She had agreed to work without pay, so the unexpected $50 check at the end of the summer meant a great deal. During her next year at school she followed the editor's advice to study typing. Later on she realized the other things she had learned—to proofread, to understand proofreading terms, what "mats" were, and how to lock a page.

Then came two blissful years at Stephens Junior College in Missouri. An English major, with as many courses as she could manage in art and psychology, she was an honor student, did art work for the publication. Then on to the University of Missouri, where she majored in advertising to prepare for advertising or public relations. Courses in basic principles and the history of advertising have helped her since to understand advertising media. She studied window display, layout, copywriting. It was all fine except that she found herself sketching dresses instead of writing copy for flour and frozen foods. An active social life brought a drop in grades and a suggestion from her father to pick a New York college close to home for her last year. Her compromise was to work in New York instead. Then twenty years old, she got a job as typist in the office of a well-known New York fashion consultant.

Interest in fashion work had grown, despite her mother's efforts to steer her away from it (her mother was a sporadic designer). Now she regrets not having taken the fashion courses in patternmaking and draping offered at Stephens. She typed hours and hours of overtime, so that her pay check was much higher than her base salary. She read with absorption the material she typed for the fashion clinics. When she heard talk in the office of starting a house organ, she volunteered to do it. Writing monthly newsy items about the staff, and drawing illustrations, was a relief from typing. Sometimes she modeled at fashion clinics. After a few months she did a little comparative shopping for hats and lingerie, and wrote reports. She followed up ads to check quality and display of merchandise.

Inexorably the typing went on. There seemed little chance for advancement, but working here had convinced her that she wanted to be in the fashion field. At the end of a year she talked things over frankly

Publishing

with her boss, who suggested that she get retail selling experience if she was serious about a fashion career. Tired out from long hours and commuting from her New Jersey home, she took the summer off before looking for another job.

She wanted a straight selling job, not an executive training program. That fall she became a salesgirl in the junior miss department of a Fifth Avenue department store. Her former boss was right. She needed that experience. She learned to identify the positive customer who knows exactly what she wants, and the customer who doesn't know and needs more help. She soon found that she had to believe in the merchandise to do a really good selling job. She learned the names and styles of many dress manufacturers. Her salary and commission averaged considerably less than her former job. Ten months gave her what she wanted.

After a summer vacation she was on the hunt for a fashion job on a magazine, or in an advertising or publicity agency. Everyone told her to learn stenography. She resisted it, assuming she'd get stuck. Now she thinks it wouldn't have hurt her. She was tired and discouraged. Finally she was interviewed by a firm that published several fashion magazines, passed a typing test, and soon after was hired by the merchandise editor as a file clerk at a rate lower than her store job.

The editor's advice was: "Read every piece of paper you put in the files and you'll know more than anyone in the department." The first day, a file cabinet almost toppled on her in her zeal to get started. But she survived to follow the editor's advice. It was a revelation. There were letters from well-known people, gripes, outlines of fashion programs, merchandising plans, and promotions. She learned every day. Gradually she started to revise the files "so it would be simple enough for me to find things." Six months later her editor raised her salary, complimenting her "on the best filing system we've had." Besides filing, she typed, distributed mail, and prepared eight "dummy" books for all the editors. Three months before publication the editors planned the layout, the number of black-and-white pages and color pages, the allotment to each department. N.J. collected the copy, illustrations, credits, and ads from each department and pasted them in the dummies. The completed dummy looked almost like the finished magazine.

When she'd been there a few months, she planned a long spring weekend visit to her college. She was taken aback by a letter from one of her professors. He had heard she was coming. Would she please talk to his classes about magazine work? She began to collect material, jot down notes on "what makes a fashion magazine." Information she gained from the files and preparing the dummies was invaluable. Without quite realizing it, she had worked up a sizable booklet on how her magazine was produced, and had learned a great deal in the process. When she asked for permission to use it at her college, the editor was enthusiastic, later used it herself for a speech.

When N.J. returned, she had to make a presentation to all the editors at a staff meeting. She was scared and embarrassed. Perhaps it was a factor in her promotion shortly after to the credit office of the merchandise department.

When the magazine shows a picture, not an ad, of a dress, suit, piece of jewelry, it gives editorial "credit" to the manufacturer and one or more of the stores where it will be sold. The credit office follows through on every detail. N.J. was in constant touch with manufacturers to check on the items mentioned, on delivery dates to the stores. She was also in touch with buyers and fashion staff in the 500 stores throughout the country that carry the magazine's "credit" merchandise. Once the magazine was off the press, each item had to be in the stores ready for customers. She worked with retailers, manufacturers, fabric houses. She learned how to talk to manufacturers, to understand more of the stores' merchandising problems. The scope was tremendous, the details overwhelming. Sometimes she worked on three issues at the same time—proofreading the one going to press, telephoning about the new one in work, planning for the issue ahead of that. It was nine breathless months of telephones, telegrams, working out final details, often till 7 or 8 at night. Her salary had been raised after she was in this office six months. She never told a soul that she didn't like it and was afraid she'd be stuck there. She was amazed when her editor said she knew N.J. was ready for a transfer.

Her editor thought her art ability would be useful in the promotion office of the merchandising department. Here promotion programs are developed to push the merchandise given editorial credits. She worked on charts of all the pieces to be promoted, listing full information on each item. She might write six or seven letters to stores about the fashion highlights of one dress. Her retail experience was helpful in preparing written material aimed to give the salesgirl in the store ideas on how to sell *this* dress, the new silhouette, or a particular designer's clothes. She helped write slogans, suggested window displays with sketches that the stores could use. She worked on a monthly supplement for manufacturers, giving information on markets throughout the country. With it all there was typing and retyping. She enjoyed her eight or nine months

Publishing

in that position. When the personnel department offered her an opportunity for more writing as secretary to the beauty editor, she wanted the chance but left the merchandise department with regret. She had been there almost two and a half years.

There were many letters to readers answering their questions on care of skin, hair, and nails, and how to be beautiful. Soon she wrote most of them herself. With the editor's help she wrote copy for a column. The writing experience was good. She respected her editor but there was an intangible personality conflict between them. She was tense and miserable at the end of a year when the personnel department discussed her job with her. She hoped for a transfer to the fashion department, where a secretary was leaving. It looked hopeless because she didn't know stenography. Unexpectedly the fashion editor, a remote figure to N.J., waived that requirement because she liked N.J.'s reputation on the magazine.

She was assigned as secretary to two editors, sportswear and accessories. Before she started, the fashion editor faced her squarely with, "We're giving a fashion show in three weeks. It must go like clockwork. Can you do it?" Grimly N.J. said yes and plunged into a whirl of activity where she struggled through those three weeks mainly by herself. The brand-new accessories editor knew nothing about shoes and turned that over to N.J., who blazed her own trail through the files and trade publications for the sources they needed.

When the sportswear editor got her own secretary, N.J. concentrated full-time on shoes and accessories. She learned the manufacturers in each price line, the style leaders, the special importance of shoes and accessories, and the need for coordinating them with other fashion branches. She did the correspondence, typed copy, followed up with manufacturers. Gradually she took on more responsibility and was on her own in the department for two months after the editor left. The new editor sent her out in the market visiting manufacturers and stores to select merchandise for the magazine to feature. At the end of a year and a half in the department she was enthusiastic about accessories. Then another new editor took over. Instead of secretary, N.J. became her assistant—her present job.

Their year together has been marked by mutual respect and liking. They share market coverage and make joint plans for the department. N.J. welcomes the responsibility of doing an independent job. Primarily she watches the fashion trends in accessories, her eye out for new ideas, always relating them to color, line, silhouette in the other branches. Half the time she is out in the market covering millinery, handbags, jewelry, belts, scarves, umbrellas, leather novelties, luggage (shoes are now in a separate department).

In September she starts scouting for material that will be in the January issue. Often the manufacturers are not ready with their samples. She may get them to develop her ideas. Recently she liked the shape of a handbag that seemed just right for the current silhouette in dresses and coats, but the colors and fabrics were not coordinated with the trend. She found the fabric and colors she wanted. When the manufacturer made up some samples, he liked them too, and put them in his line. She featured one in the magazine. She attends fashion shows of dresses and sportswear, of high-fashion imports as well as accessories, frequently getting ideas for a handbag from the line of a skirt or from an "important" pin to go on a new neckline. She may browse for two hours in Tiffany's, or Lord & Taylor's boutique.

The magazine shows accessories with the dress, coat, or suit featured. It's her job to select them and have them at the photographic "sittings." She must know the individual preferences of each fashion editor. One wants large hats with her gowns, another resists them. There is much detail and follow-up work in getting manufacturers' merchandise to and from her office. She may need twenty or twenty-five hats, as well as scarves, gloves, handbags, and a wide selection of jewelry to cover the sittings. If she sends six rhinestone pins to the studio, the fashion editor may select one. This one gets the editorial credit. Her little black book with a sketch and description of each item prevents the nightmare of giving credit to the wrong manufacturer. Surprisingly, she doesn't write her own copy. It's done by the copywriters' department. Often she rewrites it her way, but they can change that, too!

Over the six years her salary has risen respectably. Recently she turned down a job offer with much more money to do accessory advertising for an advertising agency. It's good to know her experience qualifies for other jobs, but she wants to stay with the magazine. She hopes to be an editor and thinks she has a future here. She's enthusiastic about her work, feels creative and useful in finding good fashion merchandise that many women can afford. There's enormous satisfaction when the editor accepts N.J.'s judgment about a new fashion item or suggested trend. At the low end is the detail work of the credits, and the worry about keeping track of all the merchandise sent in to her. She's worked hard all the way, done a little more than was expected. "In the long run," she says, "those extra things you do pay off."

Publishing

Still a country girl at heart, she's finally learned to enjoy living in her native city, where she shares an apartment with other women in fashion work. She's managed to attend some evening art courses in the last two years. At twenty-eight, she knows fashion is her business. Her hopes for the future combine marriage and a fashion career.

J.B. / Sportswear Editor

J.B.'s path was straight to a job that combined two of her major interests—writing and fashion. As a child she sketched and made very grown-up dresses for her dolls. She liked clothes and fashion, but never thought of working in it. Writing was her goal. After high school graduation in Summit, N.J., came Boston's Simmons College. Her journalism program included courses in copywriting, editing, feature writing, layout, graphic arts. She faced the practical problems of a journalist as editor of the college yearbook and technical editor of the paper, planning layout and writing captions. The college required work in industry to supplement the courses. In the spring of her senior year she spent three weeks as copy girl for a fashion trade newspaper in New York. Her feet hurt at the end of the day, after she'd picked up and delivered copy to all departments, but she learned the paper's large organization and met everyone.

Upon graduation, with her B.S. degree, she promptly returned to the paper, accepting the same copy girl assignment for her training period. One month later she was writing stories for the house organ. Then she was assigned to the fashion department as copy reader. She found errors, checked punctuation, counted headlines. She had to rewrite stories sent in by reporters, evaluate their importance, and then write appropriate headlines. She unified material, with a lead or over-all headline to tie together scattered stories. In three months her salary had been raised.

Later on, she summarized results of market surveys made by editors through the newspaper's countrywide bureaus. A highlight for her was the survey she made at Vassar on college girls' clothes preferences. The newspaper carried her report. Technical training in college in caption writing, editing, and layout were all useful. This assignment continued for a little over a year. She began to feel that competence on this job held her back from a chance to do reporting. There were openings in the accessories market and then in hosiery—neither came to her. Later she was glad when the lingerie market broke.

IS THE FASHION BUSINESS YOUR BUSINESS?

A year and a half after she had started as copy girl, she was assigned as lingerie fashion editor. It was a medium-sized market gaining in fashion importance. Soon she discovered it was far from easy to meet the responsibility of reporting trends and resources. It demanded ability to select important items, but also a broader view of the market as a whole, and its general trends. There was so much for her to learn about fabrics, styling, construction of the garment. She worked hard to make this market come alive on paper, worried about doing it well. Coverage was shared with the lingerie news editor who reported news items and information about people.

With the help of the assistant to the fashion editor, who headed all fashion departments, she was soon going out into the market. She grouped manufacturers by price lines, shopped the resources just like a buyer. What was new? What items were being ordered and reordered? She checked with stores and their buyers as well as manufacturers. Three days out of five she was in the market. Writing, layout of her material, meetings with the fashion editor and the other market editors in the department absorbed the rest of the time. Her enthusiasm for fashion grew. The first story with her by-line appeared two months after she was on this new assignment. (The fashion editor gives by-lines for special stories.) After six months on the job, she was promoted to women's sportswear, a bigger market. She couldn't turn down this challenge, but would have liked a full year in lingerie. Her salary was increased in the sportswear assignment.

The sportswear market was divided in two. J.B. covered knitwear, swim wear, and leather goods, and her senior took high-styled, volume, and junior sportswear. This assignment lasted ten months. J.B. thoroughly enjoyed it. Did she want an opening in the corset market? No. She got it—a strong person was needed!

It was a letdown after the excitement of sportswear. No chance to be breezy about foundation garments. Copy had to be circumspect, even sedate. It was highly technical and she learned a great deal. The discipline, she thinks, was good for her—both in gaining technical information and in writing. Besides, she finds it an advantage to know as many of the fashion fields as possible. There was an enlightening trip to Cleveland and Chicago, to visit store buyers and discuss coordination of foundation garments with outerwear. Her salary had risen, too. All in all, it was a productive year.

When both sportswear editors left, J.B. asked for the senior assignment to report the high-style, volume, and junior markets. She agreed to give up her planned vacation trip to Europe to get the job.

She's out in the market three days out of five, or sometimes part of every day, covering from fifty to seventy-five of the main houses regularly. Half a dozen she visits as often as ten times a year. She seeks the current trend in color, fabric, and silhouette, makes predictions for the coming seasons, points out outstanding items and new designs. She works with top designers, tries to get sketches of their designs in advance. If they permit, she has an artist from the paper come up to sketch the garments. She uses her knowledge of sketching in her own notes, as quick reminders of points she wants to make.

Merchandising and display angles are part of her reporting job. She's a steady attender at manufacturers' fashion shows, sometimes loiters in stores watching and listening to customers. Once she thought she might be able to arrange a part-time sales job at Christmas to have direct contact with customers, but she couldn't combine it with her regular work. Some day she'd like to take courses in fabrics and apparel construction to improve her fashion knowledge.

Back in the office she gets her material down on paper. Types it, of course. (Thank goodness for the college typing course.) She works independently. If she has doubts, she talks them over with the fashion editor. The editor has shown confidence in J.B. by doing less and less direct supervision of her work during J.B.'s four years in the department. Staff meetings give her a chance to exchange ideas with the other market editors. She arranges with the fashion artists in the department to go to manufacturers to sketch garments she has picked. Sometimes she has merchandise sent to the office. It's her job to tell the artist the type of figure or mood she wants represented. She works closely with the sportswear news editor, sharing information and coverage.

She can write with enthusiasm because she's enthusiastic about fashion, especially sportswear. It's challenging to describe a new collection without using clichés, to capture a new color or silhouette with an arresting word, to write a story that will suggest to a buyer ways of promoting the merchandise.

Deadlines, headlines, dummies, layout—all are very much part of her job. Most departments have space allocated once a week; but sportswear appears every day. Wednesday is the big day, when 10 to 25 pages are divided between the news and the fashion departments. Except for half a page she's guaranteed for Wednesday, she never knows the exact amount of space she'll get. She prepares a dummy, measuring copy and sketches, writing the headlines, and deciding on size of type. The dummy goes to the copy desk. She must tailor her writing to the space allocated. No matter how she plans, last-minute changes may eliminate a story or cut it in half.

For her big day on Wednesday, the deadline is Monday. She works till 7:30 or 8 Monday nights. Most of the other eighteen people in the department leave earlier, but J.B. finds it less frustrating to push her deadline to the limit when decisions on space are surer. Four or five times a year there are full sections on sportswear. Each Friday night before one is due, she's there late pounding the typewriter. Usually she works from 9:30 to 5:30 with weekends free.

This combination is for her—fashion and writing. She loves the sportswear market. It's stimulating to work with the top designers who relate fashion to everything—to the history of art, architecture, anthropology and sociology. She enjoys writing, creating a vivid, clear word-picture of her market.

There are headaches, too. Laying out the dummy is often tedious. Pressure of deadlines can be nervewracking. There is the frustration of having your favorite story cut or eliminated! And the unexpected copy errors creep in and spoil a beautiful phrase. Yet migraine and ulcers are not for her, although they are considered a badge of the trade. At twenty-six she likes her work and is satisfied with her progress. Her quiet unaggressive manner belies the legend that only a hard-hitting reporter gets the news. She gains the confidence and respect of designers and manufacturers, so that they will give her advance information about their plans. Her unaggressiveness helps, she thinks. She works with them slowly, doesn't ask for everything at once. Gradually she is getting what she wants. The best way to impress a firm, she says, is to do a competent job. Then that firm and the next one, too, are easier to tap for news.

Most important for her is to do a job well for her own sake. The high standards she's set have reaped high job satisfactions, including the chance to work independently with a minimum of supervision.

Her own fashion look has improved on the job. Now she gets higher-priced clothes wholesale.

Her comfortable salary means pleasant living. New York isn't as wonderful as it seemed four years ago, when she first moved there, but she enjoys the opportunity for lots of theatre, ballet, and opera. She enjoys, too, her small dinner parties with writer friends in her Greenwich Village apartment.

Looking way into the future, a step up could be associate fashion edi-

Publishing

tor, supervising the market editors and writing. Then—fashion editor. Even outside the paper she's confident her experience is marketable— on a fashion magazine, in advertising, publicity, merchandising. Freelance fashion writing is another possibility, especially after she's married. She could tackle a woman's page, for she's interested in food as well as fashion.

There's an immediate dream she's determined will come true: the not-yet-taken European trip. She feels secure enough to ask for a six month's or year's leave of absence. She's convinced it would add to her value as market editor. Best of all she'd like an assignment to one of the paper's European offices, but if that's not possible she'd try some freelance fashion writing to supplement the money she's saving for the trip.

Chapter 7

Engineering and Management of Apparel Production

PRINCIPLES of industrial engineering and sound administration are the same in the hard goods and soft goods industries but the hard goods field has taken the lead in applying them. In this age of diversification, specialization, and higher costs, more and more apparel producers find they must use modern engineering and management methods. This chapter is devoted exclusively to apparel production, because opportunities for engineering and management careers here have grown enormously. Often overlooked because it's a developing field, it needs special emphasis. This does not preclude the importance of engineering and administration opportunities in other branches of soft goods, such as the large fabric producers and retailers.

The engineering approach is to find the best method of producing the item at the lowest cost and fastest time, maintaining standards of quality. Always seeking the most effective ways, it is never stymied by tradition, by "we've always done it this way" or "it would be impossible to change because the operators wouldn't like that method." The engineer breaks down into their component parts the items to be produced and the

Engineering and Management of Apparel Production

organization itself, studies their needs and problems, and relates them to the total picture.

Usually engineering is considered a service or staff function, making recommendations to be carried out by management and those in the line of operation. Inevitably the two are closely related, often fuse. The engineer may become a plant manager. Where engineering is introduced, those in management jobs must understand and accept it if the program is to be successful. It is the scientific approach that is important, not a rigid classification by job title. While engineering methods are more easily adapted to large organizations with volume production, the approach can be used even in a small plant, and to some extent with styled products as well as the more stable. Management's attitude will determine if the questioning, analytical approach of engineering can be introduced.

A management student at the Fashion Institute of Technology took a job with a small underwear manufacturer in New York City as general assistant in the production department. Although there were only sixteen sewing machine operators and a total staff of twenty-three, he had an excellent opportunity to apply his engineering training. The two partners of this new business, eager to introduce modern methods, accepted many of the young engineer's ideas. New attachments for the machines, a changed setup in the shipping department, redirection of flow work, rearrangement of plant layout, piece-rate system of payment instead of time-work basis—all were put in operation. A student in the same class worked as engineer in the engineering department of a large women's garment manufacturer. The department had thirteen engineers. Quite different was this organization from the smaller underwear factory. Yet basically the two students used the same approach.

Engineering is basic to the production program of Rosenau Bros., Inc., a large children's dress company with five plants. Over 1,000 sewing machines manufacture more than 7,000,000 dresses a year. The cutting room has more cutting space than two standard collegiate basketball courts. The fifteen tables combine in length to almost three-quarters of a mile. In the finished dress stock room there is enough space for over one-half million dresses. Two thousand dozen dresses are added daily, but the turnover is so rapid that there is never overcrowding.

The International Ladies Garment Workers Union established its own management-engineering department in 1941, to assist in improving the manufacturing techniques and operating methods of all branches of the industry with which their members were connected. Long-term projects include developing a library of standard data for labor operations in every branch of the women's garment industry. Short-term projects consist of services such as assisting in piece-rate settlements where there are disputes or problems. The department assists manufacturers who want its service to evaluate their production methods and their piece rates, and to make recommendations for improvements. Often the union's engineering program stimulates the employer to hire an engineer or to use a consulting engineering firm.

Current trends in the industry point toward an increasing need and demand for engineering and for progressive management. The tendency toward larger firms means volume production, where engineering methods can be applied to optimum advantage. Diversification of products requires streamlining and careful advance planning. High costs and competition demand elimination of waste and full utilization of facilities, so that the margin of profit is reliable. The consumer affects the picture by increasingly demanding quality standards in the garments he buys. To maintain and improve standards without increasing costs (the consumer does *not* want to pay more), the efficient plant is the only answer.

There have been many developments in types and finishes of fabrics. Permanent press, for example, was produced by Koratron Co. in 1963, the result of research and experimentation to develop this miraculous finish. The specially treated fabric required special methods with the machines and equipment that turned the fabric into a finished garment. Engineering was important in the development of the finish and in the adaptation of production methods to utilize a fabric with this new property.

The future may show startling changes in assembly methods of production. Electronic and chemical welding as substitute for sewing sounds farfetched, yet some experimentation on this has been done. With further developments in fibers and finishes, perhaps we will soon talk of the well-welded dress. Here again the engineer plays a key role.

Automation has already made a significant contribution in the development of computer programs affecting control of production, stock control, and detailed analyses of sales and costing. Some advances have been made in computerizing for pattern control and the grading of the pattern. Although it will not affect the style factor, automated equipment will increasingly be part of the sales, merchandising, and production functions.

If the guaranteed annual wage is adopted in our economy, full utilization of workers' time will be an obvious need. Long-term scheduling and planning to avoid seasonal gaps in production will need the guidance of enlightened managers and engineers.

With keener competition to attract and hold labor in the industry, there is increased need for progressive management to improve working conditions and personnel methods. By 1970 great strides have been made by some companies. Others are awakening to this need.

Need for engineering has expanded and will continue to do so. Engineering consulting services have increased their clients. They search for able, experienced engineers so that they can meet the increasing demand from industry. Because of the shortage of experienced engineers, they will occasionally hire an outstanding trainee. A consulting firm may send one or more engineers to the client company to work for months at a time, evaluating the entire organization from plant location to distribution and marketing methods, suggesting and installing changes, training staff to carry them out after the consultant leaves. Sometimes the client hires a junior or resident engineer who will continue at the plant permanently to follow through on the consultant's recommendations. Broad analysis of a company becomes a management consulting service rather than engineering only. Sometimes they give more limited service, working on special problems of plant layout or machine equipment. The consultant's role obviously means traveling, for he serves many clients rather than just one. More staff engineers and managers with an engineering approach are being hired by the large and medium-sized companies. Most of these opportunities require willingness to relocate, since factories in this industry spread throughout the country.

What, then, does the engineer actually do? He decides on the manufacturing method that will best serve the type of garment to be produced, particularly weighing the factors of style and volume. The complete garment system centers in New York, where the old-time skilled operator has worked this way for years. The engineer studies the garment itself. A garment may be broken down into as many as forty sections, or only seven or eight. His operations analysis will determine the methods used, types of machines, flow of work, and even his plant layout.

Time study of the workers will give him data for methods analysis and for labor costs, as well as the basis for setting wage rates. Motion studies enable him to analyze the elements in each job separately and in relation to one another, attempting to find improvements in movement and method. He knows, for example, that economy in handling and avoidance of waste movements is far more important than the speed of

IS THE FASHION BUSINESS YOUR BUSINESS?

the machine. The generally accepted percentage of sewing time is 15 to 30 percent of total production time. The remainder is handling. Thus careful analysis of methods used in receiving, pressing, finishing, and distribution of the garment is essential to cut costs. Production controls to regulate flow of work and see that delivery dates are met on time, to maintain inventory needs and yet not be oversupplied with goods, are important in his planning.

Location of the plant, its layout, lighting, fixtures, and worker facilities, are all his business. The purchase of modern machinery and equipment appropriate to the needs of the products to be manufactured is a major part of his responsibility.

Job evaluation is applied to the job, not the individual. It analyzes the job, grades worker characteristics and requirements to determine its value in relation to other jobs. It is the basis for determining wage rates, for setting selection standards in employment.

Training, supervision, generally sound personnel practices play a large part in the engineer's planning. Out-of-date is the caricatured "efficiency expert" who treated the worker like a robot. The modern engineer is vitally concerned with people. Unless he knows how to work well with them, none of his plans will be effective.

Perhaps most important of all, he's a communicator. He must convince all levels in the organization, from top management to the worker in the line of operation, that his ideas are sound. Unless they cooperate to carry them out, his services have little value. Clear, concise written and oral reports sell his ideas.

Functions Performed in Engineering

SELECT THE PLANT LOCATION:
Determine labor supply, cost of land and buildings, location in relation to buying and selling market.

DETERMINE THE PLANT LAYOUT:
Place equipment and machines, and arrange relationship of departments, to insure the smooth flow of work through the plant.

PLAN THE PHYSICAL FACILITIES AND FIXTURES:
Determine type of building needed, lighting, colors, fixtures, etc. Arrange facilities for workers' needs and comforts.

SELECT THE PRODUCTION METHOD SUITED
TO THE ITEMS TO BE MANUFACTURED:
Use complete garment system for high-styled garment (very few).

Engineering and Management of Apparel Production

Use processed flow or product flow system. Work is broken down into sections or operations. In processed flow, the work for several items or products goes to the specialized sections; in product flow, the sections are all for the same item.

Use straight line system only for very stable products. (Limited application—few in operation.)

Use short line or unit system for stable and medium-styled lines. It combines the progressive bundle (a section system with well-planned flow permitting flexible plant layout, e.g. movable machines) and straight line methods.

PURCHASE MACHINERY, EQUIPMENT, SUPPLIES:

Buy machines and attachments to effect maximum production at high quality.

Design new folders and attachments and arrange to have them made.

ANALYZE OPERATIONS:

Break down garments into sections.

Analyze machinery and attachments needed. (An attachment to a machine may combine several operations, or improve and simplify them.)

Through trial or check runs arrange sequence of operations and chart the operation flow.

TAKE TIME AND MOTION STUDIES:

Do motion studies to analyze the fundamental elements of a job, attempting to find improvements in movement and method.

Take time studies with stop watch (wink counters and other devices are used, too) to determine time required by an average qualified experienced operator to do a specific, standardized job at normal effort level.

Use time studies to set piece rates, in methods analysis and to develop standard data (the accumulation of information about the same operations).

SET PRODUCTION, QUALITY, AND COST CONTROLS:

Develop controls to arrive at smooth production without waste of materials or labor. Controls provide information on lots put into work, stage of completion, production of each operator. Also inventory controls, material usage, quality control.

Develop forms and records.

ESTABLISH A WAGE STRUCTURE:

Develop wage incentive plans.

Use job evaluations as basis for establishing wage classification for individual jobs.

ANALYZE COSTS:

Figure costs of labor, materials, etc.

PREPARE BUDGETS.

DEVELOP PERSONNEL POLICIES
AND PROCEDURES:

Establish programs for recruiting, selecting, hiring, and training personnel; for supervisory development.

Do job analyses and job evaluations.

ANALYZE THE ORGANIZATION OF EACH DEPARTMENT
AND OF THEIR INTERRELATIONSHIPS:

Evaluate strengths and weaknesses of each department and of the total organization.

COMMUNICATE PLANS AND RECOMMENDATIONS:

Make written and oral reports to management.

Explain plans and recommendations to staff at all levels to gain their understanding and cooperation.

REQUIREMENTS FOR ENTERING THE APPAREL ENGINEERING FIELD

College training is recommended. Programs lead toward degrees in industrial management or industrial engineering (there are two-year and four-year programs). Good math background. Specialized courses applying engineering principles to apparel manufacturing are helpful. Recommended courses are: principles of management, organization of business, production planning and control, time and motion study, methods analysis, plant layout, cost accounting and estimating, statistics, purchasing, wage plans, personnel methods and procedures, cutting and sewing room management, machines and attachments, patternmaking, draping, fabrics.

Personal requisites: analytical approach, initiative, ability for clear concise written and oral expression, ability to work well with other people.

How does the beginner get his start? Once he's had some training to help him develop the analytical, engineering approach, he can gain from experience in any type of plant. Perhaps he starts as a junior engineer in the engineering department of a modern plant. Supervised by a senior engineer, he will have a chance to learn from good methods and procedures already established. If the factory is old-fashioned with poor equipment and outmoded methods of production and distribution, he can learn by seeing what not to do, and by planning improvements he

Engineering and Management of Apparel Production

would suggest. If the production manager or owner is receptive to his approach, he has a fertile field. Almost any change he makes may be an improvement over the methods in operation!

If, as frequently happens, the boss turns a deaf ear to the "frills" of these modern ways, the young assistant can continue to learn from the errors being made so that he will know what not to do on his next job. If the unreceptive attitude continues indefinitely, he will want to change to a place where he can learn more positively and perhaps have a chance to put some of his ideas into practice. Yet sometimes a slow and easy approach with the conservative employer may bring gradual results. One small improvement in an operation may awaken his interest in other new methods. A young management student working for a small manufacturer in New York found his boss interested in the engineering approach but unwilling to make any expenditures because business was bad. Yet wherever the student could make a suggestion that cost little or nothing to install, the employer was willing to try it. As a result of taking time studies of the cutting operations, he hammered a nail in the table next to each cutter for him to hang his long ruler on, and thus avoid the many steps back and forth for it. Cost—nothing. The employer and cutters were amazed that they had overlooked this simple device for saving time and energy in all their years in the plant.

Trainees often start as junior engineers, assistants to the production manager, or general assistants in the production department. The job will vary, depending on the needs of the plant and the attitude of the plant manager. The beginner may perform the regular duties of a floor boy, distributing work to operators, collecting finished garments, and watching the flow. If he is really in training as assistant to the production manager, the latter will give him an opportunity to sit in on planning and scheduling and gradually learn more of the management problems. Distributing work on the floor is an excellent way to learn the operations and get to know the individual workers. Maintaining production records is another good entry job. So are beginning or assistant jobs in production control, inventory control, the cutting department, or the sewing room. But one of the best ways to start is as a junior engineer under the supervision of a senior engineer or chief engineer.

A few organizations have training programs, usually informal and geared to the individual, giving the trainee time to observe and learn in each department before getting a specific assignment. The goal of these programs is to develop future managers, executives, and engineers. The training will attempt to develop the man's individual abilities and interests, as well as assign him where the organization needs him. Thus one man might end up in engineering, another in sales or merchandising. Other firms take junior engineers with training into their engineering departments to work under a senior engineer. He may get a

specific assignment as time study man. Practical training in this area is of great value. Time study is a fundamental tool in demand.

Gradually the beginner will get more responsibility. Perhaps his next step is to supervise a small unit of workers or, if in the engineering department, to work on problems independently with minimum supervision. From general assistant in the sewing department he may be promoted to assistant to the production manager.

In all the steps he takes, he is establishing himself with the people in the plant, gaining their respect and confidence. He learns to explain why he is timing them with a stop watch and to reassure them that it will not jeopardize their jobs or earnings. He learns, too, to make his recommendations clearly and concisely, based on facts that he can verify —and to do it effectively in writing. The more he knows about needle trades operations the easier it is for him to work with all departments concerned. Knowledge of patternmaking and draping and of the designer's problems will stand him in good stead when he attempts to make changes necessary for putting the item into mass production. Knowledge of fabrics and their reactions to different speeds and types of machines and needles will give him a head start in the sewing room. If he can sit down at a machine to show an operator how to perform an operation, he will do more to gain her confidence than telling her he has a master's degree in engineering.

Engineering and Management of Apparel Production

Many of these opportunities lead to positions of plant manager, with responsibility for actually running a plant. Some organizations have several plants operating almost autonomously, working on separate products, each doing the cutting, sewing, and finishing for the particular item assigned. Others specialize functions, with cutting and finishing in one plant, sewing done in others. Sometimes the sewing operations are given to "outside" manufacturers or contractors. Production coordination of the various factories is usually done by a general manager in charge of production. He might have an assistant who would travel to the plants as trouble shooter. In New York, where some manufacturers use many contractors, there is need for production coordinators who know quality standards to supervise the contractors' work.

The consulting engineering firms seek good training, preferably some experience, and a personality that will ably represent the firm. They are very selective in taking trainees. An able beginner with good training may get started as a junior engineer assigned to a plant as resident, under the supervision of a senior engineer who visits the plant periodically. He may be there six weeks or six months and then be reassigned to another client.

Flexibility about location is a definite asset to one seeking a career as engineer or plant executive. More and more companies are setting up plants away from the large apparel markets like New York. Often they maintain sales, design, and production control offices in New York with production done elsewhere. Someone assigned to the production control department in New York might miss out on a promotion later on if he were unable to move to a plant.

Attitudes are especially important in this field. Management's cooperation and acceptance of the engineering approach will make a major difference to the beginner entering the organization. Equally important is the young engineer's attitude. In his eagerness to apply his engineering principles, he must be careful not to be brash, to go slowly at first to sell the program and to establish himself with the people in the plant and with management. He must recognize too that every one of his ideas may not be brand-new and may even have been tried before, perhaps unsuccessfully. He will be wise to try to learn from those skilled workers in the plant who know their operations thoroughly rather than assume that training and information will come only from him. His ability with people is as important as his technical knowledge, often more so.

OPPORTUNITIES

Opportunities far exceed qualified people available to fill them. The improvements in technology, the growth of large companies, the expansion of business to keep up with population growth and consumer demands are all factors. Too few recognize that the apparel and allied industries have need for technically trained future executives who will have responsibility thrown at them as soon, or perhaps even sooner, than they expect it. Advancement in these industries is usually faster than in hard goods because of the more recent transition to technical planning and, too, because of the shortage of trained people to meet the demand.

In general, there are more engineering opportunities in the volume industries, where style is not too heavy a factor. Men's shirts and work clothes are examples of the more stable garments, as compared to the styled women's dresses, coats, and suits. Yet engineering has been introduced successfully into the styled branches, too, particularly when the operation is a large one with volume production. All branches of the industry have need for good managers.

In the first chapter I urged readers to assume that all the jobs and fields described in the book are open to them on the basis of their qualifications alone. It is particularly significant in this chapter. As in other industries, men predominate in positions of engineering and production management. For the young woman interested in this career, however, there are many possibilities to be explored. She will have to overcome the surprise and resistance of those who are sure that a woman would never want to be an engineer or production executive. On the other hand, some think she may have special qualifications just because she is a woman. The general manager of a large women's wear factory, an engineer himself, thinks that a bright woman engineer could contribute her reaction as consumer to the garment as well as her technical knowledge, could test out some of her theories by actually wearing the garment herself. Women encounter little resistance in costing and production control departments. Many large firms have these offices in New York City or other apparel centers, centralizing production information in relation to orders, deliveries, piece goods, trimmings, and supplies for all the factories. Women must open their eyes to these opportunities to break the traditional patterns.

EARNINGS

Management trainees' and junior engineers' starting salaries range from $6,500 to $9,000 a year, depending on their technical educational background, their maturity, and flexibility in relocating. The salaries of experienced engineers range from $10,000 to $15,000, and those of plant managers and chief engineers fall in a range of $12,000 to $30,000. Directors of manufacturing may earn from $20,000 to $50,0000.

JOB TURNOVER

There is nothing unusual in job turnover for this group. On the whole, seasonal factors do not affect the engineer or manager. He is retained even during slow periods.

B.G. / Engineer in Apparel Manufacturing

In high school he did well in his academic program, and looked forward to attending a liberal arts college with teaching probably his goal. A cousin's enthusiasm for his engineering and management major at the Fashion Institute of Technology in New York awakened B.G.'s interest. So he applied for admission to this two-year college, as well as to the four-year liberal arts programs of New York University and Brooklyn College. Acceptance at all three made him face squarely a choice between his original plan and this new possibility of training for industry, indeed a specific industry—fashion and allied fields. He decided on the latter primarily because members of his family in the fashion industry supported his cousin's position that engineering opportunities were new but growing in this industry. Besides, he could continue his college training elsewhere if at the end of two years he still wanted to pursue a teaching career.

He was not quite eighteen when he entered The Fashion Institute of Technology. His visits to garment manufacturing plants soon convinced him that the industry needed young engineers to supplement the experience of the old-time production managers. Particularly interesting to him were courses in plant layout, time study, analysis of production methods, production control, organization of the cutting and sewing rooms. All have been specifically helpful on his jobs. Even the pattern-making and draping courses were helpful, although he preferred the engineering subjects. The statistics course has proved its value over and over again. Most important, he gained the engineering approach—to question, to analyze existing methods, always seeking the best procedures.

In his last semester he spent his college work-study period with a New York children's snowsuit manufacturer. B.G. was assigned to the Lancaster, Pennsylvania factory (there were two plants), to make an engineering survey of each department with recommendations for improvements to bring down production costs. He gained practical knowledge of production in a medium-sized plant (about one hundred workers) and applied his engineering training. Equally important, he had to consolidate his ideas and recommendations in writing, both for the employer and for his engineering seminar in college. Analyzing the material and writing it up took considerable time, but it clarified his thinking and made him aware of the engineer's need for clear, concise, well-organized reports. Experience in industry has underlined their importance. He graduated with an Associate in Applied Science degree granted by the State University of New York.

Healthy draft bait at nineteen, his prime concern was to gain good experience in industry before he went into the Army. A large manufacturer of women's foundation garments (corsets and brassieres) offered him a job assisting their one engineer. The salary was low, in fact the lowest offered to any of the management graduates. The chance to learn was excellent. B.G. took it. "It was one of the most significant decisions I've ever made. The experience gained was so much more important than the salary. It's paid off."

For the first three months he was in training under the engineer's close supervision, mainly taking time studies. They analyzed the twenty to twenty-five operations in each style and then timed them. He began to learn what was fast, slow, and normal, and to "level" an operator (determine her pace). He took independent rates and checked them against those of the experienced engineer. On the basis of their time rates, they were able to set prices to be paid to the workers, who were on a piece-rate wage schedule. After three months he was able to take time studies on his own, although the engineer still checked them. He rotated among three nearby factories in New York, New Jersey, and Connecticut. At Christmas his salary was raised. Eight months of good experience preceded his departure for the Army.

Engineering and Management of Apparel Production

For two years his military assignment was in a city he liked, where he seriously considered relocating after his Army stint. Ten months before his discharge, he followed up job contacts arranged through his college placement office. The head of the engineering department of a large firm manufacturing women's foundation garments was interested in his training and experience. Would B.G. like to work immediately on a part-time basis adjusted to his Army schedule? This was more than he'd hoped for. He was assigned to independent projects that he could work on whenever he came in. Usually he put in twenty to thirty hours a week. His hourly salary wasn't high, but with the Army paying all his expenses, it was clear profit. Most important, he was enjoying the work and gaining valuable experience. He had a chance to visit two or three of their eight modern air-conditioned plants, complete with medical service, cafeterias, and libraries for their 2,000 employees.

His first project was to study wage rates in the cutting room. A newly established incentive system had brought workers' complaints that rates were low. After one month's analysis of methods and rates, he agreed that rates were too tight and raised them 18 percent. Next came a stretch of time study to set rates on new styles that would be put into production.

Then for five months he was assigned the job of cutting expenses, increasing output, and meeting the complaint of lack of space in the receiving department, where raw goods were received and dispersed to the eight plants. The department's staff of fifteen worked pleasantly, casually—and inefficiently—together. After analyzing the operations and individuals' jobs, his first recommendation was to assign specific responsibility. As a result, work was completed promptly with less time wasted. He set up a sorely needed inventory system, with steel bins that kept the goods organized and classified and at the same time saved space. A new plant layout made additional space-saving possible. The department's annual budget was reduced from $31,000 to $25,000 as a result of his changes. Careful notes from the beginning of the project gave him material for his monthly written reports and for the major report at the end. The reports got his recommendations across and helped sell them. "A good report," says he, "is money in the bank." He's learned to show savings at the beginning and to keep it concise. When he was discharged from the Army he was offered a permanent job with the company. It was tempting because he liked the work, the people, and the firm itself. However, he decided he did not want to relocate there, was eager to be closer to New York after his two years away. Back at home in New York, he accepted a job in a New Jersey town eighty miles from New York, to work for a lingerie factory employing 150 people. His move to this town was short-lived. As assistant plant manager, he was to apply his knowledge of engineering to the factory. Although he made proposals for new machinery and equipment, the firm could not—or would not—afford the money to put his recommendations into effect. Three months later he followed up an ad for industrial engineer with the foundation company where he had worked before the Army. He had not reapplied to them upon his discharge because he thought he'd be pegged at the low salary he'd received earlier. He returned as industrial engineer at a salary three times more than he'd started with three years before. (The firm's salary policy had been revised since he left.) Not only was it an increase over the lingerie job, but he could cut his expenses by living at home with his family. Besides, he liked the firm and his assignment. Seven months later he was convinced it was a good move. He had been granted two raises without asking for them.

The chief engineer, with B.G. and another, do the engineering for three plants of about 1,000 employees. First they set methods on new styles. After the design has been approved by the production department for costs, the engineers break down the sequence of operations, usually twenty to thirty for a garment. Are special attachments to the machines needed? Can some operations be combined? B.G. works with the individual operator, the quality control department, and the plant manager. He writes a methods analysis after analyzing each operation. Check runs of five to ten dozens go through the production line to test the methods and get all the bugs out. Frequently the sequence of operations is changed. Speed is of no consequence at this stage. Once the methods are set, the first large cutting of three to five thousand garments is made. After the operators are familiar with the style, B.G. takes time studies of all operations. These studies are the basis for setting piece rates, the engineer's next step. If the workers complain about the rates, the union engineer (International Ladies Garments Workers Union) enters the picture. B.G. welcomes this as an aid in handling complaints. When the union engineer finds the rates are fair, the dispute ends quickly.

Although he considers good math background, supplemented by on-the-job training, enough for a time-study man, without more complete engineering training, B.G. finds time study itself an essential tool for the engineer, especially in his early period. It's helped him learn the problems of each plant. It's developed his analytical ability. Later on he hopes that expansion of the department will mean time-study people or trainee engineers who can collect time-study data for the engineers to use. B.G. wants to devote more time to broader engineering phases. Recently he spent six weeks on a survey of the cutting department. His analysis of machinery, equipment, and utilization of space resulted in $8,000 savings. He thinks this type of analysis will increase, and probably mean a more direct relationship to production. He welcomes a chance to have both engineering and management responsibilities.

Along with the engineering approach and technical knowledge, there are other essentials for success on his job. Ability to get along with people can't be overemphasized. B.G. must sell himself and engineering to the plant manager and to each worker in the plant. He learned early, after one or two mistakes, to keep his mouth shut unless he was sure of what he was talking about. Airing his views became less important than backing up his points with solid facts, gained by close observation and study of the problem. Often the plant manager resents the engineer as a trouble-maker, or considers him the fair-haired boy out to get all the credit for himself. Or the operators assume that he will set unfair rates. His first job is to win their confidence. No matter what, he can't be a yes man. When B.G. believes in something, he stands pat and backs up his position with facts. His boss respects him for this, even when they disagree.

Report-writing is a vital part of the job. It points up recommendations for the particular project, it sells the engineering program in general, and can effectively demonstrate the engineer's own achievements. Perhaps his last raise was connected with his report on the cutting room, clearly showing a substantial saving for the firm.

There are frustrations and difficulties—usually in relationships with people. Tact is often the engineer's most prized tool. Yet the satisfactions are high. It's a challenging game to B.G. to find out what's wrong and apply basic engineering principles to reach a solution.

He sees all the catalogues from machine and equipment companies to keep up-to-date on new or changed items. He reads such trade publications as *Apparel Manufacturer* that present management and engineering problems and suggested solutions. *Factory*, a publication concerned primarily with electrical and hard goods industries, stimulates him to relate their problems to the needle trades. The basic engineering principles are the same.

His night courses at Pace College in management, banking, and finance will lead to a degree in business administration. His job gives him engineering experience, so he selected business courses rather than engineering. A specific goal in working towards his bachelor's degree is to be able to teach engineering subjects in college at night.

The future looks bright to him. He's glad he picked engineering in the apparel industry. The field is wide open. He likes his job and hopes to be there for some time. There might be a step up to chief engineer, although not in this firm, where his boss is young and well-qualified for the job. Looking ahead five years, perhaps he can make the dream come true of having his own consulting engineering firm. He will make sure that he has strong experience behind him and has developed a good reputation in the field. At twenty-three, with a year and a half full-time and ten months part-time experience, he thinks he has made concrete progress as an engineer in the apparel industry.

Two days after I interviewed B.G., he called to report a promotion. In two weeks he was to take over as plant manager of the firm's Newark, New Jersey, plant. Here all the raw goods are received, cut, and shipped to plants in New York, Connecticut, and Puerto Rico to be sewed and then returned to Newark for pressing, examining, and shipping out to customers. B.G. will be responsible for running the Newark plant, supervising its 200 employees, and coordinating production schedules and shipments with the other plant managers. He has been told that his present salary will be increased in six months and again six months later, bringing him to a considerably higher level. He had not expected to achieve so quickly his hope of rounding out his engineering experience with management responsibility. And he approaches it with humility—it's a big job.

Chapter 8

Top-Level Jobs

TOP-LEVEL jobs present an interesting dilemma. Management claims that these openings are hard to fill because of the difficulty of finding top-notch people. Yet those in executive positions seeking to break through to top management posts find it a tough jump, with a real problem in locating these openings.

The jobs referred to are at the policy-making level, often held by officers of the company. The job titles include president, vice president, assistant vice president, division manager, general manager, comptroller, treasurer. The functional areas they would cover are design and product development, research and development, sales and merchandising, general administration, manufacturing, industrial relations.

CONDITIONS AFFECTING TOP LEVEL JOBS

The apparel and textile industries have a history of small enterprises started by eager, aggressive individuals who alone determined the scope and nature of their businesses. Many of these men were forceful and dynamic; these characteristics were reflected in their businesses, which grew and prospered to become some of the well-known firms in the industry today. What is the nature and structure of these firms now compared to their early days? Where the businesses have survived, they are larger. Most of the pioneers who started them have died or retired, although a few remain, still dominating the business with the same methods they used when it started. For the most part, where family ownership continues, it is usually in second- or even third-generation hands. For the textile industry the expansion from the smaller companies to the very large started considerably before a similar growth in the apparel field. The size of the large textile firms far exceeds that of almost all apparel manufacturing.

The trend toward mergers and public ownership, away from the family-owned structures of the past, has increased rapidly for the textile, apparel, and retail industries, as indicated in an earlier chapter. The effect of mergers on top-level jobs varies, of course, with the organization established after the merger. Sometimes, to be sure, there are consolidations of jobs. Some functions can be combined so that, for example, one treasurer or comptroller may execute more efficiently the functions that were handled previously in separate companies. On the other hand,

the merger may permit the expansion of some functions and hence of the related top management responsibilities. If a recently acquired company is well known for its excellent product development, the additional financial resources as a result of the merger may permit further expansion of this already successful phase of the business. In many situations the individual companies retain substantially the same structure with its full complement of departments as before the merger. The merger has permitted greater financial leeway, broader investments, absorption of tax losses. On the whole mergers have not decreased the opportunities for top-level jobs; in some cases there have even been increases. A spokesman for a major corporation that is representative of the trend of mergers and acquisitions, estimates that 300 people in the employ of the corporation make $25,000 a year or more. Money is not the sole

Top-Level Jobs

determinant of a top-level job, but salaries at this scale are at least indicative of positions of a high level of responsibility.

The effect of poor business conditions on top-level positions is paradoxical. During the recession of 1957-58, the number of management men looking for new jobs increased substantially, with more executives finding themselves unemployed. Yet a study by the American Management Association showed that openings at the policy-making level had increased during this same period. The expressed reason for the increased unemployment was that many of the men previously holding the jobs had been mediocre, able to get by only when things were going smoothly. Their positions had to be filled by strong replacements. Unexpressed was the fact that these high-salaried jobs were scrutinized more carefully, a change in top management being recommended with the hope of restoring prosperity to the business.

A combination of factors brings a more professional approach to industry problems and is reflected in top-level responsibilities. The growth of companies, the fact that more of them are now publicly owned than in the past, the wider financial resources and, at the same time, the highly competitive situations demanding expert cost consciousness, have demanded careful appraisal of operations and often introduction of new methods. Improvements in the fields of engineering and marketing have affected these industries as well as hard goods. The apparel and textile industries have emerged from their period of youth (their history spans no more than 75 years) into the more mature one where they are willing to adopt some of the professional advances that already exist in other industries.

Nepotism had long been a major factor, especially in the apparel industry, in reaching top management. Although it still exists in some smaller companies, there has been a major change in the larger ones. The increase in size and the expansion of public ownership have required professional management, with opportunities increasing for able executives. The more sophisticated stage of the industry has also affected those relatives in top management. They are better prepared through education and awareness of the new needs in business to introduce modern methods of management, to delegate authority, and to expand the responsibilities of other executives.

The new president of a company that manufactures men's and boys' knitted shirts, doing a $25 million volume of business, is a forty-one-year-old man who entered the apparel field fifteen years ago as an engineer. With full recognition of his ability, his progress is a tribute to the opportunity for reaching top-level positions in this field.

Upon completion of his military service, he resumed his interrupted education at Princeton, graduating as a mechanical engineer. Then came three years as an industrial engineer in textile fibers for Du Pont and a year as an engineer in the farm machinery business. In the Pennsylvania town where he worked, he met socially a contractor of women's underwear. Discussion of the contractor's production problems and a job offer brought him into the apparel business. In his fifteen years with this firm, which expanded and merged with a larger company, he advanced from engineer to production manager to plant manager to general manager to vice president of manufacturing. He managed deliberately to learn as much as he could about merchandising, sales, and the financial operations of the business. Then an executive search agency found him for his present position as president. He comments, "When I came into the apparel business, I didn't care what the product was if I could get a chance to work on engineering problems and be given freedom to grow. I got just that. I am convinced that the financial opportunities and potential for growth to top management are greater in the soft goods industry than in hard goods."

QUALITIES AND EXPERIENCE SOUGHT

From my observation and conversations with chief executives, management consultants, and executive search people on this subject for the industries this book deals with, I find some agreement and even generalizations about traits and qualifications sought. Yet it is clear that managers interpret these traits individually; recognizing this is most important in considering any listing or analysis of qualities.

It is a paradox that in this day of specialization, of requirements for highly specific experience, the top-level executive is expected to have wide knowledge about the industry and a *broad outlook* to understand facets of the business in addition to his own specialization. The top-level man must see the impact of his area of responsibility on the rest of the business, the interaction of all the divisions. The late Barry Golden, well-known chain store executive, said that a top merchandising executive would have to understand store management operations as well as merchandising. In 1960 Mr. Golden predicted that some day a person without previous retail experience could become president of a group of stores, provided, of course, that he was sales-minded and had the necessary knowledge and experience in the fields of management, costs, and investments, which today are so vital to the retail business. By 1969 his prediction was a reality. The president of a large leading specialty store with several branches came to this position from publishing. The president of another large retail operation came out of the advertising field. Still another had been a top executive of a food company. The chairman of the board of a well-known corporate retail organization had been an executive of a huge soap business. In recent years there has been increasing emphasis on the need for business to broaden its outlook in relation to its community responsibilities. Large retailers, for example, have appointed vice presidents specializing in urban affairs and community relations.

In considering a man for a top-level position, the chief executive seeks a *record of achievement,* evidence of success. What has he accomplished? Is there evidence of achievement at various levels of his development? Has he progressed with increasing responsibility?

He looks, too, for evidence of the man's own *quest for self improvement* and self development. This may take the form of additional education, of extensive reading, of experimentation with new ideas.

The overworked words of *maturity* and *emotional stability* are consistently quoted as important qualities sought. Hopefully, the man has developed to the point where he understands himself well enough to use his strengths fully and control his weaknesses. The mature executive will have the strength to admit a mistake. In Perrin Stryker's articles in *Fortune* on "The Meaning of Executive Qualities," he concluded that emotional stability is really synonymous with emotional maturity. He found that a major disturbance to an executive's emotional stability stems from the conflict between his drive to get a job done and the often frustrating need to proceed patiently and even deviously to get it done. "The kind of tolerance for frustration a good executive seems to develop," says Stryker, "is a product of experience and self-understanding that have taught him to control those feelings which do not contribute to the accomplishment of a job."

Drive, the intangible quality that, almost more than any other, defies precise definition, is one of the demands for top executives. To the president of one company it means "dynamic qualities of leadership, ability to work with others." To another executive it is "ambition and push to get a job done regardless of obstacles." Perhaps it might be stated as the self-propelling force that keeps the person motivated to work with consistency toward goals of high achievement.

Initiative, too, is consistently stressed. Top management hopes to find executives who are self-starters, able and ready to take action and start programs and projects as required.

The ability to work with other people is so obviously important that it is usually considered one of the main factors in record of achievement. This is undoubtedly because it is recognized that the top-level executive is dependent on the actions of others for fulfilling his responsibilities. Will he be able to delegate responsibility and give effective leadership? It is essential to predict if he will get along with his subordinates, with his co-executives as well as with the chief executive.

The quality of *creativity* is, of course, considered an outstanding asset. It is sought by many chief executives but actually not by all. Some executives are eager for new ideas and a new approach and they will seek these in top-level executives they hire. There must be a climate to encourage creativity, a willingness to accept failure at times. For those chief executives who feel that change is good business in this world of increasing competition, this quality will be important.

It goes almost without saying that the chief executive seeks some *intellectual qualities* in his top-level people. Again these qualities are reflected and evaluated in the candidate's previous achievements. Charles E. Summer, Jr., in discussing "The Managerial Mind" referred to the "factual attitude," through which the necessary facts are assembled before decisions are made, and to the "quantitative attitude," which recognizes the value of objective measurement when that is possible. He referred to qualities of logic: to the theoretical attitude of developing new concepts from the problems and events in the business situations; to the truth and precision of his conclusions; to the consistency of his decisions. He included the qualities of timely action and of judgment as necessary elements of the "managerial mind."

The importance of a man's *character* evokes less agreement among leaders than other traits discussed. All agree that the chief executive seeks loyalty to himself and to the business. He wants a man who will tell him the truth and who will not undermine him either to those in the business or those outside. In these respects he expects ethical conduct. However, beyond this, the consultants with whom I discussed this were frank to say that in their experience rarely did the chief executive concern himself with the general matter of character and the man's ethical concepts as related to industry practices. This depends, of course,

Top-Level Jobs

entirely on the chief executive's own standards and goals. One company president said to me, "I'm concerned about the character of the man I'm hiring. A man who makes policy must think straight." He wants to know the methods this man would use in coping with problems of competition with rival firms, of dealing with suppliers, of handling the question of "gifts" received from business associates seeking favors. Here the president is clear on the standards he sets for himself and his business so that it is important for him to gauge the ethical standards and concepts of a prospective executive.

Harvard Professor Myles L. Mace wrote in *The Growth and Development of Executives*: "The lack of criteria as to what a good executive is, and the lack of uniformity in executive positions, would seem to deny the validity of any single list of personal traits." Furthermore, although the basic importance of personality traits and intellectual abilities is recognized, there are no generally accepted meanings for qualities, such as judgment and initiative, sought in an executive.

Opposition to the use of personality traits in appraising executives has developed among some management-training directors. The late Moorehead Wright of General Electric claimed that you cannot base management development activity on personality traits. General Electric's management students were being taught to observe and report on the way a manager works and responds to situations, rather than trying to judge the quality of his individual traits. Mr. Wright stated: "Men of widely divergent personalities are successful managers. Therefore we are wrong when we appraise and select people on the basis of 'traits.' It would also establish a dangerous uniformity." Perrin Stryker, in his series of articles "On the Meaning of Executive Qualities," disagreed with this opinion. He claimed that it *is* by personality traits that managers judge other managers. Yet managers interpret these traits individually, thus negating the danger of uniformity.

John K. Hemphill levelled the charge that little evidence had been found that successful use had been made of the considerable research put into the development of lists of personality traits needed in executive jobs. He suggested that similar criticisms might be made of most psychological tests and appraisal procedures. Instead he recommended the job description approach that had been worked out by the Educational Testing Service with the help of a number of companies, including American Telephone and Telegraph Company and Westinghouse Electric Corporation. This approach was concerned about the dimensions of a job, including the less tangible job characteristics such as personal demands and social restrictions, all of which are part of the job. The study was based on ninety-three executive positions. Ten dimensions of managerial work were arrived at, including: providing a staff service in non-operational areas; supervision of work; internal business control; technical aspects of products and markets; human, community, and social affairs; long-range planning; exercise of broad power and authority; business reputation; personal demands; preservation of assets. Within each dimension was a list of position elements, responsibilities, demands, restrictions, and characteristics that had been developed after considerable research. The executives on these jobs then rated these elements to indicate what part of his job each of these elements represented. This analysis provided information on similarities and differences among various executive positions as well as knowledge of the characteristics and demands of the individual positions. It was important, too, in showing the judgment of men in these top level positions as to their own concepts of their jobs. This must have been enlightening to the chief executives who may have had other concepts. This study is helpful in emphasizing the need for more information about executive positions and some of the practical uses to which this information could be put. A title tells us practically nothing about the characteristics of a managerial position. Hemphill stated, "Potential management ability cannot readily be identified without knowledge of the common denominators of executive work." He pointed out too that the lack of a personal quality that might lead to failure in one executive position might not disqualify the individual for other executive positions. Further studies and research can add to our knowledge of the nature of executive positions.

With it all we are aware that the job content and demands vary with individual companies. Certainly decisions on the hiring of top level executives continue to be made primarily by the judgment of the chief executives. Therefore the individual standards of these executives, their attitudes and goals determine the qualities they seek. For example, many executives have a strong preference for order and integration, rejecting ideas that do not fit into a pre-established pattern. Somebody has diagnosed this as "hardening of the categories," which does not permit the acceptance of information that cannot be easily classified and filed into pre-existing categories. This type of executive will not be looking for someone who is really creative. On the other hand, a more progressive chief will be wary of hiring the man who over the years has become more conservative, with a "why disturb things as they are" attitude, as this may stunt the growth of the company.

Top-Level Jobs

METHODS OF FINDING TOP EXECUTIVES

Chief executives spend considerable time and effort to find qualified candidates for their top-flight jobs. Their decision to hire comes hard, as they know the importance of these policy-making jobs to the business as a whole. No previous experience or background will exactly match the demands of this new job. The very assessment of the complex set of qualities on which the chief executive bases his opinion requires thought and much judgment. Undoubtedly he will want to consider more than one candidate before coming to a final decision. He will use several sources.

First, he will explore the personnel within his own organization. This, to be sure, is not always the case. Some executives are not aware of the potentialities of some of the able people working for them, or are so aware of weaknesses that they assume, sometimes erroneously, that any new person coming into the organization will be stronger. Where, however, there is a promotion-from-within policy and where the head of the organization has given his executives opportunity for growth and self-development, he will take inventory of those who could be considered for the upper level job that is open.

If the chief executive finds no one within or if he wants to consider outside applicants as well, he will undoubtedly explore possibilities in the industry and sometimes in other industries as well. There are several avenues he uses. He may have heard of someone with an outstanding reputation, working for another organization, whom he would like to consider. He may get in touch with him directly, or have an intermediary do so. Or he may ask people in the industry in whom he has confidence for their recommendations. Manufacturers, for example, may get suggestions from their suppliers of piece goods and trimmings, who have contacts with key people in firms throughout the industry. Manufacturers, professional associations, retailers, magazine editors and publishers, trade associations, and sometimes even bankers who serve these industries are prime sources for hearing about competent people and indirectly often fill the function of employment agent for the top-level jobs.

Some chief executives turn to executive search agencies. In consultation with the agency, the executive will give the names of key people he has heard of who might be possibilities, as well as sources for other leads. The agency then follows through on these leads, as well as its own, and screens applicants very carefully for the chief executive to interview.

In addition to these methods that are probably most frequently used, executives sometimes advertise, often on the business page rather than in the classified section of newspapers. They may communicate with college placement offices that keep in close contact with alumni and sometimes specialized agencies in which they have confidence. Sometimes they meet people socially whose personal traits seem so desirable that they want to explore the possibility of the opening with them.

The Job Seeker's Role

PREPARING HIMSELF

How can the ambitious executive prepare himself for the hoped-for move to top management? Chief executives, management consultants, and executive search men agree that the man wanting to move to the top *must* have his own program for self-development. This is quite separate from any formal plan of executive training sponsored by his company.

His ability to increase his understanding of himself is primary. Observation and study of other executives will help him to evaluate strengths and weaknesses and to apply the same critical awareness to himself. He can scrutinize his need for further experience, additional training, broader professional contacts, and the very hard area of developing or controlling some of his personal traits. His goal should be to strengthen the specialized technical knowledge he needs and also to broaden his background to be ready for the demands of top level responsibility.

Recognizing that the apparel, textile, retail, and related fields are strongly sales-oriented industries, he must study the impact of this on his area of specialization and see the implications to the company and to his own job. If he is not especially sales-minded himself, does he nevertheless understand the immense pull of this motive in his company and in the industry? A successful manufacturing executive, for example, must be prepared for this—or he won't be successful for long.

Cost consciousness, with its corollary, cost control, is increasingly important to top management. Undoubtedly he has some responsibility for this in his own division or department, but perhaps he can widen his scope to learn more. If information on new methods, new techniques, technological advances in cost control is not available in his own organization, there are outside sources he can tap.

Top-Level Jobs

Knowing himself and his ambitions, his interests, weaknesses, and strengths, his course of action will vary at different stages of his career. At one stage he may find it wise to change jobs in order to add to or broaden his experience. This may be within the same organization or in another firm. He may select educational programs, specialized courses and technical seminars to enrich his background and stimulate his thinking. Programs of the Harvard Business School or the American Management Association, for example, that are not limited to the industries we are primarily concerned with here, get varying response from chief executives and consultants. But all agree that the man who exposes himself to such programs is, at the very least, showing interest in broadening his scope. Keeping up with the technical and professional reading in the field is essential. Trade publications, professional business and technical articles and books should be a consistent part of his business life. And if he reads similar publications related to other fields and industries, he may be stimulated to apply some of the ideas to his own area. Similarly, membership in professional organizations related to his work may mean the exchange of ideas, keeping abreast of new developments, and the maintenance and broadening of important contacts. Speaking on programs for these professional organizations and writing articles for them and for trade publications give him opportunities to develop and clarify his ideas and to obtain some public recognition for them.

The axiom of "doing a good job" is elementary, yet obviously nothing is of greater importance. This includes taking advantage of opportunities to contribute thoughtful, well worked-out suggestions and, when problems develop, to think them through and express his ideas for their solutions.

METHODS OF LOOKING

Ideally he may be looked for when he isn't even seeking a change. Yet often a person may feel ready for the upward move when he hasn't been tapped. The general principles of job hunting apply, of course, but it may be well to explore methods specifically for this group. Assuming that he is employed, he must be extremely discreet in the steps he takes. The contacts he has made may be helpful to him now in alerting him to possible organizational and personnel changes and developments that may lead to new openings. Careful reading of the trade press and business pages of the daily papers may give him information of this nature, too. For the type of opening he seeks, he will want to find, if possible, personal contacts to arrange for him to meet the management representatives where these possibilities exist.

Management consultants and executive placement agencies do handle top management jobs. Most frequently they find their candidates through their own search and through leads from key people in industry. The unsolicited application to their offices is not their prime source. Yet the consultants I have spoken to agree that they look over the letters and applications and send for those applicants who seem to have some qualifications for their openings. Realistically, they send for a small percentage of this group. Yet certainly it is a source that the top management seeker should consider. Of obvious importance is effective written material—letter of application, résumé or summary of background.

He should take advantage, too, of any other source in his community that could expand his contacts. Some of the local public employment offices and college placement offices have excellent relations with industry, resulting sometimes in news of opportunities even at the policy-making level. A widespread direct mail campaign may be hazardous for the man who is employed and wants to exert caution and discretion in his search, but it is a technique open to the one who is not employed. Not typical, but certainly evidence of the results of careful planning and the fact that it *can* happen, is the example cited in a *Fortune* article of a sales executive who spent five weeks studying published reports on a large number of companies to determine the appropriate "market" for his interests. He sent 225 letters, received 180 replies, 30 interviews and 16 genuine job offers. The one he accepted paid nearly 25 percent more than the job he had left. The job seeker should keep his eye open for the advertisements sometimes placed for these positions, remembering that in such publications as the large daily newspapers, they are apt to appear in the business rather than the classified sections. He should consider, too, placing ads for himself.

Decisions in hiring top-level personnel are made slowly. Hence, the job seeker should be prepared for a long period of searching, waiting, analyzing before, hopefully, a satisfactory move develops.

FACTORS TO WEIGH

The man climbing to top management must face squarely the element of risk. Because he is at the policy-making rather than the direct action

Top-Level Jobs

level, evaluation of his work is based primarily on the actions or results of those who work for him. When things are going well, he will get credit but often with the recognition that "he has excellent people working for him." In bad times he may simply receive full blame. We found an increase in unemployment among top executives when business was poor, with chief executives and boards of trustees evaluating results with heightened care and scrutinizing the high-salaried brackets with an eye to consolidation of functions. This is a general factor he must accept but he can estimate the degree of risk in an individual company by looking into the history and reasons for turnover of the firm's top echelon.

He should know his own interests and goals well enough to seek connection with an organization that will fulfill rather than frustrate them. If he thrives on pressure and fast pace, does the prospective company function this way or is the atmosphere one of slow deliberation and quiet tempo? If his goal is for greater opportunity for creativity, experimentation and independent action, will the chief executive encourage this or prefer "tried and true" methods? If he is concerned about integrity in business practices, does the firm's reputation meet the standards he seeks? There are sharp differences in these intangibles which become increasingly important to the rising executive.

Certainly he should examine the realistic problem of family relations to estimate the effect on his responsibilities and growth with the organization. There is no general rule as the situation obviously varies in individual companies.

If the job seeker is a woman, she will know that opportunities at top management levels are few and far between for her. She will find a strong prejudice in favor of men for the high-echelon jobs. There are encouraging exceptions, to be sure, and gradually a small number of competent women are achieving recognition at this level. This should not curtail her efforts but instead give her the realistic approach and courage to keep after her goal in the face of this attitude.

In one of his many articles, C. Northcote Parkinson, of "Parkinson's Law" fame, was commenting on reactions to success. "The man or woman who achieves any sort of success is usually lucky; but not quite so lucky as others are prone to imagine. Luck is often the belated reward for unusual persistence, and that is a virtue of which not everyone is proud."

Chapter 9

For Women Only

A JOB is only one part of one's life. No one knows it better than a woman. Anatomy and tradition clamor for her attention. She's the baby producer. Neither automation nor atomic energy can take her place.

Fifty to seventy-five years ago the idea of women working outside the home was revolutionary. Financial need might drive some poor souls to such a course. Dedicated females with a career glint in their eyes, and suffragettes, were "radicals" to suggest that women could be part of the labor force. Certainly it was scandalous even to think of a woman working after marriage. The choice was a career or marriage.

That's history. Now women play an active, important role in the economy of the world, are leaders in many fields of work. Even married women. At a family-life conference, Dr. Florence Kluckhohn of Harvard University declared that most men were no longer resentful if their wives worked. With the wife contributing to the family income, she said, the couple has more time and funds to enjoy the better things of life together.

The picture changes radically, once she becomes a mother. True, there are some women whose financial needs demand that they work regardless of emotional conflicts. Without this pressure, it becomes a matter of choice. Our economy and social changes affect the functions of a mother and the way she plays her role. But her feelings are as profound and old-fashioned as her great-grandmother's. Many women want to take care of their babies themselves. Even if they have worked, they have no conflict about staying home. Others want to stay home with

For Women Only

their children, too, but at the same time miss the stimulation they gained from their work. Perhaps they want to return to work once their children are older. Still others want to combine babies and full-time work and manage to do it. It is a highly individual decision. The one constant is the woman's love and concern for her children.

Social changes have made it possible for a woman, just as a man, to find individual expression in work and creative activity. Once she's a mother she faces many conflicts if she hopes to combine home and work responsibilities. She may face equally difficult problems in giving up work. In an excellent book, *The Many Lives of Modern Woman*, Sidonie Gruenberg and Hilda Krech say "we must find different kinds of answers for different kinds of women and different kinds of families." The title is apt. A woman has many lives. Her needs and interests vary with her family situation. For years she may be completely absorbed, busy, and stimulated, caring for her home and children. But as the children get older, she finds she has more free time. Her interest in outside work becomes intense. There may be resistance from husband and family. Perhaps she has let her skills grow rusty, lost touch with her field of work during her years at home. Even if she doesn't have to overcome these problems, she may want part-time work to give her enough time to meet the needs of her family and home. Industry will accept her if she is qualified, but how often will it adapt to her need for a part-time schedule? Many individuals have worked out special arrangements. Some employers have discovered an untapped source of labor supply among part-time workers. Much more can be explored in this area, of value to industry and to women. Dr. Kluckhohn suggests that society should prefer a happy mother who is home half the time to an unhappy one who is there all day.

IS THE FASHION BUSINESS YOUR BUSINESS?

All in all it is a complex problem, different for each individual. One, nevertheless, where thinking and planning may help you over the humps. While it is difficult to predict your reactions ten or twenty years in advance, you can prepare to face some decisions. Does the field of work you are choosing lend itself to a flexible schedule if you want it? Once you've retired, are there ways you can keep abreast of what's going on in the field you worked in? Can you keep up your skills through volunteer work? Or learn new skills, develop other abilities in community work? You may never want to return to industry. Finding answers to these questions may stimulate you in other ways, help you discover how you can maintain your interests and enrich your life. I explored some of these questions with a group of married women graduates of the design curriculums of the Fashion Institute of Technology.

Over 90 percent of them were at work in the industry immediately upon graduation. Three years later half of them were married and one out of two had retired from industry. The proportion of those leaving industry increased over the years, as did their families. Had they given up their interest in industry? We asked them.

Most of them wanted to combine work in industry with their home responsibilities. They'd thought this through with their husbands, and considered family needs. Three-fourths of them were using or wanted to use their training and experience in the fashion industry. The one-fourth working were mainly full-time workers without children. The others, half of the group, were at home now, but wanted to do part-time or free-lance work.

Here is the study in more detail.

Most of the 116 graduates in the study were mothers—84 out of 116. Mothers of one, two, or three offspring. They had 102 children with 11 more en route. They were busy! Yet three-fourths of them wanted to combine work in industry with their home responsibilities. When we added 18 women who were interested in working in the future, the percentage jumped to 85 per cent. Two-thirds of those interested in working wanted part-time or free-lance work so that they could also be at home with their children. Their husbands backed them up. Both husbands and wives were determined that the children not be neglected. Nursery school, grandma, household help would cover for the mothers when they were away from home. They wanted jobs as designers, sketchers, illustrators, or related fashion work. Undoubtedly the job of mother had stimulated them as designers, too, because many of them wanted to design children's wear.

For Women Only

ONE-FOURTH OF THE GROUP WAS ALREADY WORKING. Most of them held full-time jobs. But these were the women who had not yet had children. A few mothers had worked out satisfactory part-time or free-lance arrangements.

ONE-FOURTH WAS NOT INTERESTED IN RETURNING TO WORK, immediately. However, 18 of these 30 qualified their answers by "not interested at present," "will want to return in two or three years," "in six years," "undecided," "after my family is independent," "perhaps in the future." Comments on husbands' reactions and their own desires ran the gamut of attitudes. Here are some of them:

"Only because of economic necessity would I return to work. My husband and I consider my role of wife and mother of prime importance and a full-time job."

"Since the child would have to be placed under someone else's care, both my husband and I feel it would not be advisable to work. Other factors?—I *enjoy* being a full-time mother."

'It is impossible for me even to consider working as my husband works all around the clock. My children need constant care as they are very young. Also my husband doesn't like the idea of my working now or any other time."

"I cannot go to work. Husband is against it."

"I'd like to work part-time or free-lance in three or four years. I could not consider it until the children are old enough to attend school. They keep me jumping 36 hours a day now."

"My husband has always encouraged my work. I would of course need household help. I will eventually return to work as soon as I have completed having a family and raised them through their formative years."

"By the time my child will be ready for nursery school, another will be on the way. I would not undertake work until my family will be of school age. My husband feels decidedly different. He's completely in favor of my returning to work."

"I would like to do some free-lance work (sketching and designing) because I like it so much, but my husband is absolutely opposed to my doing any work. He wants me home to care for our two children. That is

181

IS THE FASHION BUSINESS YOUR BUSINESS?

my duty as a mother. However, I still interest myself in fashion. I am arranging a fashion show for an organization I belong to. I am chairman, responsible for the program. I make posters for my club, sew drapes, slip covers, dresses. So I feel I have not lost all I learned."

HALF OF THE GROUP WAS HOME BUT WANTED TO WORK, TOO. Here are some of their comments:

"My husband thinks I should do some free-lance work at home, since he feels I shouldn't lose contact with the design trade."

"During the summer my husband (a teacher) would take care of the baby. If I could get some free-lance colorings now, my husband could pick them up and return them. I would do my work in the evenings. I am particularly interested in finding out if I could get work for the summer."

"Having a very young daughter (6 months) I would find it most convenient to work at home. My husband approves of the idea as he realizes how much I miss my work."

"My husband would like to see me continue my work. At present my daughter is in nursery school. The baby still demands a good deal of time. We've been out of town for quite a while and I would need some refresher courses before returning to work. It's been five years since I've worked in the field. I've been thinking about work quite a bit lately so that when this questionnaire arrived I was pleasantly surprised. It's good to know where we can get advice about returning to work."

"My husband feels I'm an individual and should decide as I please. Free-lance work will not interfere with my raising my child and caring for my husband."

"My home arrangements would be quite normal as my mother would baby-sit. It would be helpful to my husband, especially if I could work at home. I have done this from time to time since my baby was born and found it worked out quite nicely."

"My son starts school in September. I can leave him for one day a week with my mother who lives in the same building or with a neighbor. I can go down town that day to pick up work and discuss it."

"I feel that I could make necessary arrangements for household help and supervision of the children. My husband would very much like me

For Women Only

to be able to do some part-time work that I would enjoy. I have some very practical and new ideas about children's clothes which I don't find on the market and would like to translate these ideas into reality. As a mother I feel this would be appreciated by other mothers."

"Free-lance work would be most suitable but for a very good job perhaps I could work about five hours a day, two or three days a week. My husband would have no objections to my work, especially if a good portion were to be home work, since it would help us to reach our goal, a home of our own."

"Designers should do designing while rearing their children to 'keep their hands in.' My husband would cooperate as would most husbands who married ex-FIT-ers as they know that designing is part and parcel of their wives' happiness."

WERE THERE ANY OBJECTIVE DIFFERENCES BETWEEN THE TWO GROUPS OF THOSE WHO WANTED TO WORK IN INDUSTRY AND THOSE WHO DIDN'T? In comparing numbers of children for the two groups, there was no difference. (Exclusive, of course, of those who were working full-time. In that group there are very few children). In comparing husbands' occupations we found no real difference. A wide variety of occupations was represented in both.

Among the group who did not want to return to industry there were twelve who said flatly "No" in contrast to "Not at present" in giving their opinion about return to work. The occupations of the twelve husbands were: four engineers, teacher, two salesmen, vice president, piece-goods buyer, assistant buyer, power maintenance man for Board of Transportation, a worker in the automobile industry. The husbands of the women who wanted to return to work in industry were in the following occupations: seven engineers, four salesmen and a sales manager, three teachers and a school principal, accountant, advertising artist, commercial artist, engraver, research bacteriologist, stock clerk, maintenance electrician, photographer, butcher, hotel owner, store manager, office manager, three skilled factory workers, teletype technician, plastic manufacturer, lamp manufacturer, staff member of Housing Authority, two temporarily in the Army.

Clearly, then, the decision is highly individual, determined by the attitude of each wife and her husband. It is plain, too, that it is a family matter.

IMPLICATIONS FOR INDUSTRY. Industry has an untapped source of women with training and experience in fashion design. True, there are many adjustments to permit a free-lance or part-time arrangement required by these young mothers. But there are real possibilities of flexibility in design jobs that can be explored. Such arrangements are individual, will not work out at all times, for every manufacturer. But has industry as a whole been imaginative enough to recruit from this source? A few employers have. For example:

J.F. had started a successful boys' wear line for a well-known children's wear firm. She loved this field and worked until she became a mother. When a Canadian work clothes manufacturer wanted to experiment with a boys' wear line, J.F. was our best candidate. She worked out an arrangement that was satisfactory to the employer and fitted in with her family requirements. Once a week she traveled from her home in Long Island to New York City to shop, explore ideas, buy fabrics. At home she worked out her ideas, made the pattern and sewed the sample garment on her own machine. She sent to Canada the pattern and sample and the cost of fabrics and trimmings for each design she made. She required some household help to take care of her young son when she went to New York, to give her some free time to work at home and to relieve her of some housework. She claimed she was a better mother for it, that she was stimulated by the work and there was a financial profit too. The employer was extremely pleased with the results.

D.L., a textile design graduate, managed to keep 300 knitting machines busy producing her designs. She needed two half-days a week to come to the market to shop the stores, to bring completed designs to her firm, and to discuss plans for other designs. Her boss arranged appointments for customers to meet her at the office to discuss their particular design needs. She worked on the designs at home, got some household help to give her necessary time off. There were few designers available with knitwear experience, so this employer was glad to adjust to D.L.'s individual needs.

G.M. had designed children's dresses for a well-known manufacturer until she retired to have her baby. Enthusiastically she responded to our questionnaire that she'd jump at a chance to do free-lance designing. She took on a job of designing a gay line of aprons. Her free-lance arrangement enabled her to give plenty of attention to her home and baby. When she was completing the line, she paid a brief visit to her former employer, the children's wear manufacturer. "If you wanted to work, why didn't you let me know?" he asked. She hadn't even thought of asking him! Now she's designing for him again. With two full days,

For Women Only

Wednesdays and Saturdays, in the design room and some planning at home, she keeps the design room busy the whole week.

We're in a different era from the days when "Is your job more important than your husband or your child?" was flaunted at the woman who dared consider combining outside work with her home responsibilities. It's not unusual now for a woman to be recognized as an individual, not merely a sociological classification of wife or mother, ignoring her other interests or creative abilities. The young women in our study have made this clear. Family needs are most important and they have weighed them carefully. But they have retained interests, training, and skills for industry and want to use them.

Is industry interested in the woman who wants to reenter the labor market or work on a part-time or free-lance basis? In the past, rarely. But industry's need for their skills and the strong interest on the part of some women have combined to create more opportunities. Often more effort goes into finding part-time work than full-time. The woman who wants it must be aggressive in seeking it.

Designing is a field where part-time or free-lance work can be arranged. A woman can sometimes make special arrangements with the employer for whom she has worked full time. If she is starting anew, she must be sure she has kept herself up-to-date in her field. With a portfolio of fresh ideas and sketches appropriate to the employers to whom she applies, she can attempt to develop free-lance or part-time work. This includes fashion illustration as well as design and patternmaking.

Retailing welcomes the part-time worker in selling positions. The woman without previous experience can start in selling at a branch or parent store, working during the hours her children are in school or less if she prefers. Once available full time, she can advance to assistant department manager and department manager in a branch store and to other merchandising assignments in the parent store. It is increasingly possible to get part-time jobs in other than sales categories if the woman has the personal qualities required and is persistent in seeking out the opportunities. Some stores have separate platoons at night for executives as well as sales and stock workers. This is a good opportunity for the woman who wants to enter or reenter the retail field with career plans. Gaining some part-time executive experience, she is also preparing herself for a future period when she may want to transfer to full-time work in the day. Macy's New York, for example, has a shift working two or three nights a week from 5:45 to 9:45 and Saturdays.

The woman preparing to return to the labor market should answer for herself the question "What have you done while you've been at home in addition to previous experience?" Many activities have supplemented previous experience and qualify her for a job that needs to be done.

Simple? No. But we've stretched tradition so that now there is no rigid pattern. Each must work out her own solution. But a woman wears blinders if she does not think of a job in relation to her whole life.

Chapter 10

Is There a Fashion Career for You?

EXPLORE THE FIELD AND YOURSELF

Is there a fashion career for you? In the final analysis you will have to answer this yourself. There are information sources and agencies that can help in giving you material about the field, and in relating your qualifications and interests to career opportunities in them. Schools, libraries, local state employment agencies, guidance centers are logical places to start. Some may have more information than others. Tap them all.

You will benefit from counseling and guidance, not only in evaluating information about careers in fashion, but in weighing your own interests, potentialities, abilities, and temperament. Study the field of work and study yourself. If there is a relationship between the two, then plan for the necessary training and experience to qualify you. Some of the people in the case studies you've read have shown that teachers and counselors had considerable influence in their careers. Your school guidance counselor will have catalogues of schools and colleges, describing their pro-

IS THE FASHION BUSINESS YOUR BUSINESS?

grams and entrance requirements, or at least can refer you to other sources of information.

Professional and industrial groups can help. Employer associations such as the National Retail Merchants Association, and many others in the apparel manufacturing industry, can supply information on training opportunities and schools related to their branches. The Fashion Group, Inc., with several offices throughout the country, can supply information. In addition some of the fashion groups conduct courses, with leaders in all phases of fashion work presenting authoritative, practical information about this field. The job and career departments of fashion magazines are often excellent sources of occupational material presented attractively and interestingly. Particularly outstanding are *Mademoiselle* and *Glamour*. Both have a reprint service, so that you can get pertinent job and career articles that have appeared in previous issues. (*Mademoiselle*'s reprints are distributed through the Alumnae Advisory Center, 541 Madison Avenue, New York, N.Y. 10022. For *Glamour*'s Fact Sheets, write to *Glamour* Magazine, 420 Lexington Avenue, New York, N.Y. 10017.) Libraries and counseling agencies can keep you informed about new books and pamphlets on opportunities.

Extracurricular activities in school, and community activities, often help to clarify and develop your interests. So do part-time and summer jobs. Modeling in local fashion shows, jobs on the school or college magazine, part-time sales work can give experience and test your interests.

Dreams and high ambitions can best be achieved if harnessed to reality, geared to the individual's abilities and interests. Knowledge of yourself is essential. Can you work under pressure? Do you take criticism well? Does detail work irk you, or will you be able to follow through until the task is completed accurately? Do you recognize the importance of the mundane, practical problems behind every creative enterprise? Do you like variety and uncertainty, or calmness and security? Answers to these questions may direct you towards one branch or one type of job rather than another.

PLAN FOR A CAREER, NOT FOR ONE JOB

Approach the field broadly, planning for a career rather than a specific job. All the branches of the fashion industry are closely interrelated. Training and experience in one is often an asset, applied to another. An open mind and flexible goal will permit you to see your experience in relation to the total field, and to take advantage of opportunities that are not pigeonholed, not directed towards just one job. A millinery buyer of the leading fashion store in Scotland studied to be a millinery designer. Her training and three years' apprenticeship in the workroom of a famous designer was "the best possible preparation for my job. It's helped me to spot shoddy workmanship and poor fabrics and to recognize good design. Although I had not thought of merchandising when I entered the millinery field, I love it." It is generally agreed that retail selling experience is of value to every branch of the fashion industry. Inevitably it's the customer who buys the merchandise who makes or breaks the industry. Studying her reaction, convincing her of the importance of a new style or new fabric, is a never-ending process. Even the part-time or summer sales job can begin to build knowledge and background for the fashion field.

Using the broad approach, you will get the most from each job, every experience. If your ambition is restricted narrowly to only one specific job, work in other branches may seem irrelevant and dull. If assigned to one of these "other" branches, you will probably not recognize the chance to learn and broaden your experience. Accumulation of experience in diverse branches is healthy. Top jobs in the industry are held by people with broad and varied experience, often in several branches. A recent press announcement, for example, stated that B.R. had been appointed advertising and fashion director of a well-known dress manufacturing company. She was formerly associate merchandising editor of a fashion magazine. Before that, she was assistant fashion coordinator for a department store, and sportswear buyer for another.

It follows logically that training is a continuous process to strengthen and broaden your knowledge of all the branches, to keep up-to-date with the changes and advances in the field. Studies of Fashion Institute of Technology graduates show that within three years after graduation, at least half had taken additional courses.

LOOK AT THE INDUSTRY REALISTICALLY

Is it glamorous? A glamorous job is one that someone else has and that you don't know much about. Absolutely no one ever describes his own job in such terms. A realistic appraisal of what to expect in the fashion industry will save later disillusionment, and at the same time point up some of the satisfactions to be sought.

We did studies of Fashion Institute graduates to find out how they felt about the industry after they'd been in it a few years. Most were glad they selected this type of work and were generally satisfied with their progress and advancement. Yet when we asked them about the pleasant and unpleasant aspects of their work, most indicated that their jobs combined some of each. For example, were they received in industry with acceptance and encouragement, or with resentment and opposition, or both? The majority found there were elements of both acceptance and resentment. Tensions and pressures, yes, but there were major satisfactions in seeing an idea become a reality, in designing, producing and merchandising apparel for vast numbers of people. They found opportunity, too, for growth and advancement, a chance for young people with ideas and the stamina and drive to get them over.

Some knowledge comes only through experience on the job. Sense of timing, exercise of judgment are sharpened by sudden emergencies that require immediate action. Day-to-day experience on a job points up the unassailable importance of follow-through on all the steps and the mundane details fundamental to the completion of a task. You learn to see your job realistically in relation to all facets of the business. You demonstrate to yourself and others your ability to work with many different types of people.

Where are the opportunities? How important is it to be able to relocate? Unquestionably some fields demand willingness to travel or to move to another locality. Flexibility on this score will expose you to more opportunities.

Those interested in setting up their own businesses will study the pitfalls as well as the advantages of being an independent entrepreneur. High costs, and competition from the increasing number of large organizations, must be carefully considered. Equally important is the need for practical experience on someone else's payroll before tackling the precarious problems of running your own business.

DEVELOP ABILITIES AND SKILLS OF GENERAL VALUE TO ALL BRANCHES

Some general abilities, knowledge, and skills are equally useful in all branches. Ability to work with people is stressed so often that it sounds depressingly like a copybook maxim. No industry, no field of work can

Is There a Fashion Career for You?

skip its importance. The fashion industry is certainly no exception. Each person is dependent on others to have his ideas carried out. A brilliant plan can fall flat on its face if there's no cooperation or interest from those who have to develop it. If the designer's workroom staff likes to work for her, it will put up with unbelievable pressure to meet the demands of last-minute changes in the line. The junior engineer who is liked and respected by the factory workers will get the information he needs and a hearing for his suggestions. Frequent bursts of temperament are a luxury, or perhaps publicity material, for a few colorful figures well-established in the top ranks. Few can afford it.

Having an idea is important. Communicating it is, too. Clear verbal expression, ability to put words together effectively, is a contribution in every branch. The journalist holds no monopoly on writing in this industry. The engineer's written evaluations and recommendations, the resident buyer's market reports, are important elements in their jobs. Good oral presentation is part of every job. The mistakes made on the production line because "no one explained how this should be done," the indifferent attitude that "I didn't realize this was important," can be avoided, if the planner is able to interpret his plans in clear, well-thought-out instructions and explanations for all who need them.

In addition to the broad background and specialized training recommended for the various branches of the fashion industry, skill in typing is a handy tool no matter where you work. Sometimes it can be an entering wedge into a field that's hard to crack. It's a great help, too, when you want to get a report out and there's no one assigned to type it for you. Even if you don't use typing on the job, it undoubtedly has personal value. The telephone and the typewriter are important tools in the vital tasks of communication. All of us should be able to use both effectively. Knowledge of stenography is helpful (and necessary in some spots), but may require more training time than many can give. At least there's time to take a basic typing course one summer, or evenings, if it's not given in the regular school curriculum.

Knowledge of fabrics has become increasingly important in each branch of the industry. New finishes, new fibers, new uses affect the designer, engineer, producer, stylist, merchandiser, and promoter. It is essential for them to keep up-to-date on developments in the field. Awareness of the importance of fabric, as well as some technical knowledge, will help the beginner in any branch of fashion.

ANALYZE EACH JOB INDIVIDUALLY

Analyze each job on an individual basis. No generalization holds up when it comes to making a decision about one job. Punch holes in such statements as "You get the best experience in a large organization," "The individual is lost in a large firm," "Small companies give better supervision." One of our case studies liked the room to stretch and grow that he found in the mammoth retail organization he worked for. By observing the work of other departments right next to her, another, on a small magazine, gained knowledge that helped on her next job. In some large organizations, departments develop the individual characteristics of a small company. On the other hand, a small company where a beginner might expect to get a "chance to do everything" may be highly regimented by a supervisor who allocates the work rigidly without permitting diversity of assignment.

Most important for someone starting out is to evaluate the opportunity to learn. What type of supervision, of training program is there? What is the immediate boss's attitude towards training beginners, and the attitude of the firm in promoting them? Do you want to do the assignments described? Will the experience in this firm help towards the goal you have selected? Answers will vary for each job, for each individual, and will defy any generalization.

Absence of a formal training program does not mean there is no training. It will depend on the individual supervisor's attitude and approach. The prospective applicant is wise to look into this. Nor is the picture static even within one firm. Opportunity for learning, growth, and advancement will be affected by the transfer of a new supervisor into a department.

RECOGNIZE THAT THE INDIVIDUAL MOLDS THE JOB

As important as the job is the individual who holds it. Except in the most routine assembly tasks, each job is molded by the ability and personality, the strengths and weaknesses of the person in it. An ad calling for "Gal Friday: college graduate. Sharp. To assist stylist and piece-goods buyer" seeks someone to fill a definite need in the organization. Yet undoubtedly the job will be different depending on the girl who gets it. One may have greater value to the stylist than to the piece-goods buyer, or perhaps the other way around. This will affect not only her immediate duties, but her future advancement in the firm. The head of stock whose records are well organized and quickly spots changes in inventory, can develop her job into a key aid to the buyer in interpreting customer demand. The draper in the sample room, the production assistant in the factory, the showroom model, the layout artist in the advertising department, bring their individualities to bear on each job. This then imposes on each job holder the opportunity and responsibility to develop the job to its maximum possibilities.

FACE SQUARELY PROBLEMS OF MONEY, PROMOTION, JOB GRIPES

Money is something everybody would like to have more of. This indisputable fact is not the basis for getting it. Salary and raises have to be evaluated in relation to many factors. What are the salary rates in the community for your type of job? How does your training and experience stand up in relation to qualifications for the job? Borderline, average, good? What's the salary policy in the firm to which you're applying? Some of this information you can get from employment agencies, from watching classified ads, and directly from the firm to which you're applying. Once you're on the job, when do you get a raise and how much? Many factors have to be weighed. How long have you been on the job? Has your value to the firm increased? Have you been given additional responsibility? What is the firm's policy on raises? Even with these facts, salary negotiations are far from simple to handle. Some few people have the golden touch and always come out on top. The rest of us will do well to remember that money, although important, must be considered in relation to job satisfaction, opportunity to learn, job performance, and the firm's policy.

Chances for promotion matter a great deal. What are the requirements for the next step up? Can you meet them? When is it reasonable to expect there will be an opening? Will outside courses add to your qualifications? Are you willing to accept the responsibility or extra work that goes with the promotion? Exactly what and where are the possibilities for promotion in your firm? Here, too, there is need for acquiring information, and for relating promotion to other important factors.

Grievances and gripes are inevitable. Someone else gets the promotion you had hoped for. Why? You like your assignment but suddenly get transferred to another. You feel stymied on your job and see no possibility for promotion. The work has become increasingly routine and you have no chance to use the training that brought you to the firm originally.

You'd like to be considered for another department in the firm, but are afraid your immediate boss wouldn't like it. These and many more gripes pile up. The next step is often scanning the want ads, and trying to figure out how to look for another job while still on this one. Probably most people have suffered some of these anxieties at one time or another. What do you do about them?

An obvious step that an amazing number overlook is to bring up the problem to your boss. If you're stewing because you'd like a chance to do more challenging work, or because you think it's time for a promotion, he might be very interested in knowing this. Maybe he wasn't aware that you were so ambitious! Certainly he can give you some hint as to what the future can hold for you. If he paints a poor picture, then at least you know where you stand and can make your decisions based on fact. Leaving for another job for the sake of a five- or ten-dollar salary increase hardly makes sense if you haven't even asked your boss about chances for a raise. If there is a personnel department, you have another source for information and for discussing your situation.

A sound approach to problems of promotion and grievances, even money, too, is to make your pitch in terms of service to the boss. Let's make no mistake about it, business is business. You won't get your promotion, your transfer, or your raise unless it's good for the business. No more than your recommendation for improvement of procedures, your suggestions for innovations, will be adopted unless the boss thinks it will better the company. Too few people hop into the boss's seat to look at the picture before they ask for what they want. If you can convince yourself that there are facts to indicate that your recommendations or your promotion will be of benefit to management, you undoubtedly have more cogent arguments than "I'd love to be promoted."

Attitudes are fundamental in affecting your career. What is the beginner's attitude towards his first job? Well do I remember the young management student who started in the production control department of a large apparel producer. In addition to setting up the records, he had to maintain them. He complained that "any high school graduate could do this job—I didn't need college training for this." Soon he was fired for the flagrant inaccuracies in his records. He never had the chance to tackle the more advanced aspects of the work, although he had been hired as a management trainee.

Then there was the embryo textile designer who objected to helping with the department's files for a week to cover a temporary emergency. Although she understood it was just for that time, she griped and sulked when perhaps she might have concentrated on picking up information from the material she filed. When her supervisor was not available to answer each question at the moment it came up, she was convinced that she wasn't getting adequate supervision and training. Her actions expressed clearly her attitude that the sole job of the supervisor was training! The stylist's responsibility for getting a complete line styled wasn't in the picture, as far as this young beginner was concerned. Needless to say she didn't last long on the job.

Sometimes the beginner gets a bad break on his first job. He may be overworked, poorly paid, inadequately supervised and trained. First impressions count. Yet the beginner who generalizes from this experience that the whole industry is like this makes a grave error. He is off balance if he sacrifices his training and goal by giving up the field entirely. His second job may be entirely different.

Dull and routine tasks are part of every job. You may as well accept them; they have to be done. Often they add to your total learning and give background you're grateful for later. The attitude that every moment on the job will be challenging and interesting belongs to the dreamer.

You were hired to do a particular job. If you finish your work, or the activity is slack, do you seek other work? Do you resent it if suddenly you're asked to help in another department? Do you ever do the "extras" —things that are not required, but that are a real contribution to the boss or the rest of the department? Do you, in other words, set limits to your job? The one who extends himself often reaps dividends in learning more, and in getting recognition for initiative and cooperation. It's the extras, too, that sometimes bring a promotion.

Most significant, perhaps, are the standards you set for yourself. Not what the boss expects, but what you expect of yourself. The one who does a job well *for his own sake* is in a sense his own boss. He won't be satisfied unless he works close to his full capacity, even if he meets the standards set by the firm. He will do a job well, with or without supervision. If I were to permit myself one generalization about what I would look for in employing people, it would be just this—to find the individual who wants to do a job well for his own sake.

WHAT DO YOU SEEK IN A CAREER?

What is it that people seek in a career? Money is not the first thing, as so many think. Personal prestige and ego satisfaction rank first. A man's dignity is more important than his pay envelope. Management's attitude towards him is as vital as the wages it grants. Is he achieving his goal? Is his job respected in the firm and the community? Does he like what he's doing and the people he works with? Of course money counts, too, but it's not the prime goal, as many have learned.

Is There a Fashion Career for You?

In weighing decisions affecting your career, consider all these factors. Use the professional approach of getting as much information as possible, evaluating it carefully and realistically. There are no simple blueprints to help you decide. Once you've considered all the facts, make your decisions and live with them—without regrets. I wish you success in the career you select.

Chapter 11

Job Hunting

PERHAPS you have selected the fashion field for your career. You've read about opportunities and requirements, even have studied with this goal in mind. Now you want to get started. You want a job. How do you go about finding one?

AS A SALES CAMPAIGN

Job hunting should be approached professionally. Too few people realize this, permitting themselves to tackle it haphazardly and often to bog down in despair after a few unplanned attempts don't produce a dream job. The professional approach sees job hunting as an organized sales campaign, requiring knowledge of the product (i.e. yourself), analysis of markets for the product (occupations, industries, and particular employers who might be interested in "buying" the product), sales methods to be used, preparation, and follow-up. Once you identify yourself with a salesman or sales campaign director, you will be more realistic in job hunting. The good salesman doesn't expect to sell to every customer on his first contact. Nor does he rely just on one method. He tries them all. Personal contacts, direct mail campaigns, ads, even ringing doorbells—all of these methods may sell more products. He is well aware, too, of the importance of following up the customer who shows some interest even though she won't buy now.

The job hunter is, then, a sales director, planning and preparing a

Job Hunting

campaign to "sell" himself successfully. His ultimate goal is a job; his immediate aim is to get interviews that will lead to the goal. Research, planning, hard work, and comfortable shoes combine to combat attitudes of discouragement and defeatism that are the job hunter's worst enemy.

ANALYSIS OF THE "PRODUCT"

First comes careful analysis of the most complex of products—yourself. This is serious homework. Put it all down on paper. An easy start may be your own personal interests. You like to shop, to read fashion magazines, to sketch; or perhaps you enjoy making your own clothes. Music, theater, travel, or scientific hobbies may represent your interests. Whatever they are, jot them down.

Analyze your education. What were the courses you liked most, the most helpful ones, those in which you showed strength, those where you were weak? Do you have commercial skills such as typing? Consider your extracurricular activities, community activities.

Your job experience deserves careful analysis. Don't forget summer and part-time jobs. What were your duties, what did you learn on each job? What opportunity was there to gain knowledge of other occupations and of the industry? Think, too, of less tangible factors, of personality traits, attitudes, ability to get along with people, work habits. Can you take criticism? Do you work well under pressure? Are you able to meet deadlines without collapsing? Can you shift suddenly from one task to another because of emergencies, or do you work better at one consistent assignment without interruption? Do you enjoy working with large groups of people or do you prefer working alone or with one or two others? Do you need close supervision to be sure you will follow through on an assignment? Are you punctual, reliable in attendance? Are you setting limits in the location of the job; if so, what are they?

Once all this is down on paper, you have a solid base of material from which to draw for many purposes—résumés, letters for direct mail campaigns, answers to ads. At least as important is the self-knowledge you will have gained in making this inventory of your strengths and weaknesses, interests and attitudes. This "homework" is essential preparation for interviews.

"MARKETING" THE PRODUCT

Next comes marketing the product. Your self-appraisal may have helped to narrow the field somewhat from the very broad one of the fashion industry as a whole. If you've explored occupations and industries within the fashion field, you probably have some concept now of where your interests and background might direct you. Is it in merchandising, or perhaps fashion design? Now is the time to consult your library and guidance counselor to get appropriate lists of employers, of trade directories and publications, of employer associations. The classified telephone directory isn't to be overlooked. Some companies, especially large ones, may have booklets describing job opportunities and job requirements. You begin to develop lists of places you want to approach.

METHODS

What methods do you use? Like the salesman, you will try to use all of them, knowing that a combination of methods will produce more leads, more interviews, possibly a choice of jobs. One of the luxuries of unemployment is that you can apply any place you want. If you've had a desire to work for the ABC Co., go ahead and apply. The worst that can happen is a "No" response, and you'll still be right where you were before you started.

Start with your personal contacts and friends. Now is the time to think of the occupations and industries they represent. No need to be apologetic. You have a good product to sell and your friends may have leads and suggestions. In any sales campaign, it is essential to publicize the product. Certainly your friends should know you are job hunting.

Job Hunting

It is important to realize at the start that no one will get you a *job*. A friend may give you a lead or even arrange an interview for you. The employer may hire you as a result of the interview, but only because he thinks you are qualified to fill the job. A good personal contact in business need not be the president of the firm. A shipping clerk, an assistant foreman, a salesman may have practical information about job openings in his company. Even if there is no opening, he may be able to arrange an interview for you with his boss. Don't forget a former employer as a potentially valuable contact.

Be sure to visit your school or college placement office. These offices usually continue to give service to graduates even after they have left the campus. Your local state employment service is another source of jobs and of occupational and industrial information. There may be other community agencies, too, that give a free placement service. In addition there may be fee-charging agencies that have a reputation for giving good placement service (just remember you will have to pay a fee when you have been placed unless the employer has arranged in advance to pay it).

The first time you make a "cold" contact is like a plunge into an icy lake. It's not so bad after the initial shock. In the "cold" contact no one has paved the way for you, nor is there an advertisement showing there is a job opening. You have decided that there are specific companies to which you want to apply and this is one of them. This is the salesman's doorbell ringing. When there is a personnel department, it is relatively easy to ask for an interview and make application for a job whether there is an immediate opening or not. In smaller companies you ask for the production manager, the designer, the store owner, depending on the type of organization and the kind of job you seek.

In using the cold contact, it is especially necessary to remember that your immediate goal is to have an interview. Even if you make an excellent impression, it is hardly realistic to expect that there will be a job opening at the very moment that you apply. With the interview as your goal, you may be able to get past the receptionist just by asking to see the stylist rather than inquiring "Are there any jobs open?" The interview may be fruitful in giving you information about the company and its future opportunities, and sometimes leads to other companies where the interviewer knows there is an opening.

A letter-writing campaign is the cold contact approach by mail. If you have a short, highly selected list, you can type the letters. If you send 100 or 200 copies of a letter, typing them individually may be impractical; you can arrange with a printer or letter shop to have them reproduced in the desired quantity. The purpose, of course, is to get interviews. No one hires you sight unseen. Although a direct-mail campaign may bring a small percentage of returns, one answer that results in one job makes it a 100 percent successful campaign.

Now for newspaper ads. Most job hunters think of this method first. You look in the "Help Wanted" section and see:

1. ASST. SAMPLE ROOM, TEXTILE FIRM. Opportunity to learn the business. Will be trained. Advancement for right person.

   or

2. ARTIST—Layouts. Need trainee, art dept. of fashion magazine. Exp. pref. Bring portfolio.

   or

3. SECRETARY—Career opportunity in advertising with well-known fashion newspaper. Steno & typ required.

   or

4. ASST. DESIGNER—CHILDREN'S WEAR—Young, some experience. Ideas for sub-teen line. New department.

   or

5. SALESMAN TRAINEE. Retail chain. No exp. nec. Personable promotion types sought.

   or

6. MERCHANDISE TRAINEES. Dept. store. Training program. Opptys. for advancement. Call Personnel Dept. for appointment.

   or

Job Hunting

> 7. **MODEL WANTED.**
> Showroom work. Must be 5'6", size 12. Some exp. preferred. Knowledge of sketching helpful.

Can you meet the requirements? Do you know enough about the job demands? Should you answer the ad? First, read the ad carefully. Its questions must be answered, directions for applying carefully followed. You may want to use the same wording in your reply. Any job may offer chances for advancement. What are the promotion opportunities in the ads quoted above?

(1) **Asst. sample room, textile firm.** May lead to selling or executive jobs.
(2) **Artist—layouts.** May lead to more responsible jobs in art department, possibly art director.
(3) **Secretary, fashion newspaper.** A good springboard into copywriting, merchandising, fashion co-ordination, department editor.
(4) **Asst. designer, children's wear.** May lead to designing.
(5) **Salesman, retail chain.** Good experience for all phases of fashion. May lead to store-management and merchandising positions.
(6) **Merchandise trainees.** Leads to buying, management, fashion co-ordination and promotion.
(7) **Model, showroom.** May lead to apparel design, styling, merchandising.

The ad can give you just highlights. There are still many unknowns about the job. You may be undecided as to whether you meet the requirements. At times it's worth taking a chance if you only come close to the stated demands. An employer may have an ideal picture of the employee he wants and will set regid requirements. If the labor market is tight and he gets no one with the exact specifications, he may relax his demands and take someone who meets part of them. So it's worth a try. Some key words or phrases give clues that will guide you. Skills "required" indicates more rigid specifications than "preferred." "Career opportunity," "beginner o.k.," "training program" are signals for the young beginner.

In addition to following the "Help Wanted" columns, you may want to insert an ad describing your qualifications, under "Positions Wanted." (As sales director you must plan your budget to take care of this item, as well as the printing and mailing cost of your direct-mail campaign.) Your list of employer associations should be useful to you. Many of them have bulletins and publications for their members; some will insert free ads for qualified job applicants.

PREPARATION

The processes of analyzing the "product" and studying the "markets" for it are the broad base for your specific preparation before meeting a prospective "customer."

First, prepare a résumé which is a summary or abstract of your background aimed at your vocational or career goals. If you've done the written homework mentioned earlier in which your self-appraisal is down on paper, you'll have the information you need. It should include an outline of your goals and interests, your education and experience. Usually, too, there is personal data on age, marital status, and willingness to relocate.

I hold no brief for a stereotyped résumé form. At various stages in a career, a person will prepare different types of résumés. Early in his career, with very little experience behind him, he will emphasize education and training and interests. Years later his experience will probably be the core of résumé. He may present his jobs chronologically, summarizing his functions under each one. Or he may write a functional résumé in which he analyzes his total experience, breaking it down by separate functions and referring to more than one job under each heading. In this last type he will list his places of employment at the end. It is possible, too, for the same individual to have more than one résumé at the same time, when his interests, training, and experience direct him towards several job goals. Your résumé must be revised and brought up to date when you gain new experience and training, or change interests. Know the material in your résumé. It will be of great value in preparing for an interview. Have it handy, too, when you fill out application blanks. Don't search your memory apprehensively for dates when you can have the accurate information so easily in hand.

Beware of making your résumé too long or you'll have no readers. Weigh each word carefully, avoiding vague ones such as "etcetera," "various," "many." Eliminate unnecessary words. Instead of "I was responsible for supervising twelve people who performed sales and stock functions" substitute "Supervised ten salespersons and two stock clerks." One page or at the most two can give a concise picture of your background and goals.

Job Hunting

For a direct-mail campaign you will have to prepare a "sales" letter that will stimulate employers' interest to interview you. Here, too, you will rely on your written self-appraisal or résumé to provide the material for the letter. You will include highlights of information about your background related to the industry or occupations represented by firms on your mailing list. Individual letters written for selected employers can be geared to the specific knowledge you have of the firm, its organization, products, or services.

We come then to the specific research you do on the firms to which you are applying. Certainly it's helpful to know as much as you can about the prospective "customer." Obviously in some cases, such as answering an ad, there may not be time to find out much, but often with a little effort you can get some information. If it's a store, what is the general price level of merchandise it sells? Are there any brochures describing the store's training program and job requirements that you can read before applying?

If you are applying for jobs where artistic or design talent is sought, can you bring some evidence of your ability? A well-prepared, planned portfolio is an obvious asset, a necessity for many types of jobs. There are many opinions on the selection of material for the portfolio. It is wise to consult teachers, counselors, and friends in industry. Don't be surprised if they don't all agree! Your portfolio should show samples of a variety of work that you can do. Don't be afraid to include even fine-arts work, which may show the employer that you have a good sense of color, form, and design. Certainly if you know something about the firm you are applying to, you will try to include some work, if you can, that shows your interest and ability in the firm's field. If you were trying for a job in a pattern company, it would seem obvious to include fashion sketches of the current trend in clothes.

I've heard young engineers and prospective management executives speak enviously of the art or design student's portfolio. "It's so much easier to go job hunting with a portfolio; you have something tangible to talk about." Well, with a little imagination they can have portfolios, too. The engineer, for example, has made plans for plant layouts, production control and flow charts. He can bring a folder with samples of blueprints and charts to an interview and refer to them when he sees fit.

Your appearance is of course important. Preparation and careful checking can help to improve it. There are two reasons to stress this. First is the effect of your appearance on yourself. If you are looking your best, you feel more comfortable and relaxed, for that important interview.

Second, as you are looking for a job in the fashion industry, your appearance is an immediate sample of your taste and expression in fashion. Certainly it shouldn't be sloppy, garish, and uncoordinated. Check your grooming as well as your clothes. Dress comfortably.

Last but not least, watch your attitudes. Discouragement and despondency are the easiest ones to come by in job hunting. You're licked if you give in to them. Recognize in advance that conducting a good job-hunting campaign is harder than holding down a job. Know that it takes time to develop the campaign and that it's largely luck if you hit the jackpot immediately. Don't approach each interview with a do or die attitude—"if I don't get a job here, I'm a failure." Try to get as many interviews as you can, but don't look at each one as a final examination. Don't make one contact and sit and wait for an answer before going on to another. Nothing is then more discouraging if the answer is "no" or perhaps no response at all. Plan your campaign so that you tackle all possible methods. Three or four hours of pounding the pavements to keep appointments or to make new contacts is tiring. Don't demand more of yourself. The rest of the day can be spent profitably off your feet, following up your interviews, looking up other contacts.

Unquestionably this is a period of stress and strain. It's natural to feel impatient with receptionists who keep you waiting or to resent those who seem patronizing. Showing these feelings and attitudes is a luxury you can ill afford when you're job hunting. Remember that a secretary's comment about an ill-mannered candidate will quite likely be passed on to the boss. In planning your schedule, allow plenty of time in between appointments. Be prepared for the interviewer who keeps you waiting, or for the interview that may last an hour when you anticipated fifteen minutes. Space your appointments so that you won't risk being late for the next one.

THE INTERVIEW

All the preparation leads to the interview. An interview is a purposeful conversation between two people. You react differently to various interviewers, just as you do to people in social situations. Undoubtedly you will make a better impression in some interviews than in others. Expect it and don't feel unduly frustrated when one doesn't go too well. When there is good rapport and communication between you and the interviewer, of course the interview will proceed in an easier atmosphere. The skilled interviewer consciously tries to establish this rapport. The extent of your relaxation helps, too.

Don't leave the burden entirely on the interviewer's shoulders for keeping the interview going. A simple "yes" or "no" may answer the questions directed at you, but at the end of the interview you may not have been able to tell the essential parts of your experience, training, or interest. You must take some initiative in guiding the course of the interview. You can add to the "yes" answer by giving an example, or stating that you particularly liked this phase of the work or course, if that is the case. Remember that all interviewers are not equally adept in getting information from you, yet each of them will evaluate you on the basis of your replies to questions.

An entirely different type of interview develops when the interviewer leans back in his chair and says "Tell me about yourself" or "What can you do for this organization?" This is hard. Here's where your "homework" pays off. Now you can draw upon your knowledge of your own qualifications, and also upon information you've gleaned about the industry and the firm itself.

Remember that an interview is a conversation between people. To be successful there must be give and take. You will have to feel out the situation just as in a social situation when you meet someone new. Are you talking too much? Too little? Can you ask questions that will help the conversation flow more easily? You will have to rely on your judgment, tact and sense of timing in an interview just as in any conversation.

The interview should explore both the employer's demands and yours. Each will have to get information from the other. The employer is looking for attitudes, in addition to skills, training, and experience. Often these attitudes matter more than the tangible qualifications. Certainly he seeks interest in the job. He wants someone who wants to work for *this* industry, for *this* firm, for *him*.

Obviously, then, if you are interested, show it, say so. He is looking for attitudes of cooperation (and will steer clear of someone who has a chip on his shoulder), of industriousness, alertness, loyalty, ability to get along with other people. Often he seeks leadership potential. What are you looking for? You want specific information on job duties, salary, and hours. You, too, are looking for attitudes. What is the firm's attitude toward new employees? Is it willing to help you learn and develop? Is there an established training program? Do beginners have opportunities to advance? Evaluate the employer, just as he must evaluate you. If he doesn't give the information you seek, of course ask questions.

FOLLOW-UP

If the employer has made a job offer during the interview and you have accepted it, the only follow-up necessary is for you to report to work! However, the interview is often a preliminary step. Perhaps the employer has other candidates to interview. Or he may be doubtful about your qualifications and not ready to make a job offer. On the other hand, you may have other interviews pending and be unable to make an immediate decision either.

Unless the interview produces a job offer and acceptance, or a definite "no" to your qualifications, or a refusal by you of a job offer, follow-up of the interview should be considered.

In addition to applying principles of good salesmanship (follow-up of prospects is a recognized rule), use the good manners and graciousness you show in a social situation. If you've been a week-end guest, you consider it good manners to send your hostess a thank-you letter. After a particularly nice party, you may telephone the friend who gave it just to tell her what a good time you had. Now suppose you have had a job interview. Perhaps the interviewer has given you information and advice, even guidance and helpful suggestions. True, there's no immediate job offer. Yet you are appreciative of the time and interest shown. Wouldn't a thank-you letter be appropriate here? And good business, too? Perhaps you thought of something important you wished you had said in the interview. Besides you are sincerely interested in the job opportunity in this company. In addition to thanking the interviewer, you can add the information you omitted. It's an excellent chance to reemphasize your interest in joining the organization. If the employer does not already have a copy of your résumé, this is a good time to send it to him.

Job Hunting

If you have used the interview to get information about the company, you may be able to time your follow-up program effectively. If you know that the firm expects to be much busier in a month with increased job possibilities, you will call or write the firm at that time. If you have sent an immediate thank-you note after your interview, you may even state then when you will be in touch with them again. This further emphasizes your interest in the company.

What is your reaction to the employer's parting words, "I'll keep your application on file and call you if there's an opening," or "Call me in a week to see if I have anything"? A cynical attitude, like discouragement, is another enemy of the job hunter. Many applicants assume that these employer comments are merely an easy way of saying "I don't want you." Even if it's true in one out of two interviews (and we don't know that it is), you can't afford to assume that it is. Employers have frequently reported to me that applicants have not called them back as suggested, only to miss out on jobs. Applicants, on the other hand, have given me many happy examples of good jobs resulting from following up these employer comments. This does not conceal the fact that an interviewer may find it easier to say "I'll let you know," instead of "You're not qualified." You, however, have more to lose by assuming that this is the case rather than testing it out.

IS HONESTY THE BEST POLICY?

An advertising expert once told me that "honesty is the best policy" was the best piece of copy ever written. You will have to evaluate it yourself from the standpoint of ethics. What are its practical implications for the job hunter?

All agree that it's easier to tell the truth, to deal with facts you know and that can be verified. Yet frequently the job hunter blows up his experience, says he graduated from school a few years earlier than he did, gives an elaborate story to an employer for not keeping an appointment when it conflicts with another commitment. Obviously, in these situations the applicant assumes that he is improving his chances for getting the job he wants. What are the dangers in this approach? Often the employer checks some of these facts, such as graduation from high school or college or length of experience on a job. If he discovered the fiction he would wonder if he could trust your word in the future and decide not to take a chance. Another problem is the difficulty of

IS THE FASHION BUSINESS YOUR BUSINESS?

remembering the changes in facts you've made and adjusting the rest of your story to fit. Falsifying length of experience may affect graduation date, age, etc. It's hard to be a truly competent liar! There's also the very real danger of talking yourself into a job that you are not capable of filling and perhaps laying the groundwork for failure. All too often these very attempts boomerang and the job hunter finds himself rejected for a job that he might have secured by telling the truth.

Perhaps the best test is to evaluate the facts yourself and consider whether they are convincing. If you have carefully weighed your strengths and weaknesses and have called the employer's attention to what *your* background offers *him*, is it wise to risk weakening your case? Remember that the employer is at least as concerned about attitudes and, yes, character traits, as he is about your training and experience.

Job hunting is an inevitable fact of life to the millions who work. To some it occurs many times, to others less frequently but no one who has worked or will work can avoid it. The methods outlined in this chapter are not unusual nor even demanding as they are steps to finding suitable employment, a goal that affects one's whole life. Yet most people approach job hunting haphazardly and without preparation. Fear, discouragement, and laziness produce a series of myths that make job

hunting harder than it has to be. It is nonsense to believe that you can't ask questions in an interview unless the interviewer suggests it. It is not true that employers and personnel interviewers have magic formulas that produce perfect decisions for hiring. Skilled interviewers are the first to admit the frequent mistakes they make. There is as much variety in personality and skill among the people who are doing the hiring as among those seeking jobs. No one likes to be turned down, but it should

Job Hunting

be a comfort to know that you can do miserably with one interviewer but sail through and land a job with another. It is not a myth that job hunting is hard work. Tackle it as a rare opportunity to concentrate completely on what will be good for you. Often you are criticized if you are too self-centered, but job hunting demands it so enjoy it—talking about yourself, writing about yourself, thinking about yourself.

SPECIAL NOTES OF APPRECIATION FOR 1970 EDITION

Alfred Nieman, Vice President of Executive Personnel, Macy's New York; William N. Yeomans, Personnel Manager, J. C. Penney Co., Inc.; Richard J. Schwartz, President, Jonathan Logan, Inc.; Norman Hinerfeld, Executive Vice President, Kayser Roth Corp.; Mike Singer, former President, Mullins Textile Mills, Inc.; Catherine T. Fitzgerald, former Vice President for Personnel, Gertz; Kitty D'Alessio, Vice President, Norman Craig & Kummel, Inc.; Lazare Teper, Research Director, International Ladies Garment Workers Union; Andy Clores, Business Manager, United Scenic Artists, Local Union No. 829; John Galluzzi, Assistant Director, Creative Services, Columbia Broadcasting System; George Sullivan, Designer, National Broadcasting Company; Market Planning Service of the National Credit Office; U.S. Department of Commerce Library; Shelly Ruchlin, Book Division, Fairchild Publications, Inc.

(Reprinted from the 1961 edition.)

Literally hundreds of people have contributed to this book. I am particularly grateful to the subjects of my case studies who were interviewed during the summer, 1955. Much of the information they gave was confidential and personal. Obviously they must remain nameless. I am indebted to the students and graduates of the Fashion Institute of Technology for the constant flow of information they bring me. And to the college itself for permitting me to use pertinent material.

I want to thank the following for their help:

Market Planning Service of the National Credit Office; William Hauptman of the New York State Employment Service and Rashelle Goldberg, formerly of N.Y.S.E.S.; Harry Cobrin, Executive Director of the Clothing

Manufacturers' Association of the U.S.A.; Earl Barron, Publisher of Mascu-Lines and FemmeLines; Mary Campbell, Secretary of Condé Nast Publications; Muriel Hobson, Associate Job Editor of *Glamour*; Polly Weaver, College and Career Editor of *Mademoiselle*; Eleanor Williams, Fashion Director, and Sybil Yeomans, former Art Director, of Vogue Pattern Co.; Lazare Teper, Research Director of the International Ladies Garment Workers Union.

Also, Frieda Shaviro, of the Research Department of Amalgamated Clothing Workers; Forest Lombaer, formerly Personnel Administrator of R. H. Macy & Co.; Miriam Conklin, Employment Manager of Lord & Taylor; Barry Golden, Vice President and General Merchandise Manager of Interstate Department Stores; Herman Bronstein, General Merchandise Director, and Vesta Shaffer, Fashion Director, of Arkwright Merchandising Co.; Mary Bruns, formerly Assistant Manager, Personnel Group, National Retail Merchants Association; William Neil, of the Personnel Department of J. C. Penney Co.; David Schwartz, President of Jonathan Logan Co.

Also, Stan Marshall, Operations Chief of Bali Bra Inc.; Joan Quinn Coughlin, former Assistant Personnel Manager of Cluett, Peabody & Co., Inc.; Julia Sze, Design and Fashion Coordinator of Columbia Broadcasting System; Kitty D'Alessio, former Fashion Coordinator of National Broadcasting Company; William Mendelsohn, Vice President in charge of merchandising, Louis Goldsmith, Inc.; Connie Iverson, stylist of D. B. Fuller & Co. Inc.; Harry Weixel of Weixel Textile Design Associates; Virginia Spears, fashion designer; Richard Dorell, Studio Director, M. Lowenstein & Sons, Inc.; Harold Kurzman, President, Lily of France, Inc.; Bernard Davis, Management Consultant; Bertrand Frank of Bertrand Frank Associates, Inc.

And a special word of appreciation to Ellen Fried, my daughter, for her suggestions and encouragement.

SUGGESTED READINGS

I. Research Reports and Film Strips

Bank of America, Small Business Advisory Service: *The Women's Ready-to-Wear Business.*
Career Information Service, New York Life Insurance Company, New York. *Should You Be a Salesman?, Should you Go Into Advertising?, Should You Go Into Retailing?*
Educational Dimensions Corporation (films).
  Art Careers in Advertising, Career as a Copywriter, Careers in Apparel Design, Careers in Buying, Careers in Illustration, Careers in TV.
International Ladies Garment Workers Union: *Trends and Prospects in Women's Garment Industry.*
Latimer Report: *Guaranteed Wages* (Office of War Mobilization and Reconversion, Office of Temporary Construction, U.S. Gov't. Printing Office, Washington, D.C., Jan. 31, 1947.)
National Credit Office, Inc., Market Planning Service New York: *Transition Years of Men's and Boys' Clothing Industry, 1945-1947.*
———, *The Apparel Manufacturing Industry, 1967.*
National Industrial Conference Board: *Business Record,* May 1955.
National Retail Merchants Association, Personnel Group: *Retailing Has a Career for You,* 1954.
1969 Madison Avenue Europe and Madison Avenue Handbook, Peter Glenn Publications, Ltd., New York.
1969 Sheldon's Retail Directory of the U.S., Phelan-Sheldon Publications, Inc., New York.

1969 Phelan's Resident Buyers 58th edition, Phelan-Sheldon Publications, Inc., New York.

1968 Phelan's Women's Specialty Stores, Phelan-Sheldon Publications, Inc., New York.

N.Y. State Dept. of Labor: *Industrial Bulletin*, March 1953 ("Keeping an Industry Strong").

———, *Industrial Bulletin*, Aug. 1953 ("New York Leads in Swimsuit Styling").

N.Y. State Employment Service: *Guide to Preparing Your Résumé*.

U.S. Dept. of Labor, Job Analysis and Information Section, Div. of Standards and Research: *Job Descriptions for the Garment Manufacturing Industry*.

U.S. Dept. of Labor: *The Labor Market and Employment Security*, May 1955 ("The Apparel Trades in New York City").

———, Bureau of Labor Statistics, *Occupational Outlet Handbook*, (Bulletin No. 150), 1968-1969.

II. Books and Magazine Articles

Andrews, Margaret E., *The Job You Want*, McGraw-Hill Book Co., New York, 1968.

Avent, Catherine and Fried, Eleanor L., *Starting Work*, Max Parrish, London, 1965.

Beasley, Norman, *Main Street Merchant*, Bantam Books, New York, 1950.

Cahill, Jane, *Can a Smaller Store Succeed?* Fairchild Publications, Inc., New York, 1966.

Chambers, Bernice Gertrude (ed.), *Keys to a Fashion Career*, McGraw-Hill Book Co., New York and London, 1946.

Cobrin, Harry A., *The Men's Clothing Industry: Colonial Through Modern Times*, Fairchild Publications, Inc., New York, 1970.

Curtis, Frieda Steinman, *Careers in the World of Fashion*, Woman's Press, New York, 1953.

Disher, M. L., *American Factory Production of Women's Clothing*, Devereaux Publications Ltd., London, 1947.

Drake, Leonard, and Glaser, Carrie, *Trends in the New York Clothing Industry*, Institute of Public Administration, 1942.

Edlund, S. W. and M. G., *Pick Your Job and Land It*, Prentice-Hall, Inc., Englewood Cliffs, New Jersey.

Fortune, Ed. of, "Sixty-Six Million More Americans," Jan. 1954.

———, "Survey of 1700 Top Executives," Jan. 1959.

Frank, Bertrand, *The Progressive Sewing Room*, Fairchild Publications, Inc., New York, 1948.

Suggested Readings

Fried, Eleanor L., "Fashion Designer," *American Occupations Series,* No. 18, Research Publishing Co., Inc., Boston, Mass., 1959.
Gardiner, Glenn L., *How You Can Get the Job You Want,* Harper and Brothers, New York, 1962.
Glamour, Job Department (reprints):
  Biography of a Fashion, Commercial Art, Do You Want a Job in Publishing?, Fashion Jobs, Girls Who Work for Vogue Pattern, Modeling, Retailing Isn't for Sissies, The Salesgirl Is the Key to Retailing.
Gold, Annalee, *How to Sell Fashion,* Fairchild Publications, Inc., New York, 1968.
Gruenberg, Sidonie M., and Krech, Hilda Sidney, *The Many Lives of Modern Women,* Doubleday & Co., Inc., New York, 1952.
Hemphill, John K., "Job Descriptions for Executives," *Harvard Business Review,* Sept.-Oct. 1959.
Herzberg, Else, *Some Principles of Training Applied to the Retail Trade, Institute of Personnel Management,* Management House, London, 1955.
Jarnow, Jeannette A., *Inside the Fashion Business, Text and Readings,* John Wiley & Sons, Inc., New York, 1965.
Krieger, Murray, *Decision-Making in Marketing and Retailing,* Fairchild Publications, Inc., New York, 1969.
———, *Merchandising Math for Profit,* Fairchild Publications, Inc. New York, 1968.
Larison, Ruth Hooper, *How to Get and Hold the Job You Want,* Longmans Green & Co., London, 1950.
Lillard, Marion Neelsen, *Fashion Design,* No. 16 in Vocational and Professional Monographs, Bellman Publishing Co., Cambridge, Mass., 1955.
Mauger, Emily M., *Modern Display Techniques,* Fairchild Publications, Inc., New York, 1965.
Merriam, Eve, *Figleaf, The Business of Being in Fashion,* J. B. Lippincott, Philadelphia, Pa., 1960.
Parkinson, C. Northcote, "His Law Transforms Parkinson," *The New York Times* Magazine, July 10, 1960.
Raudsepp, Eugene, "On Becoming More Creative," *The Management Review,* Aug. 1959.
Samson, Harland E., *Advertising and Displaying Merchandise,* South Western Publishing Co., Cincinnati, 1967.
Saunders, Dero A., "Burlington Weaves a New Pattern," *Fortune,* Dec. 1954.
Saunders, Dero A., and Parker, Sanford S., "The Sunny Outlook for Clothes," *Fortune,* April 1954.
Small, Verna, "The Young American Buyer," *Mademoiselle,* Sept. 1954.
Stryker, Perrin, "Which Route Is Up?," *Fortune,* 1955.
———, "On the Meaning of Executive Qualities," *Fortune,* June, July, Sept., Nov., Dec. 1958.

Summer, Charles E., Jr., "The Managerial Mind," *Harvard Business Review*, Jan.-Feb. 1959.

Thompson, Edward T., "The Executive Job Market and the Recession," *Fortune*, April 1958.

Williams, Beryl, *Young Faces in Fashion*, J. B. Lippincott, Philadelphia, Pa., 1956.

Willing, Jules Z., *How to Land the Job You Want*, Signet Key Book, New American Library, New York, 1954.

Index

Abraham and Straus, 18
Accessories, 7
　Design, 20, 24
Advertising agencies, 28
Africa, 7
Allied Stores Corporation, 17
Amalgamated Clothing Workers of America, 15
American Furrier, 135
American Management Association, 167, 175
American Telephone and Telegraph Company, 171
Animal fibers, 10
Apparel Manufacturer, 136, 163
Apprenticeship system, 14
Argentina, 10
Art Students' League, 125
Asia, 7
Assistant designer, 24
Avenue of the Americas, 14

Back Stage, 29
Bags (women's), 7
　Design, 20
　Designer, 48-51
Ballet, 27, 29
Belts
　Design, 20, 24

Bendel, Henri, 25
Bergdorf Goodman, 25
Beta Gamma Sigma, 71
Black college students, 18
Blass, Bill, 20
Blouses
　Design, 20
Bonwit Teller, 25
Boot and Shoe Recorder, 58
Boutiques, 13, 17
Boys' wear, 7
Branch stores, 67
　Executive case history, 79-83
Brassieres, 8
　Design, 20
Brazil, 10
Bronx High School of Science, 41
Brooklyn College, 159
Burlington Industries, 17-18
　Foundation, 18
Buyer, *see also* Merchandising, 16
　Defined, 55
　Functions, 58-59
　Seasons, 55-56, 64
　Retail
　　Assistant, 62, 72
　　In buying offices, 72-74, 76
　　Salary, 61, 66
　　Training programs, 64-65

219

INDEX

Buyer (cont'd)
  Wholesale, 74-77
    Fabric, 74
      Piece-goods, 75-77
    Salesman, 77
    Trimmings, 75-76
Buying offices, 16

California Apparel News, 136
Canada, 10
Cardin, Pierre, 20
Cassini, Oleg, 20
Casual attire, 6
Catalogue firms, 17
Catalogues, school and college, 187-188
Chain stores, 16-17, 62, 72
Chicago, 14
Children's wear, 7, 8
  Design, 20, 24
  Designers, 41-45, 180
  Stylist, 114-116
  Textiles, 32
Christmas, 105
City College of New York (C.C.N.Y.), 89
Clerical, merchandise, 70
Coats, 20
  Men's, 23
Cocktail gowns, 24
Cole of California, 7-8
Colombia, 10
Colorist, 32
Columbia University, 126
Commercial factoring, 10
Comparison shopper, 71
Condé Nast, 134-135
Consumer Distribution Committee, 18

Contractor, 11
Coordinates, 20
Copenhagen, 7
Copyists, 19
Corsets, 20
Costume Institute, *see* Metropolitan Museum of Art
Cottons, 33
"Croquis," 26, 30, 32
Custom houses, 11
Cutter, 4

Dacron, 8, 74
Daily News Record, 13, 18, 21, 58, 116, 136
Dallas, 14
Dayton Corporation, 17
Denim, 74
Department Store Economist, 136
Department stores, 7, 16-17, 61-62
  Buyer case history, 83-89
Design, apparel, 19-29
  Custom, 25-26
  Functions of designer, 21-22
  Job turnover, 34-35
  Pattern companies, 26-27
  Ready-to-wear, 23-25
  Requirements, 22-23
  Salaries, 34
  Showings, 23-24
  Specialization, 24
  Theatrical, 27-29
Designers Guild of Ladies Apparel, Local 30, I.L.G.W.U., 15
Detroit, 17
Discrimination, employment, 4
Draper, 24
Draperies, 32, 33

Index

Dresses
  Design, 20
  Junior, 35-41
    Design, 23, 24
Dressmaker form, 21
Du Pont, 168

Easter, 105
Educational Testing Service, 171
Edwardian shirts, 7
Eighth Avenue, 14
Elna, 105
Embroidery, 43
  Design, 20
England, 7
Esquire, 131
Evening coats (men's), 7
Executive placement agencies, 176

Factory, 163
Fairchild Publications, 136
Fashion Group, Inc., The, 118, 119, 188
Fashion Institute of Technology, 34-35, 38, 41, 43, 46, 48, 51, 149, 159, 180, 189, 190
Fashion publications, 17, 128-147
Florence, 7
"Follow-up" boy (or girl), 74
Footwear, 7
Fortune, 169
Forty-second Street, 14
Foundation garments, 7, 8
  Design, 23, 24
Fox, G., and Company, 61
France, 10
Furniture coverings, 32
Furs, 20

Galeries Lafayette, 8
Garment center, 14
General Electric, 171
Genesco, Inc., 13
Gentlemen's Quarterly, 131
Givenchy, 20
Glamour, 37, 58, 131, 134-135
  Top Ten College Girls, 134-135
  Fact Sheets, 188
Gloves, 20
Golden, Barry, 168-169
Gray goods, 10
Great Britain, 10
Greenwich Village, 137, 146
Gripes, 193-195
Growth and Development of Executives, The 171
Gruenberg, Sidonie, 179

Harper's Bazaar, 42, 58, 131
Harvard Business School, 175
Harvard University, 178
Hats (women's), 20, 24
Head of stock, 70
Hemphill, John K., 171-172
High School of Music and Art, 51
Home Furnishings Daily, 58
Hosiery, 7
Hudson, J. L., Company, 17

Infants' and Children's Review, 44, 58, 135
Ingenue, 131
International Alliance of Theatrical Stage Employees, The, 27
International Business Machine, 124
International Ladies Garment Workers Union, 15, 60-61, 149-150, 162

221

INDEX

Ireland, 7, 12
Italy, 7

Jobber, 16
Job hunting, 198-211
    Ads, 200, 202-204
    Attitudes, 206
    Follow-up, 208-209
    Interview, 207-208
    Letters, 200, 201-202, 205
    Portfolios, 205
    Résumés, 200, 204
Job promotion, 193-196
Jonathan Logan Corporation, 12-13

Kayser-Roth Corporation, 7-8, 13
Kluckhohn, Dr. Florence, 178, 179
Knitwear, 20, 30
Kovatron Co., 150
Krech, Hilda, 179

Lancaster, Pennsylvania, 160
Lewis, R. Duffy, 55
Libraries, 187
Longchamps, 50
Long Island University, 79
Lord & Taylor, 42, 53, 117, 142
Lowenstein, M., & Sons, Inc., 34

Mace, Professor Myles L., 171
Macy, R. H., & Co., 65-66, 185
    SOTH, 67
Mademoiselle, 58, 131, 134
    Alumnae Advisory Center, 188
    College Board of Editors, 121, 134
Magnin, I., 42
Mail-order houses, 16-17, 72
Management consultants, 176

"Managerial Mind, The," 170
Mannequins, 110
Manufacture of apparel, 11
    Engineering, 14-15
    Mass production, 11
    Relation to national economy, 9
    Seasonality, 16
    Trends, 11-14
    Unionization, 15
Many Lives of Modern Woman, The, 179
Marketing, 16-17
Maternity clothes, 20
Men's wear, 20, 25
Men's Wear Magazine, 131
Merchandise manager, 76
Merchandising, 55-94
    Affected by suburban trend, 7
    Earnings, 78
    Executive, 3-4
    Job histories, 79-94
    Job turnover, 78-79
    Retail, 60-74
        Buying offices, 72-74
        Functions of buyer, 58-59
        Requirements, 59-60
        Specialization, 59-60
    Specialists, 16-17
    Wholesale, 74-77
        Merchandise manager, 76
Mergers, 166
Metropolitan Museum of Art, 41, 46
Minneapolis, 17
Model, 24, 46-48
Modern Bride, 131
Money, 193, 196
Montclair State Teachers College, 83
Mothers' Day, 105
Movies, 27

Index

Museum of Modern Art, 123
Myers, Charles F., 17-18

National economy, 9
National Retail Merchants Association, 188
"National Slacks Week," 105
Necchi, 105
Neckwear, 20
Newspapers, 17
New York City, 10, 14
New York City Commission on Human Rights, 18
New York Stock Exchange, 12
New York University, 159
Nightwear, 7, 20
Nylon, 8

On the Meaning of Executive Qualities, 169, 171
Opera, 27
Orlon, 8

Pace College, 163
Palm Beach Co., 13
Paris, 7, 8
Parkinson, C. Northcote, 177
"Parkinson's Law," 177
Pattern companies, 26-27
Patternmaker, 4
Penney, J. C., Co., Inc., 68-69
Permanent press, 8, 150
Pfaff, 105
Philadelphia, 14
Placards, 111
Planning and promotion, 95-127
  Advertising, 111
    Art, 107-109
      Layout, 108

      Paste-up, 109
      Photographs, 108
  Case histories, 114-127
  Children in, 105-106
  Consulting services, 101
  Copywriting, 106-107, 112
  Director, 106
  Display, 109-111
  Fashion promotion, 102-104
    In practice, 104-107
    Requirements, 103-104
  Functions, 97-99
  Job turnover, 114
  Packaging, 106
  Publicity, 113
  Requirements, 99-100
  Salaries, 114
  Shows, 106
  Styling, 112-113
  Textile, 117-120
Playboy, 131
Posters, 111
Princeton, 168
Production, apparel, 148-164
  Case histories, 159-164
  Engineering functions, 152-154
  Job turnover, 159
  Opportunities, 158
  Requirements, 154-157
  Salaries, 159
Promotion
  In practice, 104-107
  Requirements, 103-104
  See also Planning and promotion
Promotion director, 106
Public ownership, 166
Publishing, fashion, 128-147
  Functions, 129-130
  Job case histories, 137-147

223

INDEX

Publishing (cont'd)
  Job turnover, 137
  Magazines, 131-135
    Fashion pages, 135
  Newspapers, 135
  Requirements, 130-131
  Salaries, 137
  Trade publications, 135-137

Qiana, 8

Rainwear, 20
"Repeat," 30
Research, fabric, 8
  Design, 10
  Manufacturing, 10-11
Retail Industry Affirmative Action Program, 18
Retailing of apparel
  Career opportunities, 17-18
  Marketing, 16-17
  Promotion and publicity, 17
  Relation to national economy, 9-10
  Seasonality, 16
Retailing, 60-72
  Branch stores, 67-69
  Buying offices, 72-74
  Buyer, 55-56, 58-59, 60-72
    Assistant, 62, 72
  Central buying offices, 62-63
  Chain stores, 62
  Clerical, 70
  Comparison shopper, 71
  Department manager, 63
  Department stores, 61-62
  Discount operations, 62
  Head of stock, 70
  Salaries, 61, 66
  Salesperson, 71

  Specialty stores, 62
  Stock boy (or girl), 69
  Unit control clerk, 70
  See also Merchandising
Retailing Society, 90
Rhode Island, 68
Robert Hall Clothes, Inc., 10-11
Rochester, 14
Rome, 7
Rosenau Bros. Inc., 24-25, 149
"Rub off," 40
Rugs, 32

St. Louis, 14
Saks Fifth Avenue, 25
Salary, 5
Salespersons, 71
Sales trainee, 4
Samplehand, 20
Scandinavia, 7
School guidance counselor, 187
Schwartz, David, 12
Schwartz, Richard, 12
Seasonality, 15-16
Seventeen, 37, 58, 92, 105, 131
Seventh Avenue, 14, 41
Sewing machine operator, 4
Shirts (men's), 20, 24
Shoes (women's), 7, 20
Shopping centers, 7, 62
Show Business, 29
Shower curtains, 32
Shull, Leo, Publications, 29
Silks, 33
Simmons College, 143
Simplicity Patterns, 105
Singer, 105
Sketcher, 24, 46-48
Skirts, 20

Index

Snow wear, 20
SOTH, 67
South Africa, 8
Southern Garment Manufacturer, 136
Spain, 7
Special-occasion clothes, 6
Specialty shops, 16-17
Sports jackets, 6, 20
Sportswear, 6, 8
   Design, 20, 23, 24
      Junior resident buyer case history, 89-94
State employment agencies, 187
State University of New York, 160
Stephens Junior College, 138
Stock boy (or girl)
   Retail, 69
   Wholesale, 76
Stores, 136
"Strike offs," 32
Stryker, Perrin, 169, 171
Stylist, 33
Subteen or preteen department, 7
Suburbs, 6-7, 62
Suits (men's), 20, 23
Suits (women's), 20
Summer, Charles E., Jr., 170
Supermarkets, 7
Swimwear, 20
Synthetics, 8, 10, 33, 74
Syracuse University, 120

Tailored clothing (men's), 6
Television, 27, 28-29
Textile converter, 10, 118
Textile design, 30-34
   Converters, 30, 33-34
   Free-lance, 30-31
   Functions of designer, 31-32
   Job turnover, 34-35
   Requirements, 32-33
   Salaries, 34
   Stylist, 51-54
   Woven designs, 30
Textile Economics Bureau, 8
Textile jobbers, 10, 11
Theatre, 27-29
Thirty-fourth Street, 14
Tiffany's, 142
Ties (men's), 6
Tobé-Coburn School for Fashion Careers, 120, 121
Top-level jobs, 165-177
   Job seeker's role, 174-177
   Methods, 175-176
   Qualifications, 168-172
   Recruitment, 173-174
Top Ten College Girls, 134-135
Tot 'n' Teen, 42
Trade magazines, 17
Trainee, 3
Trouser Institute of America, 105
Turtleneck shirts, 6

Underwear, 7, 8
   Design, 20, 24
Underwear Review, 135
Unions, 15
Unit control clerk, 70
United Merchants and Manufacturers Inc., 10-11
United Scenic Artists of America, 27, 28
University of Missouri, 138
University of Wisconsin, 117
Uruguay, 10

INDEX

Vanity Fair Mills Inc., 13
Variety, 29
Vassar, 143
Vegetable fibers, 10
Venezuela, 10
Vertical mill, 10
Vogue, 42, 58, 92, 131, 135

Wallpaper, 32
Wall Street, 95
Western Apparel Industry, 136

Westinghouse Electric Corporation, 171
Wholesaler, 16
Window dressers, 111
Women, 178-186
Women's Wear Daily, 8, 21, 40, 41, 42, 44, 58, 91-92, 116, 121, 126, 136
Woolens, 30, 33
World War II, 8, 9, 16
Worth Street, 10
Wright, Moorehead, 171

About the Author

Is the fashion business her business? If you're talking about Eleanor L. Fried, author of IS THE FASHION BUSINESS YOUR BUSINESS? editions one through three, the answer is a loud, clear affirmative. The right verb might be "immersed."

Eleanor Fried admits to almost 35 years of experience in the employment field, including a dozen years with the New York State Employment Service and the rest as Placement Director for State University of New York's Fashion Institute of Technology (FIT) which produces a goodly number of creative people for the many fashion fields, particularly merchandising, textiles and apparel.

Some of her professional associations are the National Vocational Guidance Association and the American College Personnel Association of the American Personnel and Guidance Association and the Personnel Association of New York.

She is known for her down-to-earth approach to the fashion business. So her career advice can be taken at face value, sans frills. She relaxes with her husband, Sylvan Furman, in their Berkshire home in the woods. And claims a "hobby" her granddaughter, Rebecca, her daughter Ellen's first offspring.